BEYOND RITUAL

In *Beyond Ritual*, Siobhán Garrigan uses Habermas's theory of communicative action to suggest two things: first a method by which theology can access the ritual symbols by which faith is formed; and second a metaphor of intersubjectivity with which theology can propose an interpretative, rather than an instrumental, understanding of sacramentality – and thus of God. Through fieldwork studies of both 'marginal' and 'mainstream' Christian Eucharists, Garrigan develops the conversation between Habermas's philosophy and Christian theology, showing how ritual interactions form – and challenge – our very idea of God.

After rehearsing some of the main conclusions of recent liturgical theology and ritual studies, Siobhán Garrigan strikes off on an imaginative path of her own. Convinced that liturgy is social practice rather than words on paper, with dynamics of its own rather than merely the application of theology, she analyzes the actual liturgical celebrations of some actual congregations in present-day Ireland. What make her conclusions especially interesting are that, in her analyses, she creatively employs certain elements of Habermas' theory of communicative action, and that among the liturgical celebrations she analyzes are those of some marginal groups. Altogether a creative and provocative contribution to our understanding of what does take place – and of what should take place – when the Christian liturgy is celebrated.

– Nicholas P. Wolterstorff, Noah Porter Professor of Philosophical Theology,
Yale University Divinity School, USA

Siobhán Garrigan uses the philosophical categories of Professor Habermas to explore the interpersonal dynamics of the eucharist. She then uses these new analytical tools to observe what actually happens in specific masses and a feminist liturgy. She thus opens many new possibilities for the academic exploration of the complexities of Christian worship.

James F. White, Bard Thompson Professor of Liturgical Studies,
Drew University, USA

To
Janet Walton

Beyond Ritual

Sacramental Theology after Habermas

SIOBHÁN GARRIGAN

ASHGATE

Published by
Ashgate Publishing Limited
Gower House
Croft Road
Aldershot
Hampshire GU11 3HR
England

Ashgate Publishing Company
Suite 420
101 Cherry Street
Burlington, VT 05401-4405
USA

Ashgate website: http://www.ashgate.com

British Library Cataloguing in Publication Data
Garrigan, Siobhán
    Beyond ritual : sacramental theology after Habermas
    1.Habermas, Jürgen - Contributions in philosophy of religion
    2.Sacraments - Philosophy
    3.Sacraments (Liturgy)
    I.Title
    234.1'6

Library of Congress Cataloguing in Publication Data
Garrigan, Siobhán.
    Beyond ritual : sacramental theology after Habermas / Siobhán Garrigan.
        p. cm.
    Includes bibliographical references (p.) and index.
    ISBN 0-7546-3611-9 (alk. paper)
        1. Theology--Methodology. 2. Sacraments--Catholic Church. 3. Habermas, Jürgen.
    4. Critical theory. I. Title.

BR118.G32 2004
234'.16--dc22   2003059505

ISBN 0 7546 3611 9

Printed and bound in Great Britain by TJ International Ltd, Padstow, Cornwall

Contents

Acknowledgements

This is my first book. First books in theology tend to owe a great deal to those who have given the author her idea of God, and so I thank the many people who did this through teaching me how to worship and how to pray. In particular, I thank my parents, Phil Garrigan and Tony Garrigan, who have dedicated their lives to the church, to education and to their children. I thank my dad also for his music and my mum for her intelligent conversation, both of which have been crucial in forming the understanding of God stated in this book.

I also thank especially Sinéad Garrigan Mattar, my sister, who gave me an extraordinary amount of encouragement when I moved from social work to academia. Her detailed reading of the doctoral thesis which was the forerunner for this book transformed both the thesis and me. Liam Tracey and Ann Loades were, respectively, director and examiner of that thesis and their careful reading of it and suggestions for its development have been very helpful and are much appreciated.

To the friends in Ireland with whom I have eaten, played music and shared life during this turn to things academic, I give wholehearted thanks. The Brady family - all 32 of them, Nicole Massey, Dave Benson, Meike Blackwell, Ed Hopkinson, Erico Uehara, Sarah Davy, Selina Guinness, Colin Graham, Gary and Catriona Hastings, Cathy Wadell, the Gannons, Jenny and Mike Bernard, and Benita Stoney. I also thank Owen Garrigan and Tony Brown, Paddy Garrigan and Karen Verden, Christine Keating and Catherine Keating, Charbel Mattar and his girls, Orla and Eleanor, Richard Armstrong and his family, and Renata Dwan, for coming all the way to the west to share in the whole mess that is book-writing.

To my companions from the Emmaus community in Coventry, to Mary and Allen Edwards, to Todd Alwine, and to my wonderful students in Theology and Religious Studies at GMIT, Galway, I offer many thanks. The ideas and theories I share in this book started as hunches only through my work with them. I also thank my colleagues at Yale, whom I met in the final stages of this book's completion, particularly Martin Jean and Ludger Viefhues, who read parts of the manuscript, and Nick Wolterstorff and Bryan Spinks who read it all and offered generous encouragement as well as helpful suggestions. To Callista Brown, for the sheer quality of her assistantship, and for her patience, I offer heartfelt gratitude.

Two people I thank most of all. My beloved, John Brady, who has supported this project in ways I cannot begin to account, and about whom words fail me. And my teacher, mentor and friend, Janet Walton, without whom I would not be doing this work at all. As a mark of respect and a token of love, and with enormous gratitude, I dedicate the book to her.

New Haven, CT.
Easter 2003

Introduction

Successful ritual requires successful communication.[1]

In this book, I use Habermas's theory of communicative action to suggest two things: a) a method by which theology can access the ritual symbols by which faith is formed; and b) a metaphor of intersubjectivity with which theology can propose an interpretative, rather than an instrumental, understanding of 'sacrament'. The effect of combining the two in fieldwork studies of both 'marginal' and 'mainstream' Christian worship is a suggestion of *radical intersubjectivity* as a key contemporary way of speaking of God. My hope is that such a theological claim can act as a vital counter-point to the twin dangers threatening worship in Ireland and the UK, whereby ritual becomes quietly sectarian, on the one hand, or arcane, on the other.

A research question is usually the product of an academic context. The leading question for this book, however, arose when one of my colleagues at the Emmaus community house in Coventry, a man who had been homeless for years, said after one of our daily morning meetings that it had been, 'Brilliant, like a sacrament'. Despite the Christian connotations of the name Emmaus, it was not a religion-based community and many of the people who lived there, like Jim, had no church background, so I was intrigued by his choice of simile and asked him what he meant: 'You know, special, like everything coming together for a little while. It was nice to be with everyone for once, more common-purpose-like, as if we were being helped. I don't know, you can't really put it into words, can you.'

Jim's description of 'sacrament' coincided with my reading both ritual theory and critical theory for the first time. In the former was the claim, popular among liturgical theologians, that human ritual behaviour, by virtue of its rituality, conjured a type of power that other genres of behaviour did not, and this led me to ask whether there was a peculiar power in a thing called ritual - be it morning meeting or temple sacrifice - and did it determine the manner in which we were to relate to God and to one another? Was it this power that sacraments harnessed? And, if so, was this power benign, or could it fail? In the latter came a challenge to the very concept of 'sacrament' by simple virtue of the explicit anti-metaphysical premises of critical theory. Both sat uncomfortably with my hunch that Jim's use of the word held insights about the quality of human interaction - and divine revelation - that were well worth engaging in a post-modern world.

---

[1]   L.A. Hoffman, *The Art of Public Prayer: Not for Clergy Only* (Washington, DC: Pastoral Press, 1988) 63.

With Habermas's particular contribution to critical theory, contrary to the popular consensus at the time that his work was anti-religious, I sensed a useful conversation between a contemporary philosopher's interests and those of theology. With his notion of a 'communications community' came the possibility of an explanation of the workings of (ritual) power and social justice; and with his 'linguistification of the sacred' came a sounding-board for the question of what a sacrament is and whether its power is intrinsic to that of ritual and/or to that of society as a whole. Such a conversation between philosophy and theology (as it is done in worship and as it is written in the academy) is vital if we are to take a sense of the sacramental, and thus a sense of a related-to God, into the twenty first century. It is also vital if Christian worship is to be a fully socially-engaged activity at the heart of a just society and not a leisure pastime in a society of profound iniquity.

Beyond Ritual sets out the beginnings of this conversation in three parts. As an interdisciplinary study, there will be readers who are not familiar with the recent theological reflection on ritual and sacrament which forms the backbone of current liturgical thinking and Part I is designed to afford these readers access to the later parts of the study. It is also written for those who are familiar with this work but who might be interested in a nuanced telling of the tale. The way the tale is told is, in the first chapter, grounded in developments in Roman Catholic thinking (although the study moves to a cross-denominational view as it reaches its conclusion). However, if the location of the study of sacrament within 'liturgical theology' makes perfect sense to you; if your notion of the '*ordo*' already includes feminist and non-text-based rites; if the methodological question of how we access ritual is one you have struggled with in your own work; or if you are familiar with the question of the relationship between ritual power and social justice, then you might prefer to begin at Chapter Three.

Part I comprises two chapters: the first anchors the diverse interdisciplinary, theoretical *and* practical content of the book in the question of what a sacrament is, and it locates the methodology for the initial investigation of this question in sacramental theology, although it subsequently realigns this with liturgical theology. This methodological shift seeks to address the current theological insistence that sacraments should be regarded as acts rather than as texts, technical procedures, or articles of faith.

Closely allied to this insistence is a common identification of worship as ritual, understood as a distinct and unique genre of human behaviour. In Chapter Two, the notion of 'rituality' and what it 'does' becomes a lot less certain. It is in Chapter Two that the questions which originally inspired the study (what is a sacrament; what is the relationship of sacrament to ritual; what is ritual's relationship to society?) are met with the identification of a major methodological barrier inhibiting the work of theological scholarship, presented in the form of the question: how can ritual knowledge be accessed?

Opening Part II, Chapter Three proposes that the epistemology of Jürgen Habermas may offer one answer to this question of access because it suggests that by uncovering the universal validity claims conditioning discourse, one can make explicit that which is ordinarily implicit in dialogue. In presenting the methodological aspects of his thought, and beginning to adapt them to a theological application, this chapter also considers Habermas's insistence that such a methodology only has relevance in the context of a social justice-oriented discourse. His objection to a global capitalist ethic's 'colonisation of the lifeworld' is compared to Christian theology's privileging of an emancipatory manifesto of social liberation.

Discerning a direct parallel between Habermas's identification of a 'context-transcendent' ethic of justice in all instances of communicative action and Christian theology's metaphor of the realm of God, the fourth chapter investigates the theology of Christian eschatology, asking how, if not in communicative action, this realm is to be achieved. Having established that the relationship between Christians and eschatology is formed primarily in worship, the argument proposes that the notion of the realm of God is formed dialogically and is, therefore, contingent on actual ritual interaction.

The consequence of this returns the discussion to the question of access: how are we to interpret Christian doctrines of sacrament, of relationship with God, and thus of God's self, if these are dependent on the constantly unique experience of interacting subjects? Theologies of experience, while opening up the possibilities of divine revelation and undercutting the domination of the esoteric idea that doctrine is divined from texts (and therefore accessible only to experts), have nevertheless failed to pay sufficient attention to the 'checks and balances' that claiming experience as authorial demands if it is not to do harm; we have yet to develop anything like the same rigour in our interpretation of experience that we have come to rely upon in our interpretation of texts. Developing a specific analytical framework on the basis of Habermas's theory of communicative action, and marrying this with the fieldwork-oriented narrative methodology of ritual studies, the second part of the fourth chapter undertakes a Habermasian theological interpretation of a Christian liturgy of the Eucharist.

While no single ritual can be seen as typical of 'mainstream' worship, I attended over sixty Sunday Eucharists at the church used in the case-study and was able to choose an example that was representative of what happened in that church, which is considered a very mainstream parish in Irish terms (Roman Catholic, largely middle class, small town, four priests, four Masses each Sunday and regular visits from the bishop). My original expectation was that when 'mainstream' worship was studied alongside 'marginal' rituals, a greater degree of theological continuity would be apparent than other authors had surmised, there never having been a full-scale study of marginal practices in a work of sacramental theology. Contrary to my original expectations, however, this initial analysis produced very little theological interpretation; indeed, what emerged was an identification not of communicative action, but of 'systematically distorted communication.'

Part III, then, starting in the fifth chapter, applies the same Habermasian hermeneutics to the liturgical theology of various 'marginal' Christian communities. Eucharistic services were chosen (despite my regret at contributing to an overly Eucharist-oriented view of worship in contemporary theology) because it is the only worship service that all the communities studied had in common. Marginal communities are chosen because, as will be seen, throughout all the disciplines incorporated in the first four chapters is a mandate to find a way of paying greater attention to the discourses emerging from marginal contexts. Although it was not possible to study the rituals of a community of homeless people, the fact that other non-mainstream communities are chosen for analysis is also a direct reflection of the original source of the research question and of my own indebtedness to the years I spent among homeless people before entering the academy. As with homeless people, those who are selected for study are 'marginal' not because they see themselves as marginal, but because they are perceived as marginal, in these cases due to their self-identification as feminist, gay, non-Catholic in Ireland, ecumenical, and geographically/economically-isolated worshipping communities.

I had hoped that all five case-studies would be drawn from Irish communities, but in the end it was necessary to travel to the U.S.A. for the feminist and ecumenical examples. This was due to the fact that similar endeavours, although present in Ireland, are as yet young and cannot bear the demands of sustained interpretation. By contrast, the communities selected in the U.S.A. are well established and are capable of accommodating the presence of a prying stranger. With the exception of the gay assembly, I worked with each of the communities studied over a two-year period.

Applying a Habermasian epistemology to the liturgies of these communities proved not only fruitful but surprising, in that there were several unexpected outcomes. Where I had expected a strong effort to distance themselves from the mainstream traditions, quite the opposite was in fact the case; where I had expected a frequent usage of the metaphor of Trinity, this was entirely relativised by the way metaphors were used in these communities; where I expected Habermas to be only minorly useful in direct theological interpretation, he proved to be majorly so; and, regarding the central subject of sacrament, it turned out that Habermas's notion of *radical intersubjectivity*, when applied to Christian worship, supplies a rich theological metaphor, as well the useful method and epistemology for which I had originally turned to it.

In terms of epistemology, this book, in common with similar interdisciplinary studies, develops a methodology in a cumulative fashion. Thus, as can be seen in the overview above, it starts by locating the discussion in current theological methodologies and, in the course of the subsequent three chapters, explains its reasons for progressively incorporating aspects of the methodology of ritual studies, anthropology and linguistic philosophy. In terms of content, the study deliberately shifts an initial focus on sacrament to a focus on the nature of liturgical interaction (from which the notion of sacrament is thought to arise). When it returns to the question of sacrament in the conclusions of Chapter Six, it does so in such a way as to highlight the tensions between the 'fundamental' theology within which conventional definitions of sacrament are formed and the consequences of taking as 'foundational' the proposed interpretative (rather than instrumental) approach to definition.

Apparent within this revised understanding of sacrament is a rejection of the concepts of numerical delineation, grace as something that can accrue, and the conventional view of ecclesial sacramental normativity, in favour of the contingency-bound but mutually-defined, radically intersubjective nature of human-divine relationships. But perhaps the most important outcome from this new understanding of worship as communicative action is an exposure of how very little attention Christian theologians have previously given to how they access the very subject of their discourse: the ritual symbols by which Christian faith is formed.

PART I

Chapter One

A Crisis of Institutions

The [present-day] crisis in Christianity is not really a crisis of its message and the content of faith, but rather a crisis of its institutions, in that these are too remote from the practical meaning of the Christian message.[1]

Christianity's 'sacraments' have long been defined as its central institutions and the way that theology today defines them is indeed 'remote from the practical meaning of the Christian message', with its accessible God of love and suffering, its imperative to forgive, its ethic of social justice and its claim that hope is greater than death. This is largely because the conventional definition of sacramentality is remote from both current philosophical norms, on the one hand, and reports of experienced praxis, on the other.

This chapter suggests ways in which studies of Christian worship practices might be used to construct a contemporary theology of sacrament which: a) is not bound by doctrinal theology's legal and technical definition of its institutional characteristics; b) seeks to reflect the practical meaning of the Christian message by articulating a new sense of inclusiveness in terms of both language and experience, particularly as this manifests at the margins of the church; and which c) reflects the impact of recent ritual theories that have precisely relocated the sacraments in the body: the body personal, the body politic and the ecclesial body of Christ.

By considering the central concept of sacrament in the dual context of its theoretical development in doctrine and (later in the book) in the practices of Christian worship, my aim is to identify a contemporary theology of sacrament based on interpretative rather than instrumental categories. To this end, I begin with the 'classic' texts of Catholic sacramental theology but move quickly to re-locate sacramental theology in a worship (as opposed to a scholastic) context. Reflected in this move is a desire to situate theology in sacramentality, to situate sacraments in liturgy (and in liturgical theology) and to use feminist theologies of worship as something of a yardstick by which to measure the effectiveness of these re-locations. The starting point for this discussion can be expressed in the question:

---

[1]   J.B. Metz, *Faith in History and Society: Toward a Practical Fundamental Theology* (New York: Seabury Press, 1980) 169. Metz maintains this diagnosis in his recent: *A Passion for God: The Mystical-Political Dimension of Christianity* (New York: Paulist Press, 1998); he hints at the need to reinterpret the sacraments as part of his appeal to Christian tradition; see: 36, 102.

If one is interested to discover what a sacrament is, where does the search start; with a dictionary, with doctrine, with the historic texts of an established rite, with participation in worship, with a tree-hug, with a cup of tea? Within theology one approach has been preferred for most of the second millennium: the systematic exposition of the church's doctrine. Thomas Aquinas set this train in motion nearly eight hundred years ago and Luther and Barth's substantial disagreements represent a change in cargo but not engine, content but not method. Aquinas's treatises on the sacraments were presented in the Third part of the *Summa*,[2] the first two parts having considered Christology and soteriology respectively. This positioning is itself indicative of the way Aquinas understood the sacraments, in that he saw these 'exterior acts of devotion'[3] as the *ethical* conjunction, or product, of the first two parts. Effectively, he deemed it essential that the believer's reception of the sacraments was pre-figured by knowledge of what they symbolised: Christ, and salvation history.

To medieval theology, such an approach represented something of a revolution. Aquinas was departing from the widely accepted early scholastic view, accredited to Hugh of St. Victor, which had emphasised the function of the sacraments as *medicinal*, favouring instead an emphasis on their *sanctifying* qualities. Aquinas thus relativised the strength of the then-dominant idea of *causality*, shifting the focus away from its status as a principle of guaranteed effect and towards its potential as an effective *sign*. Accepting that, 'It is the consistent teaching of the Fathers that the sacraments not only signify but cause grace',[4] Aquinas expropriated Augustine's *sacrae rei signum*[5] to counter the contemporary focus on causality which, he argued, had served to undermine the necessity of the actual sign.

Aquinas's resultant notion of causality nuanced the metaphysical, rather than the catechetical, impact of sacraments, characterising sacramental causality as 'instrumental' – and this was perhaps his most radical innovation. Perceiving that the sacraments were becoming obscure, Aquinas used '*instrumentum*' to rehabilitate the concept of the sacramental to the philosophical norms of his day. The introduction of *instrumentum* allowed him to argue for the efficient causality of a sign while simultaneously allowing the integrity of that sign itself[6] or, to use

---

[2] T. Aquinas, 'Treatise on the Sacraments' in *Summa Theologiae* vol.3, Blackfriars Translation (London: Burns and Oates, 1966). Abbreviated henceforth as ST III.

[3] ST III, q. 84, a.1.

[4] ST III, q. 62, a.1.

[5] The prevailing definitions of sacrament in the Middle Ages prior to Aquinas were those of Augustine, Isidore of Seville, Paschus Radbertus and Peter Abelard. For a survey of definitions of 'sacrament' from its earliest usage up to Aquinas, see: A. Ganoczy, *An Introduction to Catholic Sacramental Theology* (New York: Paulist Press, 1989). For a cross-denominational view, see e.g.: T.W. Jennings, 'Sacrament' in M. Eliade, ed., *The Encyclopedia of Religion* 8 (New York: Macmillan, 1986) 580-583.

[6] Although this drew criticism from others equally sympathetic to Aristotle/Augustine, most notably Duns Scotus, for whom grace could not be 'contained' in a sacrament as

his analogy with the Aristotelian philosophy he espoused, the sacraments could be seen as 'instrumental cause' to God's 'First cause'. By this, Aquinas could remain true to one of his guiding maxims from St. John Damascene, 'In Christ human nature was like the instrument of the divinity',[7] while allowing his radical articulation of the sacraments to benefit from the reflected light of Damascene's well-known phrase. He explained:

> The principal efficient cause of grace is God, for whom the humanity of Christ is conjoined instrument (like the hand), while the sacrament supplies an instrument that remains distinct (like a stick moved by the hand). It is thus necessary for the salvific power to pass from the divinity of Christ through his humanity and finally through the sacraments.[8]

With this Aquinas established not just the method by which reflection on the sacraments was to persist (systematic philosophical argument), but also the vocabulary (legalistic), the central concern (validity), and the key hermeneutic approach (Christological).

Karl Rahner has claimed, however, that the current age is undergoing a '"Copernican revolution" in the understanding of the sacraments, in the existential realization of the sacramental event'[9] which is reconfiguring Aquinas's categories. Rahner perceived that the modern understanding of the sacraments was predicated on a split between two worlds, sacred and profane; accordingly, human beings are stuck in the profane world, into which God (in the sacred world) can reach via (signs instituted by) Christ, and impart grace. Grace, in this view, is the currency that redeems humanity, allowing it to bridge the river between sacred and profane worlds. By contrast, Rahner suggested that today's climate is increasingly conditioned by a worldview not of original sin, where grace must be accrued to militate against the effects of that state, but one wherein:

> Grace is everywhere, as the inmost primordial divinely implanted entelechy of world and human history. Grace... is the comprehensive radical opening up of man's total consciousness in the direction of the immediacy of God, an opening up that is brought about by God's own communication of Himself.[10]

---

an effect with its cause; and Martin Luther, who agreed with the stress on sanctification, but for whom, famously, it could not be the sacrament, but only the faith of the believer that sanctifies. See: P. O'Callaghan, *Fides Christi: The Justification Debate* (Dublin: Four Courts Press, 1998).

[7] See: H.F. Dondaine, 'A propos d'Avicenne et de S. Thomas: de la causalité dispositive à la causalité instrumentale', *Revue thomiste* 51 (1951) 441-453. Dondaine notes that Aquinas quoted this phrase forty times in his works.

[8] Aquinas, ST III, q. 7, a. 1, ad 3.

[9] K. Rahner, *Meditations on the Sacraments* (London: Burns and Oates, 1977) ix.

[10] Ibid.

Rahner's revolution is the revolt of the always-already against the to-be-earned; it is the confrontation of the technical with the existential. But are its methods or conclusions actually 'revolutionary' to those of Aquinas? With Rahner the concern remains framed in terms of efficacy and validity, and both are satisfied by the argument that the sacraments are of Christ, the Word of God who is, in them, both promise and offer. Once this Word (of God: Christ) is accepted it becomes a Word of grace which simultaneously affects grace. It is thus essentially Christological and grace is still described in terms of a currency (of connection with the divine in the human Christ). What Rahner has not addressed, what his 'Copernican revolution' fails to overthrow, is the metaphysical basis of such an approach: the persistence of a duality that requires an interventionist God (albeit an always-already intervening one) to 'overcome' some sort of existential breach between humanity and its destiny in God.

Rahner's contemporaries have proceeded along similar tracks, relying on three main sources: early Christian history, patristic writings and scholastic theology in propounding a weave of relationship with God and humanity as the warp and Christ and the sacraments he instituted as the weft. There are parallels in their conclusions, but important distinctions too, and these will be briefly considered through the work of Schillebeeckx and Segundo. Schillebeeckx, a Dominican, was steeped in Aquinas's thought and his theology can be seen as mediating the 'revolution' Rahner spoke of while also presenting an authentic reading of Aquinas to a theological world in which it had become something of a caricature.[11] At the heart of Schillebeeckx's theology lies the same conviction that one sees in his patristic and medieval sources: a belief in the inextricable relationship between the glorification of God and the salvation of people which finds its focus in the worship of the church. The 'efficacy' of the sacraments for Schillebeeckx is founded not, as for Aquinas, upon causality, but on there being moments of 'encounter' between Christ (God) and the individual human being. The analogy employed is with gestures of friendship, such as an offer of a handshake, and as such Schillebeeckx emphasises a) the availability of God's grace (as Rahner did) and b) the *interactive* nature of it, for, if the hand is not grasped, if a response is not elicited, the encounter is incomplete, indeed there has been no 'encounter'.

This last point reflects one of the important shift's of the 'revolution': an awareness - of which Luther never lost sight - that sacraments do not happen just because they are instituted to do so by the hierarchy of the church or by dogmatic theology: they require the participation, the faith, of the people. It may be easy, with hindsight, to see how this was readily interpreted as a call for more participative ecclesiology and liturgical practice, especially since Schillebeeckx is well-known for his advocacy of liturgical reform (in his writings and also as a contributor to the Liturgical Movement). He is, however, less well-known for the ethical-political emphasis he gave to this work, his argument that if 'the sacraments

---

[11]   See: R.J. Schreiter, 'Edward Schillebeeckx: An Orientation to his Thought' in R.J. Schreiter, ed., *The Schillebeeckx Reader* (New York: Crossroad, 1984).

are the visible realisation on earth of Christ's mystery of saving worship' then they call for a 'real love for our fellow men... a solidarity in human experience.'[12]

With Juan Segundo, the reverse is true: he is remembered for his passionate advocacy of a sacramental theology that has the power to transmit a political message of solidarity, his famous accusation that Vatican II 'did not move from Lumen gentium to Gaudium et spes',[13] but the fact that his methodology is straight down the line systematic theology (and not ethical-political reflection) tends to be overlooked. Like Schillebeeckx and Rahner, Segundo is greatly influenced by the late-twentieth century historical scholarship into the early church, and he makes a direct comparison between contemporary ways of celebrating the sacraments and historical reports of the earliest ways:

> The Christian who approaches the sacraments today ordinarily has the feeling that he is doing something useful and even necessary for eternal life. So far as we know, the Christian living in the primitive church saw these distinctive signs of his community... not as something useful or necessary; rather he saw them as spontaneous gestures in a community that was in possession of eternal life.[14]

Putting aside questions of his sources, or indeed the relative merits of appealing to a 'primitive' form of anything in order to establish contemporary norms, the 'revolution' in Segundo's position lies in its rejection of the theological model of sacramental grace that pervades Catholic liturgical thinking: what he, coining Paolo Freire's phrase, calls the 'bank deposit' type of sacramental theology. His argument to Rahner, who influenced him greatly, would presumably be that the revolution whereby we move from needing to earn grace (put it in the bank) in order to save for the day when we can pay off our debt on our fallen cosmological location to a world in which we freely avail of an always-already available salvation, cannot happen vis-à-vis the sacraments until it happens vis-à-vis the mission of the church as a whole: 'Only a church which recognises itself by "the name of Christ", that is, by its contribution to liberation, can give a different sense to the sacraments.'[15] Segundo's qualification of the kind of identity the church ought to display (one enacting liberation) throws down the gauntlet to Rahner's more abstract elaboration of Christ as the primordial sacrament and, therefore, the church he instituted as sacrament.[16]

Rahner's rehabilitation of grace by which it is made *accessible*, Schillebeeckx's emphasis on the necessity of personal *encounter* and Segundo's

---

[12] E. Schillebeeckx, *Christ the Sacrament of Encounter with God* (New York: Sheed and Ward, 1963) 45, 208. For a fuller account of the political focus of his theology, see also his: *Christ: The Experience of Jesus as Lord* (New York: Crossroad, 1981) 629-839.

[13] J. Segundo, *A Theology for Artisans of a New Humanity, Vol 4: The Sacraments Today* (Maryknoll: Orbis, 1974) 117.

[14] Ibid., 42.

[15] Ibid., 97.

[16] The notion of church as sacrament will be considered in greater detail in Chapter Four.

enunciation of the *liberative imperative* of the Christian sacraments have all conditioned the way in which the sacraments are now regarded and practiced. The changes in the way in which sacraments are celebrated around the world over the past thirty years derive in great part from the writings of these theologians. Yet, while these changes may themselves seem revolutionary, all three writers neglect to challenge some of the more fundamental premises upon which their arguments are based: the number and names of sacraments are taken as given; the context is a starting point in Christological (and soteriological) discourse; and their worldview is of a fundamentally metaphysical nature, accommodating patristic, scholastic and Enlightenment formulations.

The theological revolution on the Copernican level, the earth no longer being seen as the anchor of the universe, may have been prophesied in their work, but has happened concretely, I suggest, with those theologians who have been more directly influenced by Heidegger, on the one hand, and those who eschew the nomenclature of sacramental in favour of 'liturgical' on the other.[17] The former, to whom I shall turn first, revolt through an attempt to overthrow the metaphysical (and thus instrumental) notion of sacramentality; the latter revolt by refusing to see sacrality limited by any particular argument about liturgical encounter, arguing that the *doing* of liturgy is our most prime form of theologising, and our most fertile ground for interpretation. We are only just beginning to feel the effects of these new galactically-relative axes.

It was not until the mid- to late-1980's that works began to emerge that specifically addressed the implications of Heidegger's post-metaphysical philosophy for some of the centuries-old foundations of reflection on the sacraments, such as number, nature, institution, validity, administration and effectiveness. The ground had shifted and it was no longer clear that the previous categories of explication were relevant, as witnessed in Herbert McCabe's question, 'Can we have a Eucharistic theology rooted in the notion of meaning rather than being?'[18] Louis-Marie Chauvet argues that it will only be possible if the subject of Eucharistic theology in particular and sacramentality in general is completely overhauled. In his *magnum opus*,[19] Chauvet sets out so to do, attempting to accommodate the concept of sacramentality to the newly discovered 'spin' of the world and I will, therefore, look at it in some depth.

---

[17] Throughout this book, the words 'worship' and 'liturgy' are used interchangeably and synonymously, rejecting the colloquial use of 'liturgical' to designate only Roman Catholic, Lutheran and Anglican traditions of practice.

[18] H. McCabe, *God Matters* (London: Cassell, 1987) 115. McCabe's use of 'being' is not to be confused with the Heideggerian 'Being'; it refers rather to the paradigms of substances and essences, thought to constitute being, in terms of which sacramental theology since Aquinas had been couched; McCabe's use of 'meaning' is a characterisation of the post-Heideggerian crisis.

[19] L.M. Chauvet, *Symbol and Sacrament: A Sacramental Reinterpretation of Christian Existence* (Collegeville, MN: Liturgical Press, 1995; original French, 1987).

Chauvet is trying to articulate sacramental theology in terms of contemporary philosophical vocabulary, just as was Aquinas in the thirteenth century. There the parallel with Aquinas stops, for Chauvet proceeds to revise Aquinas's foundations, arguments and conclusions.[20] First of all, Chauvet perceives that in view of 'contemporary awareness of the diversity of the sacraments' and 'an increasing desire to uncover the *marks* proper to Christian identity' what is called for is not a theology of *the* sacraments but 'a *theology of the sacramental*, that is, a theology which opens up a sacramental interpretation... of what it means to lead a Christian life' and he describes this as 'A *foundational theology of sacramentality*'.[21] In pursuing this goal he re-articulates the sacraments in terms of language and symbol instead of (Aquinas's) cause and instrument. Nor is it just the terminology that departs from Aquinas; instead of figuring out his doctrine of God first, Chauvet proposes that this task should be concomitant with that of figuring out sacramentality. So his sacramental theology refuses to 'express' or 'reflect' a prior examination of God but rather to accept that the latter is affected by the former, 'For as we change our view of humanity, we necessarily and concurrently change our view of God as well'.[22]

The view of humanity being carried into the twenty-first century in the western world is one profoundly affected by the events, especially the wars, of the twentieth century. It is a view which Chauvet portrays as having rebelled, as a direct result of these events, against the paternity offered to western thought for two millennia by 'The Greeks' (Plato and Aristotle), characterised as metaphysics. Metaphysics is predicated on a Platonist ontology that demands that one can only speak of another thing by means of analogy, the world and all within it being eternally split from its ideal, source, truth or destiny. What interests Chauvet is why Aquinas, given his awareness of the limitations of analogy (i.e., the sense that we can never reach the real), chose that of cause and effect. Aquinas, as reported above, realised that this analogy suited most appropriately the metaphysical worldview of the day, wherein no subjects (human or divine) are considered able to relate in any way other than as a 'productionist scheme of representation',[23] that is, via technical connections of cause and effect.

Chauvet illustrates this with one of the founding myths of metaphysics, Plato's *Philebus*, where an analogy is drawn between ship-building and loving relationships. Pointing out the way in which Plato seeks to eradicate any possibility of an element of infinity, he comments:

---

[20] Although in his later work, *The Sacraments: The Word of God at the Mercy of the Body* (Collegeville, MN: Liturgical Press, 2001; original French: 1997) he emphasises that his own work is a development of, and not a reaction against, Aquinas.

[21] Chauvet, *Symbol and Sacrament*, 1.

[22] Ibid., 2

[23] Ibid., 21.

> The entire presentation is inspired by a *fundamental desire to eliminate as far as possible whatever pertains to a becoming without end, in favour of the Good described as achieved perfection*, self-sufficiency - as that which is perfectly measured and proportioned. Everything is under the domination of 'value', of calculation, of the cause that measures, of what is 'worth more', of what offers more advantages and greater usefulness: these are all distinctions of wisdom and intellect oriented to the Good.[24]

The problem this exemplifies is that the Greeks, according to Heidegger, overlooked 'the ontological difference... between entity and being',[25] that is, the difference between the way things appear and the things themselves, the essentially dualistic framework that dictates that being is rendered objective by thought; that the things of this world are mere shadows of the realities of the 'ideal'.

When applied to God, by Aquinas, we get 'onto-theo-logy', a way of speaking about God which is utterly conditioned by the metaphysical conviction that thought precedes language. Chauvet traces two closely-spun strands in the development of this language about God in the Christian tradition, the first being the dominance of the idea that God can be spoken of only through 'analogy', the second being the terms of negative theology. Both are based on the metaphysical premise that 'God must remain "completely unknown" to us because there is no concept which can encompass both God and humankind', that is, both are based on the premise that there is a thing that exists, a concept, which we call 'God' but which in actual fact defeats language's ability to conjure. Because we need to talk about it, we employ analogy; but many of the greatest thinkers on the subject, recognising the hopeless inadequacy of these analogies, have maintained that it is better to 'keep silence' or, at a push, say only what God is not (thus, 'negative' theology).

What Heidegger enables theology to expose, argues Chauvet, is the way in which both these approaches, although designed to grant God the limitlessness ascribed to God, serve to contain, even minimise, the possibility of human appreciation of God. The difference is a subtle one: analogy is inescapable, but instead of seeing this as regrettable, limiting, we can see it as a potentially liberating conflict:

> It behoves us to accept the language and the internal conflict it presents us with: a conflict difficult to take on, and which we are constantly tempted to erase in order to insure our domination over the world; a conflict, however, from which the subject is born and sustains itself... As a doctrine validating the truth of our language about God... analogy erases the internal conflict inherent to any discourse. However this conflict cannot be resolved; rather it must be managed - and precisely through the mediation of language: once we are able to say it, we are

---

24   Ibid., 25.
25   M. Heidegger, 'L'être-essentiel d'un fondement ou "raison"' in *Essais et conférences* (Paris: Gallimard, 1958) q. 1, p 100.

able to live it as the ever-open place where the true nature of what we are in relations with others and with God may become reality.[26]

The crucial difference demonstrated by this argument is one of starting-point: subjects do not start with the knowledge of a concept (which is then partially expressed in language) but with their own subjectivity (mediated by language). So for theology, it is no longer a quest to know an unknowable God, but rather to realise 'what we are in relations with... God'. It is a recognition that all that we are is mediated by language and that theology's starting-place is 'the heart of the lack which this mediation opens up in every subject'[27] rather than any extra-linguistic pre-conscious thought. The theological discourse engendered by such a philosophical shift is one 'from which the believing subject is inseparable [for]... subjects can truly "grasp" nothing without at the same time recognising themselves to be already grasped by it'.[28]

Heidegger's - and by extension Chauvet's - problem is the intractability of the metaphysical worldview: how can an alternative worldview be explained without using metaphysical language to do so and, by using this language, constructing the 'alternative' according to the very parameters one has sought to cast off?[29] 'Are we' Chauvet asks, 'able to think any way other than the metaphysical?'[30] In trying to do so vis-à-vis theology, that is, in trying to negotiate a non-onto-theologic, he takes as his guides Heidegger's discourse on Being[31] and Levinas's discourse on the Other.[32]

From Heidegger he accepts that:

> One cannot shed metaphysics the way one gives up an opinion. One cannot leave it behind like a doctrine which one no longer believes and will no longer defend... *For even vanquished, metaphysics does not disappear.* It comes back under another form and maintains its control, as in the distinction, still in force, between being and the entity.[33]

Heidegger attempts to go beyond metaphysics, to uncover its very source, its unexplored foundation, and this he calls 'Being'. Lest it be thought of, with

---

[26] Chauvet, *Symbol and Sacrament*, 41.

[27] Ibid.

[28] Ibid., 43.

[29] A task Derrida sees as impossible, because the question itself 'cannot express itself except in the language of the Greeks'; see: J. Derrida, *L'écriture et la différence* (Paris: Seuil, 1967) 196. Chauvet rejects Derrida's position, arguing that it is inevitably impossible if one places 'the path we wish to explore on the same level as the one we wish to replace', arguing that the topic of such a question is not just a different path but a 'change of terrain'. Chauvet, *Symbol and Sacrament*, 46, 47.

[30] Chauvet, *Symbol and Sacrament*, 45.

[31] M. Heidegger, *Being and Time* (New York: Harper, 1962).

[32] E. Levinas, *Autrement qu'être* (The Hague: M. Nijhoff, 1974).

[33] M. Heidegger, 'Dépassement' in *Essais et conférences* (Paris: Gallimard, 1958) 81-82.

metaphysically-formed minds, as *'something facing humans which stands by itself* and only subsequently comes to meet humans',[34] Heidegger puts two lines through the written script of the word, crossing it out, in order to remind the reader that this is not an 'entity' in the way metaphysics has construed entities.

How is this useful to theology? Chauvet proposes that this notion of Being (and the concomitant withdrawal of Being) reconstitutes metaphysics as an 'Event' (rather than a 'Fall'):[35] an unmasking, an opportunity for conversion and *Gelassenheit* (letting-be), the consequence of which is a gradual rescinding of all judgements ('calculations') made on the basis of 'usefulness': 'In thus unmasking the never-elucidated presuppositions of metaphysics, thinkers learn to serenely acquiesce... to the prospect of never reaching an ultimate foundation, and thus orient themselves in a new direction - inasmuch as this is possible - starting from the uncomfortable non-place of permanent questioning.'[36]

Human beings, newly aware that 'it is language that speaks'[37] will, it is suggested, become aware of the instrumental conception of language to which they have been conditioned. (It is for this reason that Chapter Three considers the theory of Jürgen Habermas, with its proposed epistemology for actually recognising, and defeating, instrumental language use). They will become aware that what is 'present' to them is only so via language. But they also, newly aware that speaking is first listening, will gain an awareness of absence: the flip-side of the presence instituted by the word heard is not silence but absence. To live with this awareness the individual must learn what Heidegger calls 'the concern of the poet: ...To be without fear before the apparent absence of the god, not to run away but, starting from this relation to the absent god, remain in a mature proximity to absence long enough to safeguard the word which at the beginning names the High one.'[38]

Or, as Levinas has it, we must 'hold ourselves in the trace of the Absent'.[39] As Chauvet notes, Levinas's vision disqualifies the *'theism* of the god of onto-theology' because, along with atheism or indifferentism, in such a stance 'the presence of the absence is lost'.[40] The presence of absence is the condition in which non-metaphysical thinking can encounter God: it is difficult, it is emptiness, but 'Emptiness is not nothing; the absence is precisely the place from which humans can come to their truth [by overcoming all the barriers of objectifying and

---

[34] Chauvet, *Symbol and Sacrament*, 49

[35] 'To conceive this history as an Event is to read it ontologically as an *historic* destiny - a destiny which reveals the very essence of a human behaviour that demands accounts, gives ultimatums, compels the real to adjust itself to human needs "from the perspective of what can be calculated."' Ibid., 48.

[36] Ibid., 53.

[37] M. Heidegger, 'L'homme habite en poète' in *Essais et conférences* (Paris: Gallimard, 1958) 227-228.

[38] M. Heidegger, *Apprôche de Hölderlin* (Paris: Gallimard, 1962) 34.

[39] Levinas, *Autrement qu'être*, 51.

[40] Chauvet, *Symbol and Sacrament*, 62.

calculating reason]';[41] it requires a 'poetic' disposition to embrace or accomplish it. It also demands - and here Levinas's thought has had a particular influence on theology - an other. 'An invisible God signifies not only an unimaginable God but also a God *accessible* through justice'[42] and this is encountered not as an abstract notion of justice but as the justice with which the suffering of an other impels us to engage.

The consequence of this philosophical other for theology is, according to Chauvet, that Christian theology must be 'the study of a God whose divinity is effaced in a crushed humanity to the point of "requiring of us this body of world and humanity without which God cannot come among us in truth".'[43] Here is Chauvet's most important banner in this latter-day revolution: the body;[44] the other is not encountered as an abstract other, but as a body. Proposing 'consent to mediation' as the 'fundamental human task', Chauvet can locate the body as the sole arena of this task. It is the sole locus precisely because it is only bodies that speak and it is only through speech that human beings create/identify the world. Contra Aquinas, Chauvet argues that the body is not the 'instrumentum' that *enables* speech; it is such of itself: 'Corporality *is* the body's very speech.'[45]

Every mediation (every language act or 'symbolic joining of the "inside" and the "outside"'[46]) is mediated by the body: such is the distinctive 'economy' of human beings. Chauvet claims that 'the body is the human "way" of inhabiting the otherness of the world as home, a familiar dwelling. The body is the *binding*, the space in the middle where both identity and difference are symbolically connected under the authority of the Other'.[47] Chauvet does not, however, understand the body as a 'unique' or discrete entity (that would be to maintain a metaphysical standard). Rather, an 'individual's' body remains sustainable only insofar as it is reformed by the notion of the inherent relationality of all bodies: 'The I-Body

---

[41] Ibid., 63.

[42] Levinas, *Autrement qu'être,* 51.

[43] Chauvet, *Symbol and Sacrament,* 75. The quotation is from S. Breton, *Le verbe et la croix* (Paris: Desclée, 1981) 9.

[44] Chauvet is not alone in this focus on the body, it being a prominent feature of much contemporary theology. Speaking of this general trend, Elaine Graham writes, 'If theological values have any substance, they will exist in primary form as bodily practices - clinical, liturgical, kerygmatic, prophetic - and only derivatively as doctrines and concepts.' E. Graham, 'Words Made Flesh: Women, Embodiment and Practical Theology', *Feminist Theology* 20 (May 1999) 120. This primary-placement of the embodied and experiential *vis-à-vis* theological construction is considered later in this chapter in the development of 'liturgical theology'. See also, for example: the essays collected in L.M. Chauvet, and F.K. Lumbala, eds., *Liturgy and the Body: Concilium 1995/3* (London: SCM, 1995); and E. Moltmann-Wendell, *I Am My Body: A Theology of Embodiment* (New York: Continuum, 1995).

[45] Chauvet, *Symbol and Sacrament,* 147.

[46] Ibid.

[47] Ibid.

exists only as woven, inhabited, spoken by the *triple body* of culture, tradition and nature.'[48]

According to Heidegger, pre-Socratic thinkers were not hampered by a dichotomy between being and language; language was 'the place humans are born at the heart of the real',[49] 'the *meeting place where* being and humankind mutually stepped forward toward one another',[50] and so Chauvet resolves the question of how to overcome metaphysics, how to 'return' to a pre-Socratic acceptance of language, by locating language not *in* the body but *as* the body. 'Our approach of returning human beings to the field of language is accompanied from end to end by the body, the *body-being*. This approach has repeatedly sent us back to the *contingent mediation* of a language, a culture, a history as the very place where the subject comes to its truth.'[51] And he comments, 'It is easy to see that this fact is of fundamental importance for a theology of *the sacraments* because the ritual symbolism that constitutes them has the body for its setting... The sacraments accordingly teach us that *the truest things in our faith occur in no other way than through the concreteness of the "body".*'[52]

To demonstrate why it is that 'the sacraments' (as opposed to other of Christianity's institutions) enable this particular kind of connection, Chauvet, drawing on language theory, develops the idea of a symbol. Historically, the Roman *symbolon* was a coin which had, as part of its character, been 'split'. Each piece functioned as a separate article, but also as a 'witness to the vacant place of the Other'.[53] At once it spoke of otherness as well as likeness: it was a 'mediator' of both. Describing sacrament as symbol, the mediatory function of the historical analogy becomes the core of his thesis: 'sacraments are mediations, not instruments', that is, symbols not signs. The body, then, is 'the point where God writes God's self in us' and it is specifically the church's institution of the sacraments, Chauvet argues, that are the script where this writing appears because they 'force us to confront mediation - mediation, by way of the senses, of an institution, a formula, a gesture, a material thing - as the (eschatological) place of God's advent.'[54] Why? Because they take the form of ritual, and ritual, Chauvet argues, facilitates this confrontation with mediation in a unique way.

---

[48]   Ibid., 150.
[49]   Ibid., 30.
[50]   Ibid., 33.
[51]   Ibid., 140.
[52]   Ibid., 140-141.
[53]   Ibid., 117-118.
[54]   Ibid., 83. Chauvet had earlier drawn on Lacan's psychoanalytic theory to note the way in which we inevitably resist mediation, but proceeds to regard this as 'folly' because 'we must accept the death of the illusion *everything in us desperately wants to believe, that is, the illusion we can somehow pull ourselves out of the necessary mediation of symbols*, situate ourselves outside of discourse, and apprehend reality directly, without passing through cultural tradition or the history of our own desire.' Ibid., 82.

Rituality is 'the particular mode of expression that constitutes the sacraments' and because of this they are 'original', they are the 'Most "instituting"'... of the Church's types of mediation'[55] (the others being scripture and ethics, which were also instituted by Christ and are also 'ecclesial mediations of our relation to God'[56]). Chauvet agrees with Rahner that the sacraments are of no greater 'value' in faith than either scripture or ethics because:

> The originality of the sacraments comes only from the Church, which radically involves itself and puts into play its whole identity... However, the theological affirmation of the Church's radical involvement needs to be more closely verified in the facts, that is, in the concrete texture of the mediation which constitutes the sacraments. This mediation is ritual... Thus, if it is correct to say that the sacraments derive their unique character from the radical involvement of the Church that celebrates them, this fact needs to be verified in their concrete, that is, ritual modality.[57]

Chauvet can argue this because of his conviction that what one finds in ritual practices, as opposed to any other mode of human behaviour, is a way of speaking that directs participants back to the body: 'The body, let us be precise, is not simply a condition for rites, but their very *place*.'[58]

What the particular rituals that are called sacraments institute, Chauvet suggests, is the identity of the church.[59] They institute this not merely due to their ritual modality (this alone guarantees only institution of some sort of identity) but because the (ritually-enacted) sacraments are 'events of grace'.[60] In this development of a sacramental theology of grace, Chauvet clearly echoes Rahner but builds upon very different (anti-metaphysical) foundations. Where for Rahner, as discussed above, grace is what was bequeathed to the world by the in-breaking of God's word in Christ and is permanently available to the faithful by 'receiving' the sacraments, for Chauvet, rituals are fundamentally about identity formation and

---

[55] Ibid., 319.

[56] Ibid., 321.

[57] Ibid., 323.

[58] Ibid., 355. He specifies his reasoning thus: 'We have previously defined humanity as corporality, a concept that expresses, through the "arch-symbol" of each subject's own body, a threefold relationship: to the cultural system of the group (the social body), to its collective memory (the body of tradition), and to the universe (the cosmic body). This symbolic interrelation comes about differently for each person, depending especially on the history of each one's desire, but each is only the person each is because each is indwelt by this threefold body. It is precisely this corporality which religious rituality symbolises', 355-356.

[59] 'It is precisely in those very acts where it recognises itself as radically instituted by Christ, as existing only as received from him, its Lord, that the Church attains its identity. The sacraments as instituted are the *instituting* mediation of this identity.' Ibid., 409.

[60] Ibid., 410.

so '"grace" designates not an object we receive, but rather the symbolic work of receiving oneself',[61] a type of receiving that:

> we can express only in the symbolic labor of birth it carries out in us: the labor of the ongoing passage to 'thanksgiving' - in this way we come forth as children of God - and to a 'living-in-grace' - in this way we simultaneously come forth as brothers and sisters for others - which makes us co-respond to this God who gives grace and is revealed in Jesus.[62]

According to this view, grace no longer pre-dates human experience. Grace is the 'self-emptying love given by God' in every meeting with the other. The difference with Chauvet, of course, is that this self-emptying love of God operates not so much over the garden fence, as one can imagine with the insistent openness of Rahner's account,[63] but primarily and very specifically at the level of body-experience formed in and through the ecclesial celebration of the sacraments, that is, ritually.

   Chauvet's twin emphasis on the body and rituality will be considered later in this chapter, and the notion of ritual upon which it is based (that is, ritual as a peculiar genre of behaviour, uniquely capable of forming identity) will be challenged in the following chapter. But two additional and closely related themes, crucial to this contemporary revolution, run throughout Chauvet's work and require attention before moving on: access and method. 'Access' refers to the question posed at the beginning of this chapter in relation to sacrament: if you want to know what a sacrament is, where do you look? It is about choice of theological starting-point. For Rahner it was doctrine, for Chauvet (although he himself does not explicitly dissociate himself from Rahner in this way) it is where the body is: it is liturgy. 'Method' signals the intentionality (or self-consciousness) in theoretical approach that has characterised the past twenty years of theological scholarship, the response to the question, if one wants to know what something is, how does one proceed in the study of it? It is about process. For Rahner it was verification in tradition; for Chauvet it is about verification in bodiliness, and because bodies, he insists, are at their most visible in ritual, it is about verification in ritual.

   In the years since *Symbole et sacrement*[64] first appeared it has set the agenda for much contemporary sacramental theology and so the discussion will now turn briefly to how these themes of access and method have been subsequently treated. The results of this short survey receive specific criticism and revision in the final chapter of this book, but are mentioned at this stage so that their cadences can echo through Chapters Two through Five.

---

[61]   Ibid., 140.

[62]   Ibid., 446.

[63]   See: K. Rahner, 'On the Unity of the Love of Neighbour and the Love of God' in *Investigations* 6, 231-249; and 'Liebe' in *Sacramentum Mundi* 3, 234-251.

[64]   L.M. Chauvet, *Symbol et sacrement: Une relecture sacramentelle de l'éxistence chrétienne* (Paris: Les éditions du cerf, 1987).

Common to much recent scholarship as its point of sacramental *access* is the 'turn to language', a hermeneutical shift which privileges an explication of the sacraments based on linguistic philosophy as a means of 'overcoming' the purportedly damaging dualisms of metaphysics. As David Power comments, 'In philosophy and theology... there is the move from metaphysics to phenomenology and hermeneutics, preferring the interpretation of language to the self-assured guidance of thoughts and ideas.'[65] This 'turn' is invariably presented as a response to a) Enlightenment values (the concomitant 'turn to the subject' from Kant onwards) and b) pluralism - of religious practice and theory.[66]

Beneath these historical factors, however, lies the central preoccupation of theology as a whole in the late twentieth century: the crisis in method.[67] This crisis manifests itself in a particularly acute way in sacramental theology because it is a written discourse about an essentially un-written subject and it is perhaps for this reason that authors have found particularly rich pickings in Wittgenstein and Ricoeur, linguistic philosophers whose main interest - the relationship between thought and word - exhibits a direct parallel with that of faith and sacraments. Arguing that, 'the most important effect of Wittgenstein was to shift us from speaking of signs *of* to speaking of signs *for*,' [68] McCabe suggests that:

> There are no ideas, whether in a Platonic heaven, nor in 'the human mind' nor, I think... in the creative mind of God, there are just people, things and the way people are present to each other, and the signs by which they establish this presence, and the meaning *of* these signs, that is, the role each sign has in establishing a form of presence. ...So, there is never something else that is the meaning of the signs I use; there is only the communication, the presence that is being effected in and through these signs.[69]

The sacraments then are 'the language of the future'[70] because they are signs for the future of humanity embodied in Christ's presence: 'Christ is present to us because our language has become his body... He is a future world, but he appears as a body of this world.'[71] By this McCabe seeks to explain Aquinas's *instrumentum* by interpreting it according to a (Ricouerian) 'depth hermeneutic', a way of 'reading'

---

[65] D.N. Power, *Sacrament: The Language of God's Giving* (New York: Crossroad, 1999) 15.

[66] See e.g.: I.S. Markham, *Plurality and Christian Ethics* (New York: Seven Bridges Press, 1999); and D. Tracy, *The Analogical Imagination* (New York: Crossroad, 1985).

[67] 'To state at the turn of the century that the Christian theological academy, across departmental and denominational lines, remains preoccupied with the question of method is to utter a truism.' B.T. Morrill, *Anamnesis as Dangerous Memory: Political and Liturgical Theology in Dialogue* (Collegeville, MN: Liturgical Press, 2000) xi.

[68] McCabe, *God Matters*, 165.

[69] Ibid., 169.

[70] Ibid., 175, 178.

[71] Ibid., 117, 125.

he compares to exposure over time to Shakespeare's plays, where the text operates in the mind of the reader at successively deeper 'levels'.

Accordingly, while he can call the sacraments 'language' and say that their work is thus 'communication',[72] McCabe nevertheless maintains that our access to them requires a depth charge, an *instrumentum*, an uncommon sign: 'sacraments belong to our alienated world in which what we are really about cannot be expressed in our own language, we need a special sacred language, a magic'.[73] Others, like Chauvet and Power, as will be discussed shortly, resolve this ordinary linguistic 'inadequacy' via development of the theology of grace, particularly in the metaphor of Gift/Giving; but McCabe insists that there is a difference between grace and sacrament because of the *presence* instituted by the *body* (of Christ) in the latter. This presence he describes as a 'summons' to 'a revolutionary continuity', 'a summons to death and resurrection'[74] because 'Death and resurrection is a revolution that gets down to the structure of communication which is the body itself.'[75]

Quite clear in McCabe's analysis is the sense that language is not necessarily benign; its 'purpose' can be whatever suits the designs of the speaker, and this can just as easily be alienation as communication. He nevertheless claims that for theology's needs (to speak of God) the 'purpose' of language is communication because this is how God has modelled its use, 'communicating' with humanity via Christ (as body, presented in the language of the sacraments). It is a similar understanding that fuels Alexandre Ganoczy's attempt to construct a 'communications theory' of sacraments: the 'divine attitude of communication is basis and norm for the corresponding human sphere and not the reverse',[76] the key to understanding which, he proposes, is to take seriously Christ's designation as 'Mediator': 'He sends, receives and mediates all in one, and this on the part of God as well as on the part of man'.[77] Consequently:

> The sacraments can be understood as systems of verbal and non-verbal communication through which those individuals who are called to Christian faith enter into the communication process of the ever-concrete faith community [the church], participate in it, and in this way, borne up by the self-communication of God in Christ, progress on the path of personal development.[78]

---

[72] Ibid., 117-127.
[73] Ibid., 175.
[74] Ibid., 123.
[75] Ibid., 124.
[76] A. Ganoczy, *An Introduction to Catholic Sacramental Theology* (New York: Paulist Press, 1984) 148.
[77] Ibid., 152.
[78] Ibid., 155.

Ganoczy's contribution to the discussion is on the level of method: a recognition that the notion of mediation is helpful in enabling access to the subject of the sacraments; a perception that the human being, constructing his or her world by language, is a valid starting-point for analysing the sacraments. However, is seeing the work of the sacraments as 'personal development' really the extent of the outcome of a communications-theoretical epistemology?

For Peter Fink, the focus is taken off the individual and placed on the communication of a whole group. 'Liturgy speaks'[79] he says, and it speaks three languages: the declarative language of liturgical instruction, the evocative language of song, prayer and proclamation and the non-verbal language of human interaction in gesture and space-arrangement. Fink came to describe these three 'languages' as the result of reading *The Constitution on the Sacred Liturgy* in the light of Ricoeur's symbol theory (concentrating on what Ricoeur calls their 'multi-meaning' expressions). To reach the deeper meaning, Ricoeur argues, one has to concentrate on the apparent one. Thus Fink proposes:

> The first language speaks a literal meaning, namely what the action and interaction mean as a human phenomenon. The second language speaks in the form of myth the deeper meaning of the first. This second language can only be heard properly if the imagination is trained on the first. The third language aims to explain and illuminate the event which is constituted by the first two languages. It speaks, however, not simply to satisfy the mind. It speaks to send the believer back to worship in search of its truth there.[80]

The slant Fink thus places on language puts imagination centre stage,[81] valuing it as the key to understanding by arguing that only imagination can transform the written 'texts' of the church into a sacrament. The imagination accomplishes this 'in three primary ways: translation, adaptation and creation',[82] which he understands as the forging of symbols. Arguing that new symbols are constantly needed if liturgical (or any) language is to be understood in changing cultures, he sees imagination as thus enabling 'New symbols [to be] born by holding together symbolic pieces that previously were not held together.'[83] However, this seeming acceptance of the

---

[79] P.E. Fink, *Praying the Sacraments* (Washington, DC: Pastoral Press, 1991) 29.

[80] Ibid., 35-36.

[81] With Ricoeur, imagination is no longer talked about as 'vision' or 'seeing', rather imagination comes to be 'assessed as an indispensable agent in the creation of meaning in and through language - what Ricoeur calls "semantic innovation".' R. Kearney, *The Poetics of Imagination: From Husserl to Lyotard* (New York: Routledge, 1991) 134.

[82] P.E. Fink, 'Imagination' in P.E. Fink, ed., *New Dictionary of Sacramental Worship* (Washington, DC: Michael Glazier, 1990) 588.

[83] Ibid., 589.

widespread reformers' call for 'new symbols'[84] is rebutted by Fink's insistence that the parameters for possible 'application' of imagination operate only within the ecclesial texts prescribed for sacramental worship; which prompts the question of how symbols – and thus sacramentality - are to be formed in non-text based situations. Nevertheless, drawing attention to the imagination is an important addition to the increasing body of work that encourages Christians to 'think symbolically' as a methodological antidote to metaphysical approaches to the sacraments. As Regis Duffy explains, 'Symbolic thinking is concerned more with the larger purposes of God's mystery as revealed in Christ than with the impossible task of explaining how a mystery works.'[85]

Susan Ross likewise contextualises her work in the 'linguistic turn',[86] but criticises her male colleagues for using it to bolster the fundamentally androcentric and patriarchal 'ways in which we understand symbols, human nature, the world and how God is revealed in the world, and how the sacraments are tied to our lives as Christians in the world.'[87] For Ross, the value of accepting Heidegger's maxim, 'Language is the house of being' in relation to the sacraments lies in its furnishing a sense that 'the sacraments, as physical realities, are the very medium of our encounter with God'.[88]   Significantly, however, Ross notes that Chauvet's description of the ecclesial 'body' neglects the fact that all bodies are gendered and asks 'whether these mediatory symbols, language and culture might function differently for women than for men.'[89] Pointing out how women are excluded from sacramental ritual, as leaders and as participants, and yet how many women nevertheless find in the sacraments 'a confirmation of the sacredness of their lives and a definition of their piety',[90] Ross proposes that this very *ambiguity* of

---

[84] See, for example: Robert Hovda's call for an alternative to 'shrivelled, dissected symbols' in R. Hovda, *Strong, Loving and Wise* (Washington: Liturgical Conference, 1976) 80-82.

[85] R. Duffy, 'The Sacraments' in J. Galvin and F. Schüssler Fiorenza, eds., *Systematic Theology: Roman Catholic Perspectives* (Minneapolis: Fortress Press, 1991) 91.

[86] A 'turn' which she dates to Schillebeeckx (1957), Rahner (1974) and Tillich (1957). This reveals an important nuance: the 'turn to language' which Chauvet expounds witnesses a divergence from the work of these authors, making the case for an explicit rejection of the metaphysical foundations on which their work is based. Ross and, to greater or lesser extents, the other authors mentioned so far choose the 'turn to language' as their context, yet see this as a *continuation* of the work of Schillebeeckx, Rahner and Tillich. This nuance betrays a lesser concern than Chauvet's with the question of the foundations of sacramental theology in the pursuit of an at least equal concern with its interpretations. S. Ross, *Extravagant Affections: A Feminist Sacramental Theology* (New York: Continuum, 1998) 140.

[87] Ibid., 30. In an earlier footnote Ross exempted David Power alone from the criticism that sacramental theology has not taken account of feminist theology: p. 28, note 15.

[88] Ibid., 141.

[89] Ibid., 146.

[90] Ibid., 10.

relationship to the sacraments needs to be acknowledged as part of the language that speaks as sacrament.

In a unique attempt to construct a feminist sacramental theology, Ross takes feminist psycholinguistic and psychoanalytical theories to propose 'family' as a breakthrough category in understanding the symbolic. Because of their recognition that 'gender is a crucial factor in the construction of the symbolic', Ross suggests these theories can reconstruct sacramental theology along the family-like lines of 'relational subjectivity'. The sacraments then would not, as Chauvet suggested, 'invoke the presence of the absent God, a presence that we long to embrace without mediation, as much as they [would] intensify the ambiguous presence of God within the immediate, concrete, particular.'[91]

Starting from a recognition that, 'All reality is given to us through language that is embedded in being and culture',[92] David Power also describes a sacrament as a 'language event',[93] and thereby claims for sacrament the mediatory function of language itself. The event that is being mediated by any Christian sacrament, for Power as for Chauvet, is the Pasch of Christ. Because sacraments are language events, he argues, they enable not just an invocation of relationship but this actual past event to enter human history as a present reality:

> What is stressed here is that it is in the very medium of language that the event enters into human lives and history. It is through the very means of language, and within both the power and constrictions of language, that the Word and Spirit are present in the paschal memorial... The twofold mission of Word and Spirit comes from the Father *as his gift*;[94]

and he thus entitles his work, *Sacrament: The Language of God's Giving.* For Power, the semiology of 'gift' or giving is the metaphor which can redeem the metaphysical because it holds within its own vocabulary the power to broach the intrinsic commercialism of onto-theological thought-patterns.[95] Power thus not

---

[91] Ibid., 167.

[92] Power, *Sacrament: The Language of God's Giving,* 64.

[93] Ibid., 76.

[94] Ibid., 82-83.

[95] Facing the same problem that Chauvet presented as the need to 'overcome metaphysics', Power asks, 'Even with the turn to language, is it possible to avoid ontotheology, that is, the type of discourse which treats of God in the language of being and first cause and of sacraments in terms of causality?' (274) and argues that this can be done via 'the language of gift'. See also: D.N. Power, 'Sacrament: An Economy of Gift', *Louvain Studies* 23 (1998) 143-158, in which he cautions, 'It may carry too much baggage from its use in human orders of friendship and society for us to easily grasp the meaning of what scripture and sacrament say of divine gift.' (152) In contrast to what he posits as the populist conception of gift, Power describes God's gift in the sacraments as 'gratuitous': 'There is no proper sense in which the Church gives anything back to God. It only acknowledges the gift given and lives out of it. It is relational, Trinitarian... This is not a responsibility to be met in "justice" nor an obligation to give back, but only a

only turns to language to better describe what a sacrament is about but, seemingly, to redeem language itself, to imply that in sacraments the limitations of language consequent on its mediatory role are, for a time, themselves overcome. Split no more.

What is implied by Power is stated explicitly by Catherine Pickstock, whose extraordinary inter-disciplinary approach to the Christian sacrament of the Eucharist concludes with the claim that only in the sacrament is there meaning. She specifies, however, that this is not the case for just any 'sacrament',[96] it is only to be realised through precise forms of rituality, specifically, sacrament as celebrated according to the texts of the Medieval Roman Rite.[97] Her conclusion is reached, like Power's, by a 'turn to language' resolved in the metaphor of gift. Pickstock diagnoses western philosophy's language regarding time as having fostered a damaged sense of relation to God and one another, but sees this resolved in 'the wholly *uninterrupted* character of gift' present in the liturgy of the Eucharist. Her project, however, does not share Power's repudiation of Aquinan onto-theological

---

freedom to go forth, to live out of the communion in love that is God-given.' (156) That being the case, why and how does he describe it as an '*economy* of gift': a 'commercium', an '*intercambio*', words that surely imply a 'relationality' of involvement. Can God actually give if we do not receive? As was seen with Schillebeeckx, if the hand is not shaken, the encounter is incomplete.

[96]   C. Pickstock, *After Writing: On the Liturgical Consummation of Philosophy* (Cambridge: Cambridge University Press, 1997). Her statement that, 'The gestures of modernity and post-modernity can be interpreted as the sacraments of an infinity of lack' raises a very interesting use of the word 'sacraments', particularly as Pickstock's agenda is to locate the resolution of human meaning solely in liturgical gestures. She evidently sees that the word sacrament has a referent outside of the scope of liturgical praxis. The quotation also supports her previous assertion that 'the post-modern theory of the sign is necrophiliac' (253), seeing the liturgical sacrament, 'The Eucharistic sign' as 'able to outwit the distinction between both absence and presence' which is quite a contrast to Chauvet's Heideggerian reconciliation of absence as merely the converse of presence and, thus, an embraceable aspect of an incarnational God rather than a block to God, which can be obliterated only by 'wit'.

[97]   Like other restorationists, Pickstock considers the Mediaeval Roman Rite as the ideal form of Eucharistic celebration. See likewise: A. Nichols, *Looking at the Liturgy: A Critical View of its Contemporary Forms* (San Francisco: Ignatius Press, 1996); D. Torevill, 'Forgetting How to Remember: Performance, Narrative and Embodiment as a Result of the Liturgical Reforms', *Irish Theological Quarterly* 65:1 (Spring 2000) 33-42. It is, however, ironic that those who argue against the reforms of Vatican II should praise instead a form of the Mass, the Order of Mass of St. Pius V, which was in its day a major experimental innovation. As Cabié comments, 'Pius V was a courageous innovator, and it is an almost unbelievable paradox that some should today be invoking his patronage to oppose a reform inspired by the same spirit as continued and brought to bear at the Second Vatican Council'. R.Cabié, *The Eucharist* (Collegeville, MN: Liturgical Press, 1986) 176.

foundations or, therefore, his concern to overcome metaphysics. What she seeks to overcome is 'pagan temporality'.[98]

In her version of a 'turn to language' she distances herself from the sort articulated above, which she deems 'post-modern'. Based on her textual criticism of the *Phaedrus*, she claims that Platonic philosophy, blamed by post-modernists for the damage inflicted by dualistic categories, has been misunderstood, because it itself 'radically challenged the beginnings of a technocratic... anti-corporeal, and homogenising society undergirded by secularity and pure immanence.'[99] The damage was done, she diagnoses, not by Plato but by Descartes, with whom theology was subtracted from ontology, leading the way for the tyranny of an essentially secular epistemology. The post-modern alternative characterised for her by Derrida, 'offers no new and critical politics beyond the *impasse* of commercialism into which modernism led us.'[100] The root of the problem, from Descartes to Derrida, writes Pickstock, has been:

> The systematic exaltation of writing over speech [which] has ensured within western history the spatial obliteration of time, which in seeking to secure an absolutely immune subjectivity, has instead denied any life to the human subject whatsoever... this project of textual spatialization is equally a suppression of eternity, since time can only be affirmed through the liturgical gesture which receives time from eternity as a gift and offers it back to eternity as a sacrifice.[101]

She continues, somewhat melodramatically, 'Hence the city which seeks to live only in spatial immanence is a *necropolis* defined by its refusal of liturgical life'.

Her almost Manichean appraisal of the culture which has borne her, her extremely questionable use of her sources[102] and her ultramontane conclusions[103] notwithstanding, Pickstock presents a profound challenge to sacramental theology's flirtation with the vocabulary of symbol and language as possessing any possibility of conveying the divine. Like her compatriots in radical orthodoxy, Pickstock issues a revisionist account of recent developments in the theology of the sacraments which alerts us to certain dangers: how sacramental theology can slip

---

[98] Ibid., 221. By which she seems to mean 'non-Christian' rather than genuinely Pagan.

[99] Ibid., 47-48.

[100] Ibid., 48.

[101] Ibid., 118.

[102] See: A. Nichols, 'Hymns Ancient and Postmodern: Catherine Pickstock's *After Writing*', *Communio* 26:2 (1999) 429-445.

[103] Perhaps the most pressing constraint of Pickstock's work is that she fails to say why other forms of Eucharistic prayer are not capable of giving the access to the transcendent that she perceives in that of Pius V. Why is it *only* in this form that meaning is resolved? If form conditions function to the extent that this claim implies, what of tradition: are we to conclude that Eucharists prior to 1570 and after 1965 have been ineffective, invalid or whatever word one would use to convey not-Eucharist? Moreover, if ontology finds its home at last in the Latin Mass, what of non-Catholics: are they condemned to exist in a permanently 'split' world, ever removed from divinity?

from Aquinas's insistence on sacraments as the locus and result of incarnation into a linguistic-analysis which locates the ultimate other as the transcendent, not as our suffering neighbour; and the fundamental schism in their work between liturgy and life, between the sacred and the profane, reflected in the very scant way in which these authors treat (Christian) ethics.

This is in stark contrast to the way in which ethics emerges as a pivotal concern in all the other works cited.[104] In fact, the way that the relationship between sacrament and ethics is explored can be seen as the second most significant development in contemporary sacramental theology, after the 'turn to language'. Rather than just being due to the *zeitgeist* however, this explicit attention to ethics has arisen as the direct result of the kind of language theory to which modern authors have turned.

Nearly all modern theology is, in a sense, an attempt to come to terms with the holocaust;[105] a struggle to persist despite the knowledge that theology played no small part in that atrocity. Out of this is born an awareness of the consequences of theory; an awareness that intrinsic to any interpretation or theory itself is the person or persons its conclusions affect, an awareness that it always affects someone; an awareness, if you like, that all discourse is political. In light of this, the pressing question for sacramental theology at the end of the twentieth century became, 'Why is there so little commitment when there is so much worship?'[106] Or, to put it another way, how can it be that people are celebrating the sacraments and yet outside the church building Christians are not acting as they should, that is, working for the establishment of communities of justice, equality and love? The question can be read both ways: if, like Rahner, you believe in the need to 'get life right' for liturgy to 'work' (i.e., living a Christian life is the pre-requisite for making a Christian sacrament[107]) then how can people be neglecting the former and yet enjoying the latter? Alternatively if, like Chauvet, you believe the sacraments have a potentially paranetic function (i.e., their symbolic power will auto-transform participants into the Christian body) then why is the 'result' of sacramental celebration not social action?

---

[104] See also: T. Sedgwick, *Sacramental Ethics: Paschal Identity and the Christian Life* (Philadelphia: Fortress Press, 1987).

[105] A small but influential constituency of which is based explicitly on direct experiences of Nazi Germany. In recent years both Moltmann and Metz have traced the roots of their theology to their traumatic wartime testimonies. Moltmann does so in the context of an argument for experience-based theology, see: J. Moltmann, *Experiences in Theology: Ways and Forms of Christian Theology* (London: SCM Press, 2000); Metz tells his own story as part of his appeal for a theology founded on narratives of suffering and hope: see: J.B. Metz, 'Communicating a Dangerous Memory' in F. Lawrence, ed., *Communicating a Dangerous Memory* (Atlanta: Scholars Press, 1987).

[106] R.A. Duffy, *Real Presence: Worship, Sacraments and Commitment* (San Francisco: Harper and Row, 1982) xii.

[107] K. Rahner, *The Church and the Sacraments* (New York: Herder and Herder, 1963).

Attached to the question is a strong sense of disappointment: many Catholic theologians, like Duffy, remembering the *aggiornamento* of the Second Vatican Council, cannot understand why the widespread reform it introduced did not 'translate' into the kind of societal reform the gospels demand, nor why liturgical participation actually seemed to lessen socio-political orientation on the part of participants after, compared to before, the reforms.[108] At the heart of this disappointment, which is shared by many beyond the Catholic church, lies a dualism that has remained largely unaffected by Heideggerian reconstructionist dynamics, that of Liturgy versus Life. 'Liturgy' and 'Life' are seen are seen as two related, but separate, spheres. This dualism arises as the result of a more fundamental and persistent one, the very one Rahner was earlier reported as seeking to address: Sacred versus Profane, wherein the role of the sacraments is conceived as offering a momentary mediation between the two.

And so the question of method returns us to the question of access, and the suggestion that it must be via an emphasis on ethics, on the sacramentality of the whole of Christian life, that worship gains its sacramental meaning. Adopting the hermeneutic tools of Ricoeur, Joyce Ann Zimmerman argues that it is possible to overcome the established methodological framework that has restricted the application of liturgy to life (or indeed *vice versa*). By 'investigating the Paschal Mystery as concretised in the deep structures of its Christian ritual forms' she claims we can elucidate 'the meaning of Christian liturgy [which] is synonymous with the meaning of Christian living.'[109]

Drawing on Ricoeur's idea of the text as a document of life, she proposes that 'Liturgy is a document of Christian living. Since liturgy functions like a text, it is more readily available as an object for interpretation at the analytic moment of distanciation than is the whole of Christian living.'[110] Two issues seem unresolved

---

[108] See for example: M. Hellwig, 'Twenty-five Years of a Wakening Church: Liturgy and Ecclesiology'; and R.R. Gaillardetz, 'North American Culture and The Liturgical Life of the Church' in L.J. Madden, ed., *The Awakening Church: Twenty-five Years of Liturgical Renewal* (Collegeville, MN: Liturgical Press, 1992). This extraordinary undertaking, where the data from a survey of fifteen Vatican II-embracing parishes around the USA were analysed by a host of systematic and liturgical theologians, sociologists and ritual critics, testifies to the failure 'to connect' liturgy and life in, for example, Hellwig's remark that 'There still seems to be the sense that liturgical worship is the real business of the church and that healing, reconciliation and the service of practical human needs in all their forms are optional additions for those with that particular character or charism' (Ibid, 66); and also in the social ethicist Peter Henriot's observation that in the colloquium itself, 'There is a disturbing absence of attention ...to the link between liturgy and social concerns.' P.J. Henriot, 'Liturgy and Social Concerns' in Ibid., 117.

[109] J.A. Zimmerman, *Liturgy as Living Faith: A Liturgical Spirituality* (Scranton: University of Scranton Press, 1993) viii.

[110] Ibid., 137, note 2.

in this approach, the first regards access: how are we to 'read' this text?[111] The second arises from her confidence that liturgy is the text of Christian living: for many Christians this may be so, but for many others (as Susan Ross alerted us earlier) it is not. Either way, by seeking to elide either aspect of the dualism in a conclusion of 'synonymous meaning', the question arises of why Zimmerman did not conclude that all life *is* liturgy? Surely Ricoeur would point out that identicality of 'meaning' witnessed identicality of subject.

Nevertheless, Zimmerman's determination to address 'The methodological questions that take us beyond *demonstration of* the relationship of liturgy and life [to] ... an *ontological rationale for* such a relationship'[112] highlights the difficulty of proposing a 'liturgical spirituality' while ontology persists in staving off sacred from profane at such a profound level. Levinas's influence in the theological, ethically-motivated attempt to bridge the gap between sacred and profane can be seen in the work of several of the above authors. As Power comments, his 'key insight... is that the ethical is actually the first step in philosophy.'[113] By putting the 'Other' centre stage, as focus and test of his theory, Levinas glimpses for theology a way of making a direct identification between the 'sacred' other and the 'profane' other which, in the process, negates those categories. Chauvet comments:

> None have struggled more vigorously than E. Levinas to liberate themselves from the Greek *logos* and to challenge the Greek tradition from the viewpoint of the Jewish; that is, to challenge Being (impersonal, anonymous, violent reducer of otherness to the totality of the same) with the Other (pure eruption and rupture bursting through the 'Face', the unifying pretensions and the ultimately totalitarian essence of the Greek *logos*).[114]

But, as Richard Kearney intimates, in a post-modern climate, simply privileging the other does not necessarily lead to treating her or him according to an acceptable ethical norm. 'The Other' may inevitably remind a Jewish philosopher (like Levinas) of the demand of justice, because he or she will be steeped in their faith's covenantal demands of justice and compassion. The dilemma for ethics in post-modern society is, 'How to do justice to the other if... there is no universal concept of right or regulation to guide our interpretations?'[115]

---

[111] From the written, prescribed texts, the orders of service, in which case we face the criticism that liturgy is a dynamic reality not a written sourcebook; or from observation, in which case we share the problems encountered by anthropologists: the dilemma of the apparent impossibility of accessing what others are experiencing, which will be examined in Chapter Two.

[112] Ibid., 141.

[113] Power, *Sacrament: Language of God's Giving*, 272.

[114] Chauvet, *Symbol and Sacrament*, 46.

[115] Kearney, *Poetics of Imagining*, 211. Kearney's view is, however, challenged by the use made later in this study of Habermas's notion of the ideal speech situation, a concept

The question is no less acute for Christians, and echoes Duffy's original question, rephrased as: why, when the social justice-oriented imperative lived out in Christ's life, represented in the enactment of his death and resurrection in the sacraments, is enacted by people in their own language and in their own communities, do Christians nevertheless persist in creating and supporting societies of extraordinary iniquity and injustice?[116] Although most commentators place great emphasis on the intrinsic connection of sacrament and ethics, few have responses to this question.

The responses that have been offered invariably blame liturgy itself, claiming it is being done poorly. Some Catholics say Vatican II messed everything up and the solution lies in a return to the Latin Mass. Others say the problem arises because the various recent liturgical reforms in many denominations have not been implemented fully enough. A minority of others argue that we need to develop new forms of worship altogether. Aidan Kavanagh, whose scathing criticism of the worship of 'middle class' communities would fall into the first category,[117] articulates one of the real problems this question exposes: a 'middle class' starting-point for doing theology. It is also, as will be reported below, a non-feminist starting-point. Duffy's question reflects the concerns of mostly white theologians looking at North Atlantic[118] middle class parishes; for communities of people oppressed, the issue of 'sacrament ethics' has been framed in a very different way.

Writing in collaboration with his Uruguayan co-workers, Segundo argues:

> If the sacraments are to contribute to the creation of a community that signifies or makes transparent a message, then it is necessary that the commitment which they presuppose be accepted with the full burden of its visibility - but also with the full functionality of a message that is to be transmitted in its complete and perfect sense. In no case should it be transmitted as a divine judgement on persons.[119]

So not only must celebration of the sacraments make transparent the ethical commitments necessary to give a Christian message, they must do so in a way that accords with those commitments (rather than in a way that asserts the criteria of

---

that insists that speakers and hearers do indeed negotiate (and thus share) ethical values by virtue of the nature of language exchange. See below: 125-133.

[116] For an early treatment of this question see: M. Hellwig, *The Eucharist and the Hunger of the World* (New York: Paulist Press, 1976).

[117] See: A. Kavanagh, *On Liturgical Theology* (New York: Pueblo, 1984) 1-69. Although one of the constraints of Kavanagh's work is the lack of investigation into *why* such a seemingly abominable form of worship should have been created.

[118] The phrase 'North Atlantic' is used as a shorthand reference to northern European (British, Irish, French, German and Scandinavian) academies as well as to those whose dominant cultural historicity is in direct continuum with them: principally, the U.S.A.

[119] Segundo, *The Sacraments Today*, 85.

divine authority). Another of the early liberation theologians,[120] Tissa Balasuriya, discerns that 'the main problem [is] that the whole Mass is still a bulwark of social conservatism and not yet a means of human liberation.'[121] Underlying both quotations is a consciousness that the oppression that the authors' communities experience in society is reinforced, rather than challenged, by the sacraments of the church.

The fact that most sacramental theology is written from a white, middle-class, North Atlantic perspective may account for its tendency to be oblivious to a sacrament's ability to exclude, alienate and oppress. By focusing on the liturgies of marginal communities, in Chapters Five and Six, this study attempts to answer the criticism made by these marginalised theologians while also testing the suggestion (and challenging the idealisations) made by nearly all liturgical theologians that it is indeed at the 'margins' of the church that sacramentality is most authentically expressed.

The kinds of oppression these liberation theologians have named concern social, economic and racial discrimination. However, they neglected to address the injustices meted to women.[122] Susan Ross draws a parallel between the *Mujerista* perspective and her own, arguing that 'a critical focus on sacraments and justice needs to be attentive to injustice's multiple facets, particularly gender.'[123] She points out that the *Mujerista* theologians discovered that, as a remedy to their previous denial as part of liberationist liturgies, one cannot simply 'add women and stir', inserting women's experiences and stories into an existing ritual form, for 'when women's experiences are incorporated consciously into worship, they do not simply add on to it but also transform it.'[124] Ross thus notes that the consequence of the extraordinary changes apparent in liturgy when it does include women's experience inevitably also changes the very 'definition' of sacrament.

What is clear in these liberation and feminist sacramental theologies is an acknowledgement that the doctrinal category 'sacrament' as it is presently constructed is actually incompatible with the doctrinal desire that it serve an ethic of justice. While theologians may write about the sacraments as 'ethical heuristics',[125] these liberationist and feminist authors witness to the fact that in practice they can serve to oppress. They intimate that this has something to do with the theological definition of 'sacrament' itself. Thus Leonardo Boff comments:

---

[120] Interestingly, nearly all the original Latin and Black liberation theologies were based on biblical analysis; the feminist and later womanist and *Mujerista* ones have been based also on experience, including, in a privileged way, the experience of worship.

[121] T. Balasuriya, *The Eucharist and Human Liberation* (Maryknoll: Orbis Books, 1979) 8.

[122] See, for example: A.M. Isasi-Díaz, '*Mujerista* Liturgies and the Struggle for Liberation' in L.M. Chauvet and F.K. Lumbala, eds., *Liturgy and the Body* (London: SCM Press, 1995).

[123] Ross, *Extravagant Affections*, 177.

[124] Ibid.

[125] The phrase is Power's: *Sacrament: The Language of God's Giving*, 53.

> The sacraments are not the private property of the sacred hierarchy. They are basic constituents of human life. Faith sees grace present in the most elementary acts of life. So it ritualises them and elevates them to the sacramental level.[126] Today's Christians must be educated to see sacraments above and beyond the confines of the seven sacraments. As adults they should know how to enact rites that signify and celebrate the breakthrough of grace into their lives and communities.[127]

Similarly for Ross, what is evidenced in women's 'ambiguous' relationships with the sacraments is the emergence of a sacramental theology characterised by:

> An extension of the 'sacramental moment' beyond the moment of actual canonical reception ... [which] means a greater continuity between ritual and everyday life.[128] Feminist theology stresses the ambiguity of sacramentality ... [it] seeks a sacramentality that is grounded both in the lived experiences of women and men, and in the example of Jesus.[129]

However, neither propose that we rename any other human ritual as one of the sacraments, nor do either propose that we cease referring to the Catholic seven as 'the' sacraments (indeed they continue to do so and to expect that we know to what they are referring). Indeed, the notion of sacramentality they both advocate is still based on 'the sacraments': it still has hierarchical overtones, the 'real' sacraments being worthy of the full title, sacrament; the other life rituals and experiences being very important yes, but only 'sacramental' i.e.: *like* a sacrament. One still seems to derive its (referential) power from the other.

Nevertheless, whether employing a criteria of liberation or a metaphor of ambiguity, at the very core of any proposed redefinition of sacrament in sacramental theology, just as at the core of the non-feminist 'middle class' arguments for the irreducibility of the sacraments' ethical objective, are two constants: Christ and the church. Nearly all contemporary commentators within the field a) retain the idea of Christ and therefore church as the 'primordial' sacrament and b) have recently concentrated on explicating this in terms of a post-modernist poetics of the body. Typically, Margaret Mary Kelleher notes that: 'The purpose of the sacraments, as articulated by the Second Vatican Council is to sanctify persons, build up the Body of Christ, and give worship to God. They are presented as sacraments of faith which confer grace and effectively dispose the faithful to receive this grace.'[130] Combining this with Congar's remark that the Council had restored the *ecclesia* as the subject of liturgical action, Kelleher is left with the

---

[126] L. Boff, *Sacraments of Life, Life of the Sacraments* (Beltsville: The Pastoral Press, 1987) 7.

[127] Ibid., 5

[128] Ross, *Extravagant Affections*, 75.

[129] Ibid., 51.

[130] M.M. Kelleher, 'Sacraments as the Ecclesial Mediations of Grace', *Louvain Studies* 23 (1998) 180.

question, 'How can one understand the assembly as acting subject in the sacraments?'[131]

Criticising Chauvet for focusing on the verbal at the expense of the non-verbal aspects of ritual, she proposes that the type of interplay that occurs in the sacraments is, because of its bodily form (body of God, bodies of humans), capable of going beyond the limits of ordinary conversation. However, like Chauvet, Kelleher perceives that because of their *rituality*, a context that she sees as privileging the human capacity for holistic interaction, the sacraments can 'mediate the flow of the river of grace' such that 'the church gives birth to the church'.[132] The Church, then, is not a fixed entity but rather contingent on the sacramental calling to presence, birthing itself through the actual celebration of the sacraments.[133]

The foundation of Kelleher's synthesis is Vatican II's reconceptualisation of the sacraments as liturgical *actions*, a revision that has prompted a wide-scale turn to social scientific studies of ritual. Attention to human ritual action as a peculiar category of human behaviour is, then, a major part of the question of method. In the hands of sacramental theologians it becomes a foray into the human sciences and a 'borrowing' of a selection of apt anthropological conclusions (as seen in Kelleher's use of Victor Turner in forming her ecclesiology via worship). There are two important issues at stake here: whether and how theology should consult the social sciences; and the allied question of ritual theory, of how one mounts a theoretical presentation of a multi-faceted interaction, of how one puts people to paper. The implications of this trend for contemporary theology will be discussed below, while the following chapter will take up the issues identified above, looking in depth at the ritual theory on which theologians, such as Kelleher, increasingly draw.

Chauvet and Power's major contribution in this field is their recognition that a) sacraments are not objects, but events; b) the type of event they are is ritual[134] and c) theology has to find a way of engaging with them at this level. Their accounts nevertheless suffer from their almost exclusive reliance on the type of anthropology that defines 'what ritual does', rather than also considering those

---

[131] Ibid.

[132] Ibid.

[133] There are three main constraints in Kelleher's thesis: 1) it is based on the equality of acting subjects and this is questionable given the perception of clerical (and other forms of) power in many congregations; 2) Kelleher uses Turner as authoritative without considering his critics; and most importantly, 3) feminist authors have denied that, when they are alienated from liturgy by its language, forms, and in some cases leadership, they can be part of this birthing. These issues will be addressed further in Chapter Four.

[134] This is not to imply they were the first to draw attention to the theologian's need of a better understanding of the nature of ritual. Early advocates were Odo Casel and Romano Guardini (see bibliography); the issue entered the mainstream with Aidan Kavanagh.

ritual critics who question whether in fact it 'does' anything at all. So when Power writes:

> Sacraments have rites, indeed in some sense take place wholly within a ritual context, but they are not reducible to rites, and indeed are always in a situation in which the word proclaimed, the memory kept, the divine gift offered are 'crossing out' ritual sedimentations, as one crosses out something in a written codex by overwriting it,[135]

he is exhibiting a very sure and conservative view of what a ritual is, rather than reflecting the consciousness of inaccessibilities and paradoxes that inform much of contemporary ritual studies. Likewise Chauvet's anthropological assertion that ritual's primary function is to institute identity is stated without mention of those other studies that deny that this is necessarily a function of ritual at all, never mind its main one (such as Staal or Bell, whose work is considered in Chapter Two).

Chauvet and Power are only exhibiting the limits of the genre in which they have been trained to conduct scholarship, systematic theology. If, in the wake of Vatican II, sacraments are to be conceived as actions rather than articles of faith, if they are to be considered primarily as liturgical events, then the sort of argumentative discourse that has traditionally engendered the construction of sacramental theology is profoundly inhibited, if not redundant.

Almost all contemporary sacramental theologians acknowledge that the context in which the sacraments must now be studied is the actual liturgy of the church. Power, for example, writes: 'Even when attention to the process of interpretation distances the thinking from the act of celebration, thinking begins with celebration, is referred back to celebration, and loses itself again in the wonder of celebration... Celebration is itself a hermeneutic.'[136] And, as if to demonstrate the universal acceptance of this approach, he notes that even those post-modernists (most notably Millbank) who do not reject the language of being, nevertheless nowadays agree that 'theological discourse must find its peace in doxology'.[137] Yet neither Power nor Chauvet, neither Ross nor Sedgwick, actually describe a full worship service at the beginning, middle or end of their work. If their work 'found its peace in doxology', it did so beyond the pages they systematically composed.

The most profound development in writing about the sacraments in the past thirty years has not been the development of Schillebeeckx's modernist reconceptualisation of encounter between human/divine subjects, nor Chauvet's post-modernist attempt to overcome the subjective/objective impasse bequeathed him by metaphysics; neither has it been the appropriation of linguistic philosophy nor the intellectual promulgation of ethics. It has been the methodological paradigm shift from sacramental to liturgical theology, the claim that 'Liturgy is the

---

[135] Power, *Sacrament: The Language of God's Giving*, 38.
[136] Ibid.
[137] Ibid.

ontological condition for doing theology',[138] examination of which will occupy the remainder of this chapter.

Shifting the study of sacrament from systematic argumentation to liturgical interpretation has two immediate effects: a) to make theology engage with divine-human relations (and thus the question of God) at the level of experience (as opposed to that of proof, designation or speculation); and consequently: b) to allow the voices of women and others long omitted from the construction of theology regarding sacrament to be heard.[139]

Gordon Lathrop describes the first shift by crediting the way in which theology can no longer be understood to operate at only one 'level', discerning three levels on which theology in the current climate is being expressed: primary, secondary and pastoral. 'The liturgy itself is *primary* theology... *secondary* liturgical theology is written and spoken discourse that attempts to find words for the experience of the liturgy and to illuminate its structures;'[140] and when this attempt to find words is focused on 'specific problems of our time, these reflections may be called *pastoral liturgical theology.*'[141] This is in contrast to the conventional view of theology wherein belief, understood as a response to doctrine and tradition, was posited as primary, and liturgy was construed as the practical 'expression' of those beliefs.[142]

---

[138] This famous phrase comes from the original title of liturgical theology: A. Schmemann, *Introduction to Liturgical Theology* (Crestwood, NJ: St Vladimir's Seminary Press, 1966).

[139] Not because of the simplistic prejudice that women can only talk at the level of experience (millions are as well trained as men in the conventional ways of the academy), but because women have been saying for years that the authentic starting point for theological reflection ought to be experience; and the pioneers in this field have developed models for such exploration. See, for example: V. Fabella, and M.A. Oduyoye, eds., *Third World Women Doing Theology* (Maryknoll: Orbis Books, 1988); P.M. Cooey, W.R. Eakin, and J.B. McDaniel, eds., *After Patriarchy: Feminist Transformation of the World Religions* (Maryknoll: Orbis Books, 1990); M. Procter-Smith, *Praying with Our Eyes Open: Engendering Feminist Liturgical Prayer* (Nashville: Abingdon Press, 1995).

[140] G. Lathrop, *Holy Things: A Liturgical Theology* (Minneapolis: Fortress Press, 1993) 5, 7.

[141] Ibid., 7.

[142] Sedgwick suggests it is a question of starting-point and notes that, 'The problem... in beginning with either [scripture or tradition] is that they already presuppose the experience of faith and a community of faith.' *Sacramental Ethics*, 14. Geoffrey Wainwright, who did much pioneering work in theology's early days of taking seriously a starting-point in worship (see his 'systematic theology of worship': *Doxology: The Praise of God in Worship, Doctrine and Life* (New York: Oxford University Press, 1980)) has been criticised in recent times for maintaining the belief that there is 'a set of beliefs which undergird worship' such that *lex orandi lex credendi* is reversed (see Sedgwick, *Sacramental Ethics*, 49). For a fuller debate, see the responses to Wainwright at the North American Academy of Liturgy detailed in *Worship* 57:4 (July 1983) 290-332; and the recent *festschrift* in his honour: D.S. Cunningham, R. Del Colle and

Yet Lathrop objects to the idea that such an approach is 'conventional', arguing that his own view is the more conventional, founded as it is on the fifth century maxim ascribed to Prosper of Aquitaine, *Lex orandi, lex credendi*. In his commentary on this phrase,[143] Aidan Kavanagh emphasises its foundational perspective: worship founds belief, he argues, in the same way that foundations do a house or the virtue of the justice founds the law. Kavanagh traces the loss of such a perspective to the debates of the Middle Ages,[144] the product of which in both Catholic and Reformer camps was, 'a secondary theology... now determining rather than interpreting text and form'.[145] What subsequently emerged as the normative foundation of theology was 'a notion of *orthodoxia* not as a sustained life of "right worship" but as "correct doctrine", to be maintained by a centralised ecclesiastical authority.'[146] Doctrine had come to define worship instead of *vice versa*. Liturgy had become a matter of law, and thus to this day, the opposite of orthodoxy ('right worship') is understood to be heresy ('wrong opinion') rather than, more correctly, heterodoxy ('wrong worship').

However, as Kavanagh continues, 'There was more afoot in the sixteenth century than some disagreements over justification, the real presence of Christ in the Eucharist, and papal primacy. A sense of rite and symbol was breaking down and under siege.'[147] What transpired, according to Kavanagh, was 'a new system of worship... in which printed texts would increasingly bear the burden formerly borne by richly ambiguous corporate actions, involving water, oil, food and the touch of human hands'.[148] Theology became the study of those printed texts. By the end of the twentieth century though, awareness was growing among liturgical theologians that, to use the metaphor David Fagerberg borrows from Wittgenstein, you can know the name of a chess piece, but that is not the same as knowing its moves. Fagerberg argues that theology had to strive to overcome its long latent dichotomy between worship and theology wherein 'theology exists for academicians and liturgy exists for pure-hearted (but simple-minded) believers.'[149]

Echoing the question with which this chapter began, if one wants to know not just the name of the piece but also its moves, where does one look; whom does one ask? Fagerberg, influenced by Alexander Schmemann, proposes, 'Liturgical

---

L. Lamadrid, eds., *Ecumenical Theology in Worship, Doctrine and Life: Essays Presented to Geoffrey Wainwright on his Sixtieth Birthday* (Oxford: Oxford University Press, 1999).

[143] Or, *'legem credendi statuat lex supplicandi.'* For an alternative interpretation, see: K. Irwin, *Liturgical Theology: A Primer* (Collegeville, MN: Liturgical Press, 1990).

[144] Typified in the English Act of Uniformity, 1549 (the product of which was the Book of Common Prayer) and the Council of Trent in 1614.

[145] A. Kavanagh, *On Liturgical Theology* (New York: Pueblo, 1984) 80.

[146] Ibid., 81.

[147] Kavanagh, *On Liturgical Theology*, 108.

[148] Ibid.

[149] D.W. Fagerberg, *What is Liturgical Theology? A Study in Methodology* (Collegeville, MN: Liturgical Press, 1992) 13.

theology is principally what is transacted in historic liturgical rites and secondarily that which can be uncovered by structural analysis of those rites.'[150] Similarly, Robert Taft makes the question of 'where to look' the centre of his study and proposes that, as with literary theory, it is not adequate to look merely at the vocabulary of a text; one has to examine the syntax. Moving on from this comparison of liturgy to a text, he concludes that one has to seek out the structural forms of a liturgy for, he says, 'In the history of liturgical development, structure outlives meaning'.[151] Two issues, however, prevent this from providing a satisfactory answer to the question: Taft negates the possibility that the structure itself is 'meaning'-ful and this greatly limits possible interpretation of it; and because it is performed in an historical mode, structural analysis of liturgy as Taft proposes it returns the debate to texts alone as the objects of study.

This is the difficulty facing liturgical theology: if the subject of its reflections is to extend beyond the written texts of worship, *how* are these other aspects to be studied? How is theology to develop the sort of rigour in its interpretation of experience that it depends upon in its interpretation of texts? How is a scholar to say, so and so did this with the oil and this is what it meant to them? Whether or not 'meaning' is that which should concern us anyway is a matter of some controversy, and will be discussed in the following chapter. The crucial question at this stage is how liturgy is to be accessed, if not by its texts.

Kevin Irwin advocates a methodology which will go beyond the text, which privileges context as source, or text, for liturgical theology:

> Our thesis is that for an adequate liturgical theology one must examine the component parts of liturgical rites - texts, symbols, actions and gestures - both in relation to each other and also in light of the times and places when and where communities were or are engaged in these rites... This is to assert that liturgical rites are only adequately understood and interpreted theologically in relation to their experienced context.[152]

However, while establishing that this is a viable alternative to the argumentative theology he sees as having been inadequate to theology's task, he too neglects to say *how* this content is to be examined. He delineates the scope of his thesis by listing what he does not intend to address, and this includes, 'The formulation of a precise method derived from the social sciences for interpreting and evaluating liturgical performance... and how to assess the liturgical assembly's engagement in both liturgy and in developing theology derived from it.'[153] No-one else has addressed these either. What exists in the body of liturgical theology as it currently stands is a great deal of passion, an extraordinary change in optic lens, profound

---

[150] Ibid., 9.

[151] See: Kavanagh, *On Liturgical Theology*, 80.

[152] K. Irwin, *Context and Text: Method in Liturgical Theology* (Collegeville, MN: Liturgical Press, 1994) 54.

[153] Ibid., xii.

insight and endless assertion. How can Irwin maintain that theology's foundation has to be *experience*, yet decline to address the fact that experience is notoriously difficult to access in written discourse?

This, the question of access, is the most pressing unanswered question of sacramental and liturgical theology.[154] A scholar can write on the basis of what she experiences as a participant, sharing her own personal reactions, feelings and thoughts. She can do this collaboratively and extrapolate points of empathy and tension between various accounts. But how can she, as a scholar, understand what others have experienced in liturgy? How is she to access the very subject of her discourse?

Can she, for example, write about a liturgy she has not attended? Can she write about liturgy in a general way, or does she have to restrict her remarks to her own particular reflections on her experiences at this specific ritual with this specific community on this particular day? Lathrop attempts to overcome the problem this obviously presents by asking whether there is not a 'core' to Christian liturgy which is shared by all Christians.[155] He discerns that in the 'pattern' of worship among Christian assemblies there are certain 'shared central things' and he names these the '*ordo*' of Christian faith practice:

> Common to the different churches is the deepest structure of the *ordo* of Christian worship, the received and universal pattern or shape and scheduling of Christian liturgy. This *ordo* organises a participating community together with its ministers gathered in song and prayer around Scriptures read and preached, around the baptismal washing, enacted or remembered, and around the Holy Supper.[156]

Crucial to Lathrop's perception of this pattern is the twin discernment that the 'elements' of the *ordo* only function by virtue of their mutual 'juxtaposition': 'meeting and week, word and table, thanksgiving and beseeching, teaching and bath, pascha and year.'[157] Because, he explains, 'even the bath and the meal have needed to be set next to the Word of Christ, to be transformed by it, in order for us to see how great is God's gift of grace on, in and under materials drawn from human nature.'[158] This represents a potentially phenomenal alteration in the study of the sacraments: following Lathrop's schema, the 'words of institution' are

---

[154] Apart from obliquely in Irwin's saying what he was not going to regard, the question of access has not been raised so far in the main works of the discipline.

[155] In this he extends one of the most positive forces unleashed by this new form of theologising: a liturgical approach to ecumenism which holds the seeds of greatly improved inter-denominational practice and understanding. Geoffrey Wainwright has been a pioneer in this area too; see: G. Wainwright, *Worship with One Accord: Where Liturgy and Ecumenism Meet* (Oxford: Oxford University Press, 1997).

[156] G. Lathrop, *Holy People: A Liturgical Ecclesiology* (Minneapolis: Augsburg/Fortress Press, 1999) 106-107.

[157] Lathrop, *Holy Things*, 179.

[158] Lathrop, *Holy People*, 204.

impossible without their juxtaposition with (for example) baptism, the sermon is impossible unless it is seen alongside (for example) its location in the 'non-time' of the Sabbath. The shift is so tremendous because it articulates something that has been implicit for a long time: sacraments are whole liturgies, not pure, special, technical moments within and discrete from the 'moment' that is the liturgy as a whole.

Lathrop also sees in a discernment of the juxtapositions of the *ordo* a response to the earlier-stated question of the intrinsic connection between the sacraments and social ethics.[159] This is because the juxtapositions that make up the liturgy place a tension on ritual itself and, 'The world that is thereby created is not the status quo, but an alternative vision that waits for God, hopes for a wider order... than any ritual can embody.'[160] All liturgy has to be doing to ensure that it remains a 'force for critique' of society, Lathrop proposes, is 'simply and faithfully following the *ordo*'.[161] Faithfully following the *ordo* guarantees 'biblical grounding, universal acceptance, local exercise and the widespread trust that [gatherings] are under God's approval.'[162] Yet the problem with such an approach, apart from the fact it still has not addressed the thorny issue of how we access the *ordo* in the first place, is that it construes 'tradition' as a guarantor rather than a guide, a Rule rather than a platform. This has serious consequences for the manner in which liturgical theology addresses issues of validity and authority, and these are considered in depth in Chapter Five.[163]

The above authors exhibit an essentially fundamentalist, conservative agenda based on a belief that 'faithfully following the *ordo*' is the correct way to relate to God in liturgy. It is necessary at this point, therefore, to justify my contention that this theological shift, major as it is in terms of speculative methodology, can amplify the voices of Christian feminists vis-à-vis sacrament – voices that are usually sidelined as 'feminist theology' rather than being seen for what they are: valid and, in some cases, prophetic sacramental theologies. First of all, it must be emphasised that there are feminist authors who also believe that faithfully following the *ordo* is the appropriate attitude for worship, but who advocate that the language employed in this task must not be sexist and its leadership roles must be open to women as well as men. Gail Ramshaw is one such theologian and she comments:

---

[159] As the title of his book suggests, Sedgwick is concerned to emphasise that a move to liturgical theology in no way limits theology's central ethical concerns: 'While worship offers a privileged point of entry into the Christian life, it is not insular.' *Sacramental Ethics*, 15.

[160] Lathrop, *Holy Things*, 210.

[161] Ibid., 212.

[162] Ibid., 106.

[163] In its attempt to be ecumenical, it becomes overly reductionist.

In some churches the liturgy is particularly cruel for women. I am amazed at how many women remain in churches where they are not allowed to preside or preach, where God is unremittingly termed Father and King and He, where texts call the human community 'man', where Eve is blamed for sin. I wish the women in these churches well: I would be out of there, for I would not tolerate the cognitive dissonance between the myth I accept and the myth these rituals enact. As you might guess, I choose carefully which church I attend.[164]

For Ramshaw then, a church may have the meal, the bath, the sabbath and the word, but if these are juxtaposed with language, doctrine and ecclesial roles that alienate women, they are not acceptable. Ramshaw has, in response, undertaken pioneering work in the area of liturgical language, in an attempt to show how the male naming of God and community can be modified and greatly enriched by a fuller receptivity to the metaphors of (particularly biblical) Christian sources. She does not seek to replace male terms with female ones; rather she establishes principles on the basis of which worshipping communities might develop their own vocabulary, principles of metaphor and inclusivity.[165] Her proposals are based on the argument that the sexist language of the *ordo* was originally conceived as inclusive (to work for *all* the faithful) and metaphoric (under the awareness that all language for God is partial and ultimately inadequate); the language became rigid and exclusive over time because its meanings were confined by both clergy and laity: 'Current examination of the androcentric language in liturgy has demonstrated that "Father" and "Son" terminology has been both misunderstood by the faithful and mis-taught by the Church's teachers.'[166]

Seeing the Trinity as the central, essential, metaphor of Christian engagement, Ramshaw concentrates on its articulation:

The One is about transcendence, about being beyond the universe... The Two is about incarnation... Transcendence transforms human life. The Three is about communion, the bonded circle that animates, the shared life without which existence is meaningless. The Three affirms that the future of the One and Two is in us all... Because of the Third, the deity is part of the I-who-I-are. Because of the Second, I see in Jesus the I Am. Because of the First, I am not the ultimate I. We strive to say it better.[167]

Other feminist Christians, in striving to say it better, do advocate the use of feminine-explicit language. Marjorie Procter-Smith argues that androcentric metaphors are so much a part of our collective psyche that it will only be by using explicitly feminist alternatives that we will root out our deep-seated attachment to

---

[164] G. Ramshaw, *Under the Tree of Life: The Religion of a Christian Feminist* (New York: Continuum, 1998) 91.

[165] See G. Ramshaw, *Liturgical Language: Making it Metaphoric, Keeping it Inclusive* (Collegeville, MN: Liturgical Press, 1996).

[166] Ibid., 38-39.

[167] Ibid., 52.

the male ones.[168] Gender neutral language (or gender equable, for example, using 'mother' alongside 'father') she argues, does not have the power to actually *undo* the language of patriarchy, it just proposes a parallel. Moreover, Procter-Smith's striving is not merely to say it better, but to insist on the possibility of a radically altered notion of 'it'. Her project is in surprising contrast to the majority of feminist Christians authors who, although keen to be more open to the language born of their authentic, non-patriarchal, relations with God nevertheless still predicate Trinity as the normative metaphor of Christian faith and practice.[169] Are 'normative' metaphors necessary? It is apparent that, as with the issue of the *ordo*, even some within this liberation-oriented discourse have construed their conclusions in terms of authority and Rule rather than openness to the other of faith.

Ramshaw's comment that she would be out of a sexist church as fast as she could is also deeply offensive to those who do not share the privilege of her choices. In many parts of the world only one Christian church is on offer. In other parts, there may be a choice of denominations, but its language and leadership are equally sexist. In others, the language and leadership may be male but women believe that the 'underlying message' is neither male nor female and a twin sense of loyalty and personal identity would prevent them from abandoning the community which has long supported them. In yet others, like the part of the world in which Ramshaw resides, there may be the 'choice' of a community reformed along the lines she advocates but from which women may yet be alienated, because for some women even the forms of Christian worship, its structures, the very *ordo* Lathrop identified, are themselves androcentric and therefore limiting to women's authentic encounters with God.[170]

In common to the various feminist approaches outlined above, Mary Collins still discerns a 'feminist hermeneutic for reinterpreting redeemed and redemptive relationships' the key characteristic of which is that it 'centres on

---

[168] M. Procter-Smith, *In Her Own Rite: Constructing Feminist Liturgical Tradition* (Nashville: Abingdon Press, 1990).

[169] See: R.C. Duck and P. Wilson-Kastner, *Praising God: The Trinity in Christian Worship* (Louisville: Westminster John Knox, 1999). The desire to emphasise the centrality of Trinity in feminist discourse has warranted a special research group of the American Academy of Religion, of which Duck and Ramshaw are members. E.A. Johnson and C.M. LaCugna did pioneering work in this field (feminist interpretations of Trinity) although not from an overtly liturgical starting-point. See bibliography.

[170] Procter-Smith discerns three main 'approaches' within the feminist liturgical movement, all of which have to be represented in a study of Christian feminist worship: 'remaining within a patriarchal tradition, rejecting patriarchal authority while claiming traditional identity, or moving to another religious context altogether.' M. Procter-Smith and J.R. Walton, eds., *Women at Worship: Interpretations of North American Diversity* (Louisville: Westminster John Knox, 1993) 2.

women's experience'.[171] But, Collins asks, is the ritualizing of these experiences in their not-necessarily *ordo*-based forms really worthy of the name 'liturgy'? Do the experimental and improvisational character of these events locate them beyond the pale of liturgical theology, as suggested by the 'many classical liturgical authorities'[172] who have objected to these feminists tail-gating the word for their rites? These critics, Collins reports, 'celebrate a "right way" of being and doing, a way understood to be in harmony with a divinely revealed design'[173] and women calling their rituals 'feminist liturgy' is profoundly disturbing to them. Collins, however, uses the work of ritual theorist Catherine Bell to suggest that, contrary to the beliefs of so-called liturgical authorities, feminist ritualisers display no less a degree of continuity than their patriarchal counterparts, using ritual strategies that 'produce the past in such a way as to maximise its dominance of the present'.[174]

Implied in the criticism to which Collins refers is a deep-seated concern to preserve the universality of the church, to oppose movements that would otherwise provoke schism. While there may be such factions in the worldwide community of Christians, feminist liturgists do not recognise this among their goals; on the contrary, as Janet Walton points out: 'Feminist liturgy is ultimately not just for women, but for all people... [Its] primary goal... is to draw together *all* aspects of our relationships in ritual contexts that promote truth-telling [that is]... rooted in a dialogue between the realities of history and the expectations and potential of liturgy.'[175] The central part of Walton's book contains narrative accounts of various feminist worship services, at the end of each of which she asks what about them was 'feminist liturgy', and at the end of the book she suggests how these learnings might be applied to mainstream church worship.

None of the stories about liturgy that she tells are recognisable as what normally goes on in mainstream church worship and she is aware that they therefore 'may seem to some to be "occasional liturgies" that is, conceived, planned and performed in response to a particular need for one-time use.' Yet this would be to miss the point for, according to Walton, they are a 'widening of the circles of traditions'[176] in an attempt 'to discover how to use symbols, texts and forms that express... relationships with God, one another and our created world more accurately and more authentically. The quest is a matter of justice.'[177]

---

[171] M. Collins, 'Principles of Feminist Liturgy' in M. Procter-Smith, and J.R. Walton, eds., *Women at Worship: Interpretations of North American Diversity* (Louisville: Westminster John Knox, 1993) 11.

[172] Ibid., 12.

[173] Ibid., 19.

[174] C. Bell, *Ritual Theory, Ritual Practice* (New York: Oxford University Press, 1992) 123.

[175] J.R. Walton, *Feminist Liturgy: A Matter of Justice* (Collegeville, MN: Liturgical Press, 2000) 12, 31.

[176] Walton's view of the relationship between feminist liturgy and Christian tradition will be discussed further in Chapter Five. See below: 180-183.

[177] Ibid., 12.

How can this study then claim that for sacramental theology these Christian feminists open some sort of door? Because of liturgical theology. Obviously this is not related to liturgical theology's delineation of a specific universally acceptable *ordo*. Rather, if liturgical theology has established that theology's focus should be the liturgy as a whole, instead of its separate 'elements', then the liturgy is, in a holistic way, a sacrament.[178] Furthermore, if liturgies are to be studied primarily as lived experiences and not as historical or prescribed texts or objects, there arises a demand that actual narratives of liturgies are included as the origin of the discourse, and this makes unprecedented demand for the inclusion of Christian feminists' stories about their worship (that is, *all* Christian feminists' stories, including those for whom Trinity is not a conditioning metaphor).

Collins perceives that the reason 'feminist liturgy is less accessible for examination than are traditional liturgies' is that 'feminist ritualizing very seldom gets turned into text, either before or after it is done.'[179] What liturgical theology is exposing is that no liturgy, feminist or otherwise, can get 'turned into' text in such a way that by studying the text one can study the liturgy.

And so we see that the 'turn to language' has been joined by a 'turn to praxis'. By coming to understand through the various liturgical movements and reforms of twentieth century that sacraments must be studied as lived events, systematic and liturgical approaches have both posited as the object of analysis not text but context, the 'juxtapositions', the narratives of the experience. This turn to praxis has, however, been shown to present several challenges. To begin with, by

---

[178] Fink makes explicit the argument that the sacraments *are* the liturgy of the church: 'The Constitution on the Sacred Liturgy proceeds to speak of sacraments as *liturgy*, that is, actions of the church in liturgical assembly.'   P.E. Fink, *Worship: Praying the Sacraments* (Washington, DC: Pastoral Press, 1991) 6-7. Also, in a widely acclaimed article, Irwin proposed that it was no longer useful for theology to speak of 'sacramental theology', with all its scholastic connotations, given that the sacraments were to be studied as liturgies, via liturgical theology. See: K. Irwin, 'Sacramental Theology: A Methodological Proposal', *The Thomist* (April 1990) 54:2.

[179] Collins, 'Principles of Feminist Liturgy', 12. Collins proceeds to discuss why feminists do not write more about their liturgies and concludes that the current 'atextuality of feminist liturgy may be only a strategy and not a principle', born as part of the learning process 'where women who have been socialised to look elsewhere for authority are learning to look to themselves and to one another, not to expert authors...' (15) This may be true, but it ignores the fact that considerable writing about liturgy by women does exist but has long been simply overlooked; for example, Nathan Mitchell in a recent list of resources for the study of the Eucharist names only two women in a list of over sixty authors. See: N.D. Mitchell, *Real Presence: The Work of Eucharist* (Chicago: Liturgical Training Publications, 1998) 121-135. An alternative bibliography, which testifies to the growing volume of womens' writing on the subject in the years Mitchell considers can be found in: T. Berger, *Women's Ways of Worship: Gender Analysis and Liturgical History* (Collegeville, MN: Liturgical Press, 1999). Teresa Berger's research outlines a variety of texts, within the academy and beyond, which furnish examples of women's reflections on liturgy.

and large, 'the sacraments' are taken as a given, thus defeating the otherwise non-normative intentions of those many authors who seek to advance a broader focus on sacramentality.[180] It also needs to be asked whether, with the changed lens of liturgical theology, the term 'sacrament' has not been rendered arcane.[181] The conclusion of this book will address this tension by challenging both the givenness of 'the sacraments' and their relationship to 'sacramentality', and proposing guidelines for an interpretive rather than an instrumental approach to their definition.

The turn to praxis has also failed to say how worship experience can be accessed except, paradoxically, as text. Many theologians have begun a conversation with the social sciences in an attempt to make in-roads in this area but, as evidenced above, little impact has yet to be felt on theological methodology. The most urgent area of attention to date has, rather, been the designation of worship as ritual and the ensuing rush to appropriate the theories of the nascent school of ritual studies. In the rush, Turner's notion of the ritual process has given theology the illusion that ritual is a reducible category, an action that functions, universally, to 'do' certain things in a community, such as instituting identity via its symbols which mediate meaning.

Consequently, the dominant mode of current interpretation is one that seeks to elucidate 'meaning'. This has two problems, both of which will be discussed in the following chapter. The first is technical: the meaning of the word itself is used in a variety of distinct and non-synonymous ways: the search for meaning may simply extrapolate what a symbol 'means', or it may refer to meaning over and against a modern world that is seen as lacking in 'meaning', or it may require that liturgies are 'meaningful', that is, that they touch people at a very deep level. This is confusing, but it is not as significant as the second problem: perhaps ritual is not a meaning-oriented activity; perhaps, as the ritual theorist Fritz Staal suggests, ritual is 'meaningless'.

Another popular theological acquisition from the social sciences has been Mary Douglas's anthropological designation of ritual as communication. Like Turner's conclusions, Douglas's 'fitted' the new theological frames of symbol and language. This has led to theology handicapping itself in two ways: first, in theologians' hands the appeal to language and communication has led to an elision of the two terms. Linguistic philosophy, as will be reported in Chapter Three, not only disputes such an elision on the grounds of accuracy but alerts us to the potential totalitarian tendencies of those who pretend that by using symbol/language they are communicating.

This handicap is not due solely to the use of Douglas or any other choice of ritual critic, but also to the choice of linguistic philosopher. By choosing,

---

[180] For example, Chauvet, Power, Duffy, Ganoczy, Ross: all op. cit.

[181] David Power has written that in feminist writing about worship the distinction between sacrament and liturgy has all but dissolved. See: Power, *Sacrament: Language of God's Giving*.

predominantly, Heidegger, Wittgenstein and Ricoeur, theology has privileged a model of language that concentrates on its illocutionary force. The technology of illocution suited very well traditional perceptions of liturgy as performative, for it accented language in the performative mode. However, other linguistic philosophers (Foucault, Habermas) are critical of such an emphasis, conscious that the performative is not necessarily the communicative, and the illocutionary may therefore work to 'put in place' only the dominant symbol, to exert the power of one over another. This, obviously, poses problems for a religion which supposes there to be neither slave nor free, male nor female, Jew nor Greek; and an attempt to view liturgy in an other than performative frame forms the basis of the discussion of Chapters Four and Five.

Secondly, appropriation of Douglas's communications-theoretical approach has led to a widespread acceptance that it is the very *rituality* of liturgy that enables sacramental communication, the corollary of which is that you cannot have the sacramental without the ritual. This seems more prescriptive than the essentially incarnational nature of Christian faith can either bear or testify to. If it is via ritual that we are to access liturgy/sacrament, theology's dialogue with Ritual Studies demands far more attention than it has presently received, not least because Turner and Douglas have their critics; the following chapter seeks to address this.

This chapter has discussed the main developments in sacramental theology from the mid-twentieth century to the present time. It has identified several major shifts: some empirical, such as the desire to overcome metaphysics and the concomitant turn to language, the location of sacrament in the body and the relationship between the ecclesial body and the body politic (ethics); others methodological, particularly the demand that study of sacrament be located in the praxis, rather than the texts, of Christian assemblies. The subsequent exploration of theologies of experience and the interdisciplinary use of the human sciences to garner greater access to this experience was reported to supply both gains and limits to theology. In terms of gains, liturgical theology, construed in this study in both conservative and feminist forms, offers the possibility of a sacramental theology based on interpretative rather than instrumental categories; in terms of constraints, too little is known (and too much assumed) about the power of human ritual behaviour to support the claims theologians make of Christian worship, and theology has yet to find a suitable epistemology for accessing Christian rituals in such a way that this question of power can be addressed. The empirical issues are impossible to consider without prior attention to the methodological ones, so the following chapter will examine the emerging field of ritual studies, with an eye to developing a suitable hermeneutic for the description and analysis of Christian worship later in the book.

Chapter Two

Questioning Rituality

How but in custom and in ceremony
Are innocence and beauty born?[1]

Sacramental theologians, as was seen in Chapter One, increasingly draw on the work of scholars from the social sciences in response to the late twentieth-century re-location of theology in worship. Such references are sought to help a discipline previously based mostly on texts and textual criticism to adjust to an epistemology that favours human acts and the analysis of actions. This chapter investigates the grounds on which theology consults the social sciences in general and the emerging field of ritual studies in particular. It questions Chauvet's assertion that rituality is what makes a sacrament in the light of recent developments in ritual studies and it argues that while ritual studies affords liturgical theology a wealth of methodological precedent and experimentation, cross-cultural perspectives, self-conscious epistemologies and the articulation of some very significant issues (ritual definition, ritual power and ritual tradition/legitimacy), it nevertheless fails to answer the problem for which theology turns to it: the question of access.

The latter half of the twentieth-century saw an increasing amount of reference to scholarship from the social sciences in theological works about sacramentality. As reported in Chapter One, Regis Duffy and Susan Ross turned to psychology, Mark Searle to sociology, Chauvet and Power to linguistic philosophy, Kavanagh and Hoffman to art criticism, Driver and Mitchell to social anthropology.[2] The key shift has been a recognition of the human being, inseparable from his or her context-dependence on the living organism of the earth, as the conduit through which any and all theology is constructed. No longer is it solely a soteriological faith-claim that conditions and charts the evolution of

---

[1] W.B. Yeats, 'A Prayer for My Daughter' in *Selected Poetry* (London: Macmillan, 1962) 103.

[2] Such innovative conversations are not unique to the study of liturgy but, rather, can be witnessed in almost every theological field; see, for example: the way in which the biblical field has been transformed by archaeology (e.g., the classic, W.F. Albright, *From the Stone Age to Christianity: Monotheism and the Historical Process* (Baltimore: John Hopkins Press, 1946); the historical by sociology (e.g., J. Wach, *Comparative Study of Religions* (New York: Columbia University Press, 1958); and the systematic by psychology (e.g., W. James, *The Varieties of Religious Experience* (Cambridge: Cambridge University Press, 1902).

Beyond Ritual

Christianity; it is the *experience* of Christians. From Barth and von Balthasar in the first half of the century to Moltmann and Radford-Ruether in the second, what counts is the encounter. So theologians, realising that their ability to describe and assess encounter is weak due to their training as textual and historical-doctrinal scholars, turn to those disciplines that have concentrated on interpreting experience for assistance. Thus Kilmartin comments, 'God communicates with his people in and through history, in and through historical forms of communication. The human sciences analyze the laws governing this communication. They furnish data, which should accompany and support theological reflection...'[3]

Regarding sacramental theology in particular, Ganoczy points out that:

> All previous analyses of the sacramental economy of salvation had as their point of departure a composite picture of God, Christ, the Church and the sacraments... Today the human individual in all his personal and interpersonal reality has been added to this picture... From the vantage point of the human sciences, the human individual constitutes the point at which all sacramental theological reflection begins.[4]

However, this move to incorporate the methods and theories of the social sciences is not merely due to the general human-centred shift in late twentieth-century systematic theology. It is important to recognise that, regarding theology stemming from worship, it also has its roots in the nineteenth century with the historical investigations of the liturgical movement.

Liturgical theology in the forms with which we are now familiar did not exist prior to an engagement between theology and the secular study of rites and societies. It sometimes seems that this has been forgotten, what with liturgical theologians who portray it as a fairly 'pure' art unto itself;[5] but its foundations were laid by the likes of Aidan Kavanagh who broke new ground by applying what Erikson had to say about human development to what the church had to say in its rituals,[6] and by feminist liturgists who applied the sociological gender critique of Betty Friedan (and others) to their own experiences of church and began to develop liturgies that were more true to their experiences and desires as women.[7] In the

---

[3]   E. Kilmartin, *Christian Liturgy: Theology and Practice*. Vol. 1. *Systematic Theology of Liturgy* (Kansas City: Sheed and Ward, 1988) 18.

[4]   A. Ganoczy, *An Introduction Catholic Sacramental Theology* (New York, Paulist Press, 1989) 147.

[5]   See, for example: D.W. Fagerberg, *What is Liturgical Theology?* (Collegeville, MN: Liturgical Press, 1992).

[6]   A. Kavanagh, 'The Role of Ritual in Personal Development' in J. Shaughnessy, ed., *The Roots of Ritual* (Grand Rapids: Eerdman, 1973) 145 - 160.

[7]   For a fuller account of the roots of feminist liturgies in the U.S.A., including a critique of the way these developed in a white middle class environment which could be blind to associated issues of race and wealth, see: J.R. Walton, *Feminist Liturgy: A Matter of Justice* (Collegeville, MN: Liturgical Press, 2000) 14 - 30.

developments that ensued, from high church Catholic to experimental feminist, these new liturgical theologians appropriated the insights of the emerging ritual scholarship, particularly those authors, as with Douglas and Turner, who emphasised ritual's communicative or transformative purpose.

Speaking of the dominant current in late twentieth century liturgical scholarship,[8] Mitchell comments, 'These scholars all seem to assume that ritual's primary purpose is the social production of meaning through a culturally conditioned system of symbols. These meanings are encoded in rites (and hence available through ritual symbols) - yet ultimately, they lie beyond the participants' power to manipulate or control.'[9] This view reflects the theories outlined in the work of anthropologist Roy Rappaport, the background ethic of which is primarily concerned with legitimation (in the sense of ritual authority).[10]

Feminist liturgists, on the other hand, have picked up on theories which describe a far greater degree of ambiguity in what ritual is about,[11] while retaining the idea that rituals heighten the effectiveness of symbols, thus maintaining a broadly symbolist account.[12] Like their colleagues in liturgical studies they also, generally speaking, prioritise a notion of 'meaningfulness': firstly, due to the meaning-orientation of the symbolist mentality and, secondly, by the common anecdotal criterion of effective worship as 'meaningful'. Furthermore, feminist theology also tends to agree with Turner in its attribution of transformative power as a key constituent of ritual;[13] however, in most feminist cases, the background ethic is not legitimation, but emancipation, justice.

Mary Collins straddles both camps:

> Ritual studies are worth pursuing by researchers interested in the interplay between theology and culture precisely because ritual acts constitute a distinctive kind of religious and cultural expression, one which is corporate in its manifestations and bodily and non-discursive in its presentation of content. Those

---

[8] Mitchell describes this as a 'high church Catholic cartel' but it in fact includes Protestant scholars, notably Saliers.

[9] Mitchell, *Social Sciences*, 32.

[10] See especially: R.A. Rappaport, *Ecology, Meaning and Religion* (Richmond, CA: North Atlantic Books, 1979).

[11] See, for example: Kathleen Hughes's use of Catherine Bell in her 'Sacraments and the Ecclesial Mediation of Grace', *Louvain Studies* 23 (1998) 189.

[12] See: T. Berger, *Womens' Ways of Worship: Gender Analysis and Liturgical History* (Collegeville, MN: Liturgical Press, 1999) 126-128.

[13] It is however important to note Bruce Lincoln's criticism of both Turner and Van Gennep for their adoption of androcentric models of 'transformation'. Lincoln suggests more gender-equible and feminist possibilities. See: B. Lincoln, *Emerging from the Chrysalis: Studies in Rituals of Women's Initiation* (Cambridge, MA: Harvard University Press, 1991).

very characteristics make ritual inaccessible to ordinary theological methods, which work with texts.[14]

Common to all is a definition of ritual as a specific, unique and discrete way of acting which accomplishes things other ways of acting cannot.

Yet recent developments in the study of ritual do not always bear out these assumptions. Indeed some current thinking presents a profound critique of the model of ritual as social-constitutor/personal transformer in which liturgical theology originally found its spur. Catherine Bell opens her most recent book, *Ritual Perspectives and Dimensions*,[15] by pointing out that, 'While the activities we think of as "ritual" can be found in many periods and places, the formal study of ritual is a relatively recent and localized phenomenon'.[16] *The Encyclopaedia of Religion* agrees,[17] specifying 'recent' as the past twenty years and 'local' as the U.S.A., in its report that ritual studies first emerged 'as a distinct field within the discipline of religious studies'[18] in the late 1970s and early 1980s with the advent of a study group under that title in the American Academy of Religion and its own journal (the *Ritual Studies Review*).

Given widespread scholarly interest in the subject of ritual stemming from the nineteenth century, this seems a bold claim even when qualified thus: 'What is new about ritual studies is the deliberate attempt to consolidate a field of inquiry reaching across disciplinary boundaries and coordinating the normative interests of theology and liturgics, the descriptive ones of the history and phenomenology of religions, and the analytical ones of anthropology.'[19] Locating the work within 'religious studies' in this way overlooks the extraordinary background the study of ritual has in a much broader range of scholarly fields. While it is true that 'what is new' is the consolidation of various projects within an 'independent'[20] field, it is important to recognise the influence of what is older on how this came about.[21]

---

[14] M. Collins, 'Critical Ritual Studies: Examining an Intersection of Theology and Culture' in her *Worship: Renewal to Practice* (Washington DC: Pastoral Press, 1987) 97.

[15] C. Bell, *Ritual Perspectives and Dimensions* (New York: Oxford University Press, 1997).

[16] Ibid., ix.

[17] M. Eliade, ed., *The Encyclopedia of Religion* 12 (New York: Macmillan, 1986) 422 - 425.

[18] Ibid., 422.

[19] Ibid., 422.

[20] C. Bell, *Ritual Theory, Ritual Practice* (New York: Oxford University Press, 1992) ix. Bell describes 'the recent emergence of ritual studies' as an 'independent and interdisciplinary field of study' and credits Ron Grimes in particular for this consolidation. It is difficult to accept the interdisciplinarity of the field as a uniquely twentieth-century characteristic, given the extraordinary range of disciplines involved in

The origins of the study of ritual are concurrent with the nineteenth century interest in the origins of religion. The small cluster of scholars on the European side of the Atlantic usually identified as its earliest exponents would not have been familiar with the nomenclature of 'religious studies'[22] and yet while approaching the subject according to the conventional wisdom, or methodologies, of their various disciplines nevertheless display a degree of cross-fertilisation of ideas not dissimilar to what we now recognise as the field of religious studies. Friedrich Max Müller was a linguist, Edward B. Tylor an anthropologist, Jane Harrison a classicist, Emile Durkheim a sociologist and Andrew Lang, like Sir James Frazer, a comparative anthropologist. All these various disciplines - along with biblical studies, and the archaeology that was transforming it - pursued scholarship on the subject of ritual with such a degree of cross-fertilization among them that it is difficult to maintain the strict distinction made above about the uniqueness of today's 'ritual studies' as a branch of scholarship.

What is pertinent, however, is that there was little continuity between then and now: the late ninetheenth century's eclectic and interdisciplinary approach was pretty much wiped out with the development of an 'orthodoxy' (derived from phenomenology) which dictated that what mattered was myth and symbol, not the rite itself. This was, in turn, allied to a prevailing anthropological hermeneutic that, conceiving ritual as repetitive, pre-critical behaviour, dominated subsequent twentieth-century scholarship in the subject. Furthermore, and of particular significance for the theological interpretation of rites, with the passing of this strand of scholarship went the notion that ritual as a peculiar genre of human activity has within itself something that is essentially and uniquely expressive of God (or gods, or the transcendent).[23]

---

the study of ritual, and the degree of conversation among them, in the nineteenth century.

[21] It is also important to note that the designation 'ritual studies' seems only to be coined by American scholars, and even they are very cautious about this. Most European authors tend to retain a primary affinity to their 'home' discipline, be it religious studies, anthropology, sociology, theology or psychology, even when the subject of their investigation is wholly to do with ritual. So one cannot yet refer to it as a school or a discipline or a field. It is too disparate, and the key critics themselves resist the nomenclature. For the purposes of this study, when reference is made to ritual studies, it is to a body of work from various disciplines, within the social sciences, on the subject of ritual going back nearly two hundred years. As a form of theory it is 'emerging'.

[22] Although Max Müller, as early as 1869, argued for the appropriateness of a *Religionswissenschaft* - a Science of Religions - which would examine religion but not from theological or philosophical points of view. See: M. Müller, *Chips from a German Workshop* (1869) (Chico, CA: Scholars Press, 1985).

[23] I am grateful to Sinéad Garrigan Mattar for making this point.

The story of the development of theories of ritual through the course of the twentieth-century can and has been told in a variety of ways,[24] and contains the key debate as to what, in fact, a ritual is. Over a two-hundred year period, the definition of ritual has experienced multiple re-incarnations, many of them just in the past twenty-five years, but perhaps the most radical happened during the nineteenth century. In the first edition of the *Encyclopaedia Britannica* of 1771, 'ritual' is defined as a book prescribing church ceremonies. Its definition in the third edition (1797) is broadened to include the 'rites and ceremonies' of 'the ancient heathens', an understanding which prevails until 1852, after which time there is no entry for 'ritual' at all. When one reappears in the eleventh edition of 1910, the previous understanding of ritual as a *script* containing the instructions for religious worship (heathen or otherwise) has completely disappeared and, in its place, ritual is now seen as 'a type of practice', a universal phenomenon of human behaviour characterised by symbolic reference to meanings. One can easily detect a parallel with the evolution of the study of worship during the twentieth-century, described in Chapter One, which has moved from studying liturgies as texts to studying them as practices, what Hoffman has called 'the liturgical field'; that is, 'the holistic network of interrelationships that bind together discrete things, acts, people, and events into the activity we call worship - or better still, ritual'.[25]

Within the social sciences then, for most of the twentieth-century, the notion of ritual underwent several further alterations in definition, but they were nuances on the theme of a practical rather than a textual science. During the sixty years after the 1910 definition, anthropology settled on a cohesive set of what Bell calls 'reigning scholarly assumptions about ritual and its social role' which portrayed it as a universal phenomenon, a symbol-system, a meaning-oriented activity. There was widespread agreement as to what people thought ritual 'did' (it formed and maintained social order) and how it did this (symbolically). It was seen as a way of acting common to all peoples which was fundamentally 'fixed': repetitive, un-self-conscious, symbolic actions which, once inculturated, varied little and served as significant markers of a community's identity.

---

[24] For example, Bell (1997) discerns three major theoretical movements: first, those who thought ritual was about the ongoing expression of basic human and cosmic myths (Andrew Lang, William Robertson Smith, Mircea Eliade, Jonathan Z. Smith); second, those who thought its function was to order social structures (Emile Durkheim, Bronislaw Malinowski, Roy Rappaport, Arnold van Gennep); and third, those who thought it was primarily about symbolic communication and manipulation (Edmund Leach, Clifford Geertz, Marshall Sahlins, Pierre Bourdieu). Stanley Tambiah, Mary Douglas, Victor Turner and Claude Lévi-Strauss she locates straddling the second and third. However, Fiona Bowie (1999) draws the lines of engagement quite differently, portraying the debate as having been between 'intellectualists' (such as Eliade and Horton) and 'symbolists' (and here, unlike Bell, she includes Durkheim as well as John Beattie, Maurice Bloch and Clifford Geertz).

[25] L.A. Hoffman, *Beyond the Text: A Holistic Approach to Liturgy* (Indianapolis: Indiana University Press, 1987) 173.

No one scholar encapsulates all these elements in a single definition, indeed there are disagreements between scholars on each point, but it can be seen as the 'lowest common denominator' between a wide range of commentators, from Eliade's conception of ritual as the deposit of originatory mythology, to Durkheim's understanding of ritual as collective representation, to Douglas's conviction that its purpose is communication, to Rappaport's 'definition' of it as 'the performance of more or less invariant sequences of formal acts and utterances not encoded by the performers'. All would seem to agree with Rappaport that, 'Ritual is not simply an alternative way to express certain things... certain things can only be expressed in ritual.'[26] Rappaport's work is therefore seen as representative of the accepted view underpinning social anthropology, a perception of ritual as a universal, collective practice among human beings, designed to convey 'canonical'[27] meanings that can only be communicated via ritual forms; forms which are largely fixed, repetitive, pre-critical or even sometimes pre-conscious, and which give access to an authority (God, gods, ancestors, spirits, etc.) which conditions existence. Mitchell offers a summary of this position: 'ritual is essentially [seen as] a way to regulate social life; to shape personal and corporate identity; to review and renew values; to express and transmit meaning in symbolic word and act; to preserve tradition; and to insure cultural cohesion and continuity.'[28]

Ron Grimes was the first to credit the subsequent changes in this view to Victor Turner. Arguing that Turner altered the course of the study of ritual, Grimes writes, 'Before Turner ritual was static, structural, conservative. After Turner it is imagined as flowing, processual, subversive.'[29] This owes in large part to Turner's focus, in *The Ritual Process*, on that which is 'liminal' in personal development, be

---

[26] R.A. Rappaport, 'The Obvious Aspects of Ritual' in *Ecology, Meaning and Religion* (Richmond, CA: North Atlantic Books, 1979) 174 - 175.

[27] Mitchell reports that according to what he coins the 'conservative consensus' of twentieth-century anthropology, 'while some of ritual's messages may be indexical (consisting of variable, transitory information transmitted by participants *about* themselves - e.g., their current physical, psychic or social conditions - *to* themselves and others) its deepest and most stable messages are canonical (consisting of messages concerned with ultimate realities not visibly present but conveyed through symbols). Canonical messages are never invented or encoded by participants; they are "found" or "discovered" as already given in and by the rite.' *Social Sciences*, 33.

[28] Mitchell, *Social Sciences*, 25.

[29] R.L. Grimes, 'Reinventing Ritual' in *Reading, Writing and Ritualising: Ritual in Fictive, Liturgical and Public Places* (Washington, DC: Pastoral Press, 1993) 6. Turner's work was prolific and produced over a long time, with the result that, like Mary Douglas, he came to several points of self-contradiction. Thus, Grimes notes that, paradoxically, Turner was a staunch defender of the conservative model in his writings about his personal (Roman Catholic) faith and convictions: 'If he had adhered to his own definition, he would never have noticed most of what he argued was distinctive about ritual.' Ibid. 7.

that in periods of transition (such as adolescence), in social dramas (such as workplace conflicts) or in socioeconomic situations (such as 'the marginal people in our society' whom he sees as being potentially oppressed or ignored). By identifying and studying this liminal, or 'threshold', social experience first, and looking from there to ritual (instead of *vice versa*), Turner emphasises a creative, even transformative, notion of ritual as generative of,[30] rather than merely representative of, socio-cultural norms. Ritual thus serves not so much to put in place a particular pre-conceived social structure but to be the place at which social structure is itself worked-out.

Turner also noted that between persons in liminal stages in their lives there emerges a unique sort of bond, which he described as 'social anti-structure' or *communitas,* and he sees an inevitable paralleling process between these bonds as they manifest in both the society at large and the rituals that the society performs. These bonds are:

> Undifferentiated, egalitarian, direct, non-rational, existential, I-Thou (in Buber's sense). *Communitas* is spontaneous, immediate, concrete, not abstract... It does not merge identities; it liberates them from conformity to general norms, though this is necessarily a transient condition if society is to continue to operate in an orderly fashion. It is the *fons et origo* of all structures and at the same time their critique.[31]

With this insight, Turner introduced the idea that ritual can be as critical and subversive as it can be formal and conserving. He thereby challenged several of the established norms of ritual study: ritual is shown to be potentially creative rather than merely customary, evolving rather than fixed or blindly repetitive, dynamic rather than static, critical rather than conservative. For Grimes, this de-construction of the prevailing definition of ritual has consequences for the conclusions one draws about ritual actions: 'Gestures once regarded as innate and scenarios once treated as sacrosanct are now understood as cultural constructions',[32] and this in turn serves to challenge the ingrained belief that those who participate in ritual do so pre-critically. A more accurate account of what is going on, Grimes suggests, is 'reflexivity', which he describes as 'the awareness of performance by the one who is performing', something which, he adds, 'Does not have to precipitate the demise of ritual; it can become part of the work of ritual. It may even be that ritual is a primary cultural means whereby participants learn to comprehend and criticize the constructedness of what are taken to be cultural facts.'[33]

---

[30] He wrote, 'Ritual ... hold[s] the generative source of culture and structure, particularly in its liminal stage.' V. Turner; E. Turner, ed., *On the Edge of the Bush: The Anthropology of Form and Meaning* (Tucson: University of Arizona Press, 1986) 171.

[31] V. Turner, *The Ritual Process: Structure and Anti-structure* (Baltimore: Penguin Books, 1969) 114.

[32] Grimes, 'Reinventing Ritual', 18.

[33] Ibid.

A strong echo of this position is heard in Catherine Bell's *Ritual Theory Ritual Practice* in which she suggests that the chief activity of 'ritual' is negotiation, a 'strategic way of acting in specific social situations'.[34] Bell, however, takes the question of definition further, claiming that 'ritual as such does not exist';[35] what does exist, indeed all that exists, she proposes, is 'ritualising'. By this, Bell intends to expose how deeply and detrimentally attached ritual scholarship is to the quest for a universal definition of ritual and how it consequently sidelines seemingly local, but actually crucial issues, such as power.

Examination of the conclusions that scholars draw about 'ritual', she says, tells us more about the scholar than about the ritual.[36] She identifies the key problem as arising due to the way in which the social sciences have constituted 'ritual' as 'the object of a cultural method of interpretation' by pointing out that, 'The implicit structure of ritual theory, while effective in identifying a distinctive phenomenon for cultural analysis, has imposed a powerful limit on our theoretical flexibility, our divisions of human experience, and our ability to perceive the logical relation inscribed within these divisions.'[37] Bell's work exposes two things: first, that the themes introduced in Turner's work set today's agenda for ritual studies: ritual as performance; ritual authority deriving from invention as well as tradition; ritual as transformative power; and the methodological relationship of theory to practice which manifested in his work as the imperative for fieldwork-oriented theory.

Second, however, Bell also begins to expose the limitations that viewing ritual through these lenses present, demanding that the assumptions underlying the Turnerian endeavour - of universal practice, of relation to social order, of symbolic meaning, and of how power works - are questioned and reframed. Both sets of themes, Turnerian and post-Turnerian, will be addressed in the remainder of this chapter, with two intentions: first, to examine the grounds on which Chauvet claims that rituality makes sacrament; and second, to provide the groundwork for the methodology developed in the subsequent chapters of this study.

Theology, in seeking an engagement with ritual studies is thus consulting an 'unresolved' field, in which many of its most basic of definitions (what a ritual is, why people do them, what they achieve) are hotly contested. However, as Bell comments:

---

[34] Bell, *Ritual Theory, Ritual Practice*, 67.
[35] Ibid., 140. Bell comments in her later work, 'To anyone interested in ritual in general, it soon becomes evident that there is no clear and widely shared explanation of what constitutes ritual or how to understand it.' *Perspectives and Dimensions*, x.
[36] Definitions and theories of ritual are, Bell argues, 'vivid reflections of the questions that concern us and indicate, therefore, something of the way in which we who are asking the questions tend to construe the world, human behaviour, meaning, and the task of explanation.' *Perspectives and Dimensions*, 89.
[37] Ibid., 17.

The lack of any definite winner in the history of theory does not mean that scholarship on ritual has not forged useful tools for analysis and reflection. Ritual as the expression of paradigmatic values of death and rebirth; ritual as a mechanism for bringing the individual into community and establishing a social entity; or ritual as a process for social transformation, for catharsis, for embodying symbolic values, for defining the nature of the real, or for struggling for control over the sign - these formulations are all tools that help us to analyze what may be going on in any particular set of activities.[38]

Ritual studies thus offer a bundle of questions which challenge the methodology of any liturgical theology. Where the emerging field of ritual studies is potentially most useful to liturgical theology is in its exposure and critique of damaging presumptions and methodologies, and in its creative search for alternative approaches, investigation of which will occupy the remainder of this chapter.

Since its inception, Religious Studies has been aware of the parallel between human and animal ritual: humans are not the only creatures that ritualise certain aspects of their behaviour. Commenting that, as regards animals, scholarship has not been encumbered with the ill-defined but strong distinction that the human sciences have created between 'sacred' and 'secular' ritual, Richard Schechner notes that, 'Ethologically speaking, ritual is ordinary behaviour transformed by means of condensation, exaggeration, repetition, and rhythm into specialized sequences of behaviour serving specific functions usually having to do with mating, hierarchy, or territoriality.'[39] If only there could be such a succinct summary of its human manifestation! The point is, of course, that although early pioneers adopted and defended very similar definitions for human ritualistic behaviour, these nevertheless failed to account for the significant differences between the ways humans and animals go about creating ritual.[40] It is at this point, the actual *creating* of a ritual, that scholars like Schechner have sought to access an account of the peculiarity of *human* ritual behaviour.

Examining the creative process in order to learn more about human behaviour has its roots in Freud's 1912 work, *Totem and Taboo* in which Freud wrote:

> Only in art does it still happen that a man who is consumed by desires performs something resembling the accomplishment of those desires... People speak with justice of the 'magic of art'... But the comparison is perhaps more significant than it claims to be. There can be no doubt that art did not begin as art for art's sake. It

---

[38] Bell, *Perspectives and Dimensions*, 89.

[39] R. Schechner, *The Future of Ritual: Writings on Culture and Performance* (New York: Routledge, 1993) 228.

[40] Schechner comments, 'For... bees everything is genetically pre-determined. There is no learning or improvisation, no composition classes where new behaviours are invented and tested.' *The Future of Ritual*, 228.

worked originally in the service of impulses which are for the most part extinct today. And among them we may suspect the presence of many magical purposes.[41]

Recent comparisons of ritual and the artistic process have parted company from Freud in several respects,[42] but produced remarkably consistent results. While Schechner examined the dramatic arts,[43] others have looked to visual, musical and operatic arts, and to dance. In common to most are conclusions that place emphasis on performance, on improvisation, on volition, on interaction, and on a necessary (acquired) level of competence or technical expertise. Relating this to something called 'ritual' has not only supported Turner's claim that the ritual process 'opens up a time/space of anti-structural playfulness',[44] but has also claimed for ritual itself the nature of performance. Thus, Bobby Alexander proposes without expecting controversy, 'Ritual defined in the most general and basic terms is performance, planned or improvised, that effects a transition from everyday life to an alternative context within which the everyday is transformed.'[45]

Alexander highlights the way in which current criticism sees ritual not only to exhibit similarities with artistic performances, but to be itself a form of performance. Performance is taken as the bottom-line statement of what ritual is. This has enabled some remarkable insights, such as Grimes's categorisation of the many and various ways in which rituals can 'fail'. In devising this account, Grimes took J.L. Austin's speech-act theory and applied it to ritual, commenting that, 'Even though it assumes the primacy of language (which Grimes has ardently refuted in many other articles), it serves as an effective bridge between linguistic and performative theories.'[46] By locating ritual criticism as a form of 'performative

---

[41] S. Freud, *Totem and Taboo* (1912) (New York: W.W. Norton, 1962) 60.

[42] Firstly, they are not starting from a seeking-the-origins perspective and so do not share the automatic privileging of a 'primitive exemplar' which one sees in Freud and which is so typical of much early twentieth-century scholarship; secondly, the point of access for the scholar is, usually, as participant rather than as clinician or 'detached' observer (and the resultant commentary reflects this in a self-conscious way). At its most explicit, this can be seen for example in Schechner's description of his initiation as a Hindu Brahmin (*The Future of Ritual*), Turner's intiation as a member of the Ndembu tribe (V. Turner, *The Forest of Symbols: Aspects of Ndembu Ritual* (Ithaca, NY: Cornell University Press, 1967) or Karen McCarthy Brown's 'accidental' possession by a spirit at a Haitian Vodou rite (K. McCarthy Brown, '"Plenty Confidence in Myself": The Initiation of a White Woman Scholar into Haitian Vodou', *Journal of Feminist Studies in Religion* 3:1 (1987) 67 - 76).

[43] Schechner, an anthropologist, was also the Director of a New York theatre company. See: R. Schechner, *Between Theatre and Anthropology* (Philadelphia: University of Pennsylvania Press, 1985).

[44] Schechner, *Future of Ritual*, 233.

[45] R.C. Alexander, 'Televangelism: Redressive Ritual within a Larger Social Drama' in S. Hooker and K. Lundby, eds., *Rethinking Media, Religion and Culture* (Thousand Oaks: Sage Publications, 1997) 139.

[46] Grimes, *Ritual Criticism*, 195.

theory', Grimes can compare Austin's notion of speech acts as 'performative utterances'[47] to ritual contexts. Furthermore, he can extend Austin's acknowledgement of the fact that performative utterances (speech acts) do not always 'work' into the realm of religious studies and suggest a glossary of 'ritual infelicities' (such as 'when an act discredits or invalidates the acts of others') which alert scholar and practitioner alike to the largely ignored issue of ritual's potential to be 'infelicitous'.[48]

Several points emerge from Grimes's essay that prove pivotal to my investigation. First is Grimes's dismissal of language as an adequate object of study in ritual investigation. Like the liturgical theologians profiled in Chapter One, Grimes's position is typical of recent ritual studies in general which eschew the verbal, preferring to focus on the gestural, emotional, atmospheric, aesthetic and spatial. This has not, however, been a charted route, as Michael Aune has noted: 'Traditionally... ritual scholarship has been weak, vague, or nonexistent when it comes to these experiential, noetic and effective dimensions of participation... In fact, scholars have often declared these dimensions as simply off limits because they are both ineffable and inaccessible.'[49]

While it has been demonstrated that texts of rituals (either in the form of the scripts giving instructions for practitioners - where such exist - or the accounts written by historians) fail to offer an adequate conduit for accessing the activity of ritual as it is experienced by its practitioners, the conclusion that the verbal elements are an unproductive avenue of investigation has not, however, been supported with the same strength of evidence. Ritual scholars, in privileging the noetic, underestimate the degree to which language-use itself may be noetic. Language-use and exchange is a verbal activity, but viewing it merely as verbal reduces it to a textual comparison that serves to mask its other, experiential affects and functions.

So used are we in the west to regarding words as literature that we neglect the possibility that language, a complex bodily act, is as *performed* as any other gesture. Scripts are texts, but the words uttered in rituals, or elsewhere, are more appropriately studied as *behaviour*, not verbiage. This is not to say that the non-verbal is not important, on the contrary; it is simply to emphasise that language exchange among human beings may benefit from being understood more as behaviour and less as a text. (Such an approach, which to date has been little

---

[47]   J.L. Austin, *How to Do Things with Words* (New York: Oxford University Press, 1962). This famous book was the published version of the William James Lectures that Austin delivered at Harvard in 1955. In it Austin drew on the idea of speech acts as 'illocutionary', a notion championed by Wittgenstein, which indicated that words, by being exchanged, *put in place* the reality they describe.

[48]   Eleven years after this work was published, there has yet to be any significant development of the crucial point Grimes makes.

[49]   M.B. Aune, 'The Subject of Ritual: Ideology and Experience in Action' in M.B. Aune and V. DeMarinis, eds., *Religious and Social Ritual: Interdisciplinary Explorations* (Albany, NY: State University of New York Press, 1996) 141.

explored, will be discussed at length in Chapter Three, where a model for accessing 'meaning' via study of language-exchange will be developed not on the basis of semantics but on the linguistic philosophy of Jürgen Habermas.)

Allied to this concerted effort to avoid studying language in favour of more 'experiential' components is a presumption that such can in fact be accessed. The second point arising from Grimes's criticism is not so much the question of what, if not language, gives access to ritual, but how do such do so? This echoes the methodological barrier Chapter One discerned to be facing liturgical theology. If you want to know when there has been a ritual infelicity (or indeed felicity) how can you tell? How are we to judge when a ritual is ineffective? *How* does Grimes, or how do his colleagues, access experience - their own or that of others? Grimes's answer, informed by the methodologies of a variety of human sciences, is threefold: ritual criticism must be engaged-in as an observer-participant in fieldwork; participants in the ritual must be interviewed, before, during and afterwards; and the observer's own experiences and reactions can provide both guide and foil to their interpretations.

This is a great improvement on what has gone before, where the explicit issue of access has been either overlooked or declared impossible (as with Aune); however it is also problematic. How people respond in interview situations has been the subject of much research, with many studies devising formulae for questions that will elicit the 'truth' of an individual's perception. Yet these have been criticised by a wide range of scholars who insist that interviews can only ever afford a very partial view of their subject because the questions asked will always condition the answer given; and, more importantly, the nature of subject(s) is such that the reality of an event is constructed intersubjectively, so the event cannot be accessed by lone-subject interviews. This problem will be considered again towards the end of this chapter.

Third, Grimes's insistence on fieldwork as the locus of the study of ritual[50] is taken as a key pre-script for my own study. Although it is unusual for theological reflection to be paired with case studies, it seems that any attempt to take seriously the social sciences as a conversation partner in the analysis of worship necessarily demands adoption of this most basic tenet of anthropological procedure. Precisely how this is to be done in a liturgical theological context is developed in Chapters Three and Four.

Grimes also raises the associated issue of how observer and participant are ordinarily differentiated in fieldwork, proposing that the anthropological idea of an observer as somehow 'outside' or 'detached' is a fallacy, given that any human being present at a ritual is unavoidably involved. It is one of the distinctive

---

[50] Grimes is not alone in this; as he remarks, 'There is a growing consensus in religious studies that the criticism of ritual ought to mediate between practice and theory and that theorizing about ritual ought to be rooted in field study. Even ancient ritual texts are best interpreted in light of methods developed out of actual observation of contemporary rites.' *Ritual Criticism*, 217.

contributions of performance theory to religious studies that it has located the idea of 'action' not solely in the bodies of the actors on the stage but in the bodies of the audience members as well; a scholar then, Grimes comments, 'is merely a particular sort of audience member'.[51] Correspondingly, Grimes insists that the scholar must be 'visible' in his or her report or interpretation of an event. This, too, provides a guiding principle for the studies presented later in this book.

Catherine Bell criticises this use of performance analogies to speak of ritualising as typical of the problem, outlined above, whereby scholars conduct their investigations with a self-serving circularity:

> The increased naturalization of the outside observer that is obtained in the very definition of act as performance takes the relationship between subject and object constructed by the theorist and inscribes it into the nature of the object itself. In other words, ritual comes to be seen as performance in the sense of symbolic acts specifically meant to have an impact on an audience and entreat their interpretative appropriation.[52]

However, Bell misconstrues the purpose which performance theory attributes to performance; it is not presumed (as Bell implies) that the purpose of ritual is communication; indeed theorists such as Schechner and Grimes looked to performance theory precisely to overcome the constraints of the theory of symbols as meaning-conveyers with which Bell corrals them.[53] What performance-theorists are suggesting is not merely that the audience is impressed by the performers (as Bell has it, that they should impact on them) but that the opposite is equally true.

Thus there emerges an idea of intersubjectivity between all present, a holistic sense that while actors and audience each have their roles, all are in a sense 'performers' because all, only together, comprise the event that is a performance; and there amid this creative intersubjectivity, says performance theory, one finds the observer. It is not an attempt to 'naturalize' the observers ('gamekeepers turned poachers') because they are, by virtue of their role, already natural to that particular situation. There is not a special gallery where they could go, where they would not affect proceedings but could voyeuristically judge in peace. Besides, if they were not 'natural', the intersubjective collective (i.e., all the other actors in the ritual) would turn on them and drive them out and away.

Performance-theory's approach to ritual therefore demands the scholar's awareness of his or her location, and this, too, will be adopted as a key methodological tenet of this essay. In the case studies that follow (in Chapters Four and Five) the presence and participation of the scholar at the rites observed will be made explicit and reflected in the subsequent interpretation. It is, however, essential also to heed Bell's associated criticism that 'the notion of performance as

---

51   Grimes, *Ritual Criticism*, 230
52   Bell, *Ritual Theory, Ritual Practice*, 42.
53   See: Ibid., 43.

a critical tool for approaching certain activities comes to be used as descriptive of the fundamental nature of those activities'.[54] Returning to Grimes then, the fourth point is that studying ritual as basically human behaviour in performative mode (as opposed to other modes), while raising the crucial and still ignored issue of potential 'infelicity', may nevertheless limit ritual criticism.

Moreover, as will be reported in Chapter Three, the philosophy of Jürgen Habermas suggests that the power dynamics that are established by interaction pursued in the performative mode may be inherently oppressive. While this would account for certain of ritual's infelicities (in a way that Grimes or Austin do not), it does not account for its many successes (in a way that their schemes do), indicating, with Bell, that ritual cannot be reduced to the category of performance alone. Therefore, while adopting the observer-as-participant approach of performance-theoretical methodology, this essay will reject any underlying notion of ritual as *primarily* performative.

Fifth and finally, adopting an imperative to contextualise scholarship in practice (via case studies compiled in fieldwork) and accepting the demand for transparency of the observer in the process of this data creation and collection, Grimes argues that one cannot, however, merely 'apply' a theory to data. His method 'has been to experiment with theory, both extending its scope and exposing its limits, as well as teasing a few texts [broadly understood] with some new questions'.[55] While this sounds benign enough, Grimes's work in fact displays a deep-seated ambivalence to theory, an ambivalence typical of many current commentators in the field. Ruel Tyson, like Grimes, proposes a 'practical criticism' as a counterpoint to a perceived starchiness on the part of theory: 'If the practice precedes the theory of it and if the explication of methods presupposes a history of application, then fieldwork should precede theories of culture, including the relation between religious action and other cultural forms; and practical criticism should precede theoretical criticism.'[56]

This kind of approach is roundly rejected by Frits Staal, for whom theory is the essential pre-critical harbinger of access to any event. Contemplating what would make a scholar ascribe a definition of 'ritual' to any particular set of activities (before they even begin to 'criticise' them), Staal remarks:

> We have intuitions about what rituals are but we do not precisely *know* what they are. In order to know it we need a theory first, and not the other way around. ...Theories cannot be 'derived' from data ... they are inspired by ideas, musings and other exercises of the imagination. Once formulated they should be clear enough to be subjected to tests and experimentations.[57]

---

[54] Ibid., 42.

[55] Grimes, *Ritual Criticism*, 207.

[56] R.W. Tyson, *The Practical Criticism of Religious Action* (American Academy of Religion: Working Group on the Systematic Study of Meaningful Forms, 1975) 141.

[57] F. Staal, *Rules Without Meaning: Ritual, Mantras and the Human Sciences* (New York: Peter Lang, 1989) 62 - 63. Staal is following Bertrand Russell, whom he quotes:

Staal's argument has a significant sub-plot: the belief that Religious Studies in its adoption of anthropology (and other social sciences) has fallen into what he calls 'the Myth of the Two Cultures',[58] which manifests itself as a fundamental prejudice against the 'natural sciences' on the part of the 'human sciences' and, to a lesser degree, vice versa. In other cultures (such as Indian ones), he argues, this split did not occur, with the result that there is no ambivalence surrounding the role of theory, and he suggests that in the West, 'the general scientific method of gathering data and formulating hypotheses to account for these data can be fruitfully adopted.'[59]

Staal's argument serves to expose the degree to which a substantial amount of theorising has already taken place before one even steps into a ritual space. Theory, it seems, unavoidably conditions interpretation. His argument is that, consciously taking theory as a partner, it is possible to access what is deemed by others to be inaccessible.[60] Staal asks, given that ritual is a human activity, 'how can ritual and mantras be governed by rules that lie beyond the human sciences and the study of religion?'[61] and proposes that a 'promising point of departure for the study of [ritual] lies in the human sciences',[62] not in terms of following an already existing approach, but rather: 'If we place ritual... in the wider domain of human activities and competences and relate them to other features and characteristics of the human animal.'[63] As an experiment then, Chapter Three will attempt to develop a scientific approach (using linguistic philosophy as a guide) as a means of affording access to interpretations that the human sciences generally surmise to be inaccessible, that is: the understanding that participants themselves have of their actions.

One particular pre-governing theory that Staal seeks to uncover is the perception, prevalent in the west, that language conveys meaning. Arguing against those many anthropologists who, following Douglas, see rites as analogous with language, Staal insists, 'ritual and mantras are not language... because they originated prior to language in the scheme of evolution'.[64] Staal is not saying that language is not important, or that it is inadequate as a vehicle for studying rites; on the contrary, he seeks to emphasise both these points. His truck is with the way

---

'Instinct, intuition, or insight is what first leads to the beliefs which subsequent reason confirms or confutes.'

58   Staal, *Rules*, 421.
59   Staal, *Rules*, 433.
60   'We do not possess much in the way of a science of ritual, even though the subject is certainly amenable to precise investigation, not unlike physics, mathematics, or grammar.' F. Staal, 'The Meaninglessness of Ritual', *Numen* 26 (1979) 15.
61   Staal, *Rules*, xiii.
62   Ibid., 2.
63   Ibid., 2.
64   Ibid., 437.

anthropologists, when looking at language-use, concentrate on meanings and symbols[65] when what they should be looking at are its rules ('syntax').

In a now famous essay he rather bullishly proposed that rituals are in fact meaningless. Dismissing all previous North Atlantic approaches to ritual, he argues on the basis of Indian Vedic ritual scholarship that, 'Ritual is pure activity, without meaning or goal'[66]... 'It is an activity governed by explicit rules. The important thing is what you do, not what you think, believe or say.'[67] Accordingly, the point of *studying* ritual is not to find out what it means, but, like the Indian Sranta Sutras, to record its rules: 'Ritual systems are like language in that they are governed by rules, but unlike language in that they do not express meanings. For their study, understanding and analysis, such systems accordingly require syntactic theories that deal with rules, not semantic theories that deal with meanings.'[68]

Staal's article sent a shot across the bows of ritual scholarship. Staal, aware of the shock that his alignment of ritual with meaninglessness would cause remarked, 'I prefer a thing, like a person, to be itself and not refer to something or somebody else. For all we know, life itself may be meaningless.'[69] However, linguistic theory in the years since this article was written has itself demolished its own prior notion of 'meaning' with the result, reported in Chapter One, that it is now commonly held that the nature of symbol or meaning lies not in any purported referential quality (to conjure associations with meanings external to itself). Modern symbol theory, like Staal, discredits 'referential' notions of meaning in favour of a more contingent apparatus that knows each word or phrase only by what it itself constructs.[70] Yet the question of *how* it knows this remains a neglected subject of investigation.

Staal suggests it is known in a way similar to the Sanskrit formulation of ritual rules, yet fails to report *how* the writers of these rules accessed the information they represent as diagrams (were they observers, participants, shamans, scholars? Is the syntax they perceive the same that others would perceive of the same event?). He is disparaging of the 'generalisations' of western scholars, and perhaps rightly insofar as they have paid inadequate attention to methodology, yet he is blind to the legitimate motivation behind this 'generalisation': the very genuine doubts which western scholars have expressed regarding turning to a text (which is what Staal does) to understand a ritual. The question that remains is *how* one is to access ritual. This is the core question that ritual studies presents to this

---

[65] Although he makes an exception for Noam Chomsky. Ibid., 47 - 58.

[66] Staal, *Meaninglessness*, 9. For a criticism of this article see: H. Penner, 'Language, Ritual and Meaning', *Numen* 32:1 (1985) 1 - 16.

[67] Staal, *Meaninglessness*, 4.

[68] Staal, *Rules*, 452.

[69] Staal, *Meaninglessness*, 22.

[70] However, it does not deny meaning, or the relation between meaning and language; it just perceives it as inherent rather than referential.

thesis; it will form the basis of the discussion of Chapter Three and the Habermasian model of analysis developed in Chapters Four and Five.

The associated question is what ritual *does*. Chauvet's claim was that rituality enables mediation in a way that no other genre of human behaviour allows. What is it about ritual that does this? Staal's thesis would seem to dispute the claims Chauvet makes for ritual's power, in its supposition that ritual is 'pure activity' with 'no goal' or usefulness. However, anyone who has ever been married knows that ritual 'does' something; it makes spouses out of lovers, and many expect it does a great deal more. This is not to say that ritual is 'utilitarian', but it is to dispute Staal's idea that it has no goal. A couple approaching the registry office or the altar expect that something, a specific thing, will be achieved by doing so. Is such an idea of transformation (as purpose) limited to rites of passage (although it is highly likely that each person expects a different thing), or can it be seen as operative in other rites as well?

Comparison has been made between Staal and Talad Asad,[71] another scholar who proposes that study of rites should reject the (western) preconception of them as symbol systems. Studying (the texts of) medieval Benedictine monasticism, Asad discerns the purpose of the rites prescribed in the Rule of St. Benedict as akin to Foucault's 'technologies of the self'. Like Foucault, Asad approaches ritual via a focus on the body, on the body as a 'political field', and criticises modern definitions of ritual for placing emphasis on performance without attention to *apt* performance: 'Apt performance involves not symbols to be interpreted but abilities to be acquired according to rules that are sanctioned by those in authority; it presupposes no obscure meanings but rather the formation of physical and linguistic skills.'[72] Asad introduces the concept of apt performance to reflect the recent sociological imperative to study rites for their *embodied* practices. Tracing the lineage of this epistemology to Mauss (prior to Bourdieu, to whom the idea is more widely credited), Asad maintains that, 'The concept of *habitus* invites us to analyse the body as an assemblage of embodied aptitudes, not as a medium of symbolic meanings.'[73] This opens up the possibility of 'inquiring into the ways in which embodied practices (including language in use) form a precondition for varieties of religious experience'.[74]

---

[71]   See, for example: Mitchell, *Social Sciences*.

[72]   T. Asad, *Genealogies of Religion: Disciplines and Reasons of Power in Christianity and Islam* (Baltimore, MD: John Hopkins University Press, 1993).

[73]   Asad, *Genealogies*, 75. Mauss here disagreed with Durkheim, by proposing that in order to overcome the Cartesian mind-body dualism, 'the human body was not to be viewed simply as the passive recipient of "cultural imprints", still less as the source of "natural expressions" that are "clothed in local history and culture"....It was to be viewed as the developable means for achieving a range of human objectives, from styles of physical movement (e.g.: walking), through modes of emotional being (e.g.: composure) to kinds of spiritual experience (e.g.: mystical states).' Ibid., 76.

[74]   Asad. *Genealogies*, 76. See also: F.D. Goodman, 'A Trance Dance with Masks: Research and Performance at the Cuymaungue Institute', *TDR, Drama Review* 34:1

Asad pursues this with an extraordinary exposé of the way in which the bodily disciplines - meals, words, gestures - of the Rule of St Benedict formed religious desires, or virtues, in the bodies of the monks. The rites prescribed in the monastic programme, he writes, 'did not simply evoke or release universal emotions, they aimed to reconstruct and reorganize instinctive emotions - desire (*cupiditas/caritas*), humility (*humilitas*), remorse (*contritio*) - on which the central Christian virtue of obedience to God depended.'[75] There is a goal to ritual in Asad's view, but one that can only be understood by thorough reconstruction of the historical conditions contextualising any particular set of ritual acts. In the case of medieval Benedictine monks, that goal was communion with God, but it was not any sort of symbolic or aspirational goal, rather, 'The inability to enter into communion with God becomes the function of untaught bodies'.[76]

Asad is drawing attention to the primacy of technique, of execution, in the study of ritual.[77] From the point of view of theology consulting the social sciences this is an important concept to take on board because, as Mitchell notes, it establishes a bottom line which insists, like Staal, that 'religious reality (including ritual) must be allowed to be itself, and not simply a set of symbols that point to something else.'[78] Furthermore, Asad offers a hint about the vexed question of access that offers a methodological precedent for this essay: in his study, the point of access to rituals is through study of their interrelated embodied practices, including language in use.

There are, however, some significant attendant difficulties. Asad's conclusions - with their denial of critical faculties on the part of participants, their denial of ritual infelicities as anything other than the product of untaught bodies, their denial of creativity among ritual actors well as their denial of the body of the critic vis-à-vis his or her relation to the subject of study - seem to ride roughshod over those other ritual critics, like Grimes, who have shared his emphasis on its embodied nature.

(1990) 102-114. Goodman conducted extensive experimental research on the effects of adopting specific physical postures on mental/emotional/cognitive states.

[75] Asad, *Genealogies*, 134.

[76] Asad, *Genealogies*, 77.

[77] Wittgenstein, in line with his philosophy of linguistic illocution, commented on a magical cure described in Frazer's *The Golden Bough*, 'In magical healing one *indicates* to an illness that it should leave the patient. After the description of any such magical cure we'd like to add: If the illness doesn't understand *that*, then I don't know *how* one ought to say it.' Tom Driver remarks of this famous comment that it 'reminds us that the oddities of ritual are not greater than the peculiarities of language because, at one level, ritual is language. But Wittgenstein's remark misses the sense of ritual as obligatory, the sense that if you are going to obey a particular God or to heal a certain disease, you must do it in a prescribed way. In short, ritual is not only language but also technique.' T. Driver, *The Magic of Ritual: Our Need for Liberating Rites that Transform Our Lives and Our Communities* (New York: HarperCollins, 1991) 144.

[78] Asad, *Genealogies*, 86.

Most pertinent among these issues is the question of the role and purpose of authority in ritual. Asad concludes that the work of the anthropologist of religion 'must be primarily a matter of describing a dependence on authoritative practices and discourses, and not of intuiting a mental state laying beyond them said to be caused by ritual'.[79] What is contentious is neither 'mental states' (few anthropologists nowadays proceed in the fashion described), nor the idea of 'dependence' on practices, but the question of what makes these practices 'authoritative'. Asad said earlier, regarding the medieval Benedictines, that the practices were the result of following rules established by those in authority. This notion of an 'external' authority operative in ritual is contested by Grimes who notes the ways in which, if, as Asad maintains, ritual is the thing itself and not a referential code, then authority can (indeed should) be internal to it, that is, needing no one else's sanction.

Grimes proposes that the appeal to tradition as a justification for ritual authority, an appeal that 'it's just the way it's done', is a deterrent to criticism, a ruse to 'deflect explanation'.[80] He prefers to see the 'tradition' posited as an authority as 'a mode of active construction',[81] a means by which rites evolve and are constantly recreated by the act of doing them. He is careful to stress that this does not dismiss the idea of tradition, but rather builds on it: 'I do not want to argue that ritual cannot be traditional, only that it is also invented and that it can be creative.'[82] His argument is that because every speech act and every gesture is a unique act, every ritual therefore creates itself anew - and differently. He says the argument can thus be made that 'The authority... of ritual is dependent on - in fact ought to grow organically out of - those who participate in it.'[83] Unfortunately, he does not develop this view in further detail. Others involved in what Grimes calls 'emerging ritual'[84] have developed the idea as it pertains to Christian worship, and this will be considered in greater detail in Chapter Five. So the problematic issue is not simply authority or legitimation or validation but, as Asad has himself alerted us in his application of Foucault's theory, power.

The difficulty with Asad's position lies in its claim that the inability of a ritual to be effective is due to untaught bodies, because this overlooks the complexity of the power dynamics of 'teaching'. It also overlooks the power-relations conditioning the production of the texts which he studied as sources for this work, and it overlooks his own power-placement as anthropologist as well. As feminist ethnology has sought to demonstrate, any cultural analysis 'is composed of seriously contested codes of meaning... language and politics are inseparable,

---

79	Ibid., 249.
80	Grimes, *Reading, Writing and Ritualising*, 7.
81	Ibid., 9.
82	Ibid., 8.
83	Ibid., 46.
84	Ibid., 24. Emerging ritual, for Grimes, is the ritualisation of marginal communities.

constructing the "other" entails relations of domination'.[85] Indeed, one must ask whether the desire to render ritual 'meaningless' and to emphasise instead a certain sense of both 'givenness' and 'obligation' serves both to mask and to sustain the patriarchal nature of the rites that Asad and Staal study.

Catherine Bell criticises this way of construing 'power' as 'the simplistic misconception that power is the imposition of one person's or group's will on others'[86] as opposed to the complex multi-faceted creation of a whole society, as described by Foucault. She asks, 'How does ritual do what we keep saying it does: How does it actually inculcate cultural or political values, converting beliefs about another world into facts about this one and vice versa, and "inventing" traditions even as it purports to be transmitting them?'[87] She concludes that it does this because 'Ritual is the thing itself. It *is* power; it acts and it actuates.'[88] Bell's proposal is that, contrary to all the established theories, ritual is neither a 'referential instrument' nor a 'functional mechanism' nor an 'expressive medium in the service of social solidarity and control',[89] it, 'ritualisation', is rather 'a strategic mode of practice' and it is itself 'the very production and negotiation of power relations'.[90] Her position is thus quite akin to Asad's:

> The ultimate purpose of ritualisation is neither the immediate goals avowed by the community or the officiant nor the more abstract functions of social solidarity and conflict resolution; it is nothing other than the production of ritualised agents, persons who have an instinctive knowledge of these schemes embedded in their bodies, in their sense of reality, and in their understanding of how to act in ways that both maintain and qualify the complex microrelations of power.[91]

Undoubtedly, Bell's emphasis on ritualisation (instead of a thing called ritual), on its strategies (rather than its supposedly fixed rules) and on its effectiveness as a means of negotiation (rather than inculturation or anything else) have all radically altered the contemporary study of rituals. Her statements on power, however, demand further attention, as they fail to address several problematic issues arising from her implication that power *can* always be negotiated.

A situation of domination or oppression by definition involves one party depriving the other of an equal right to negotiate. If the purpose of ritualisation is, as she and Asad maintain, to empower ritual agency, then what of those people who are disempowered by those very practices? Nearly all the ethnographic fieldwork undertaken and published so far has been by North Atlantic scholars who look at

---

[85] D.J. Hess, 'The New Ethnography and the Anthropology of Science and Technology', *Knowledge and Society* 9 (1992) 10.

[86] Bell, *Ritual Theory, Ritual Practice*, 194.

[87] Ibid., 194.

[88] Ibid., 195.

[89] Ibid., 197.

[90] Ibid., 196. Her thinking here is much influenced by that of Clifford Geertz.

[91] Ibid., 221.

far away places or far away times. When they address questions of ritualised violence it is with some sort of distance: either through ethological comparison or study of a more 'primitive' society.

The urgency of studying ritual has to be related to the extraordinary proliferation of 'ritualised' violence in our own times and places. Chapter One asked how women could continue to participate in rituals that endorsed a form of power that supported and fostered a gender bias that was damaging to women. But there are many other instances of the ritualisation of violence, from the obvious - such as ritual abuse, to the more tangential such as the Irish struggle to come to terms with so many of its ordained ritual-leaders being involved in sexually abusing their (often young) ritual-participants, to the seemingly obscure but no less relevant, such as domestic violence: the ritualised quality of descriptions of home violence is compelling and disturbing.[92] Perhaps most urgent in our own context is the connection between religious ritual and political/para-military sectarianism. Yet ritual theory, in its use of religious studies, comparative anthropology, social anthropology, ethnology and artistic criticism has failed to address this issue for want of a) a workable critique of ritual power and b) cases studies close to home.

Bell writes that 'Ritualisation always aligns one within a series of relationships linked to the ultimate sources of power' and asks, 'What forms of power are defined in the relationships so redemptively reordered?'[93] Her suggestion of 'redemption' as the work of ritualisation (vis-à-vis power) is but one example of the way that ritual studies' insistence on power as both complex and abstract serves to idealise it and mask its systemic nature. For many people, the experience of being ritually forged as social agents has been far from redemptive. To explore this issue further, the next chapter delves deeper into the social sciences, into the philosophy of society, and fosters a conversation between theology, ritual studies and Habermas. Habermas is chosen because his work has explicitly placed the issue of the abuse of power at the centre of his project of a theory of society.

'Even to say it in one word, ritual, is asking for trouble.'[94]

Contemporary theologians turning to the social sciences for help in understanding the nature of their rituals are in for a rockier ride that hitherto imagined. The above synopsis has demonstrated that the term 'ritual' itself, as Schechner wryly remarks, has become 'trouble'. Indeed, in some quarters, the conclusions drawn from scrutinising what is intended by the word have rendered it virtually redundant.[95]

---

[92] See: C.J. Adams and M.M. Fortune, eds., *Violence Against Women and Children* (New York: Continuum, 1995). See also the many fictional accounts of domestic violence, e.g.: R. Doyle, *The Woman who Walked into Doors* (London: Jonathan Cape, 1993).

[93] Bell, *Ritual Theory, Ritual Practice*, 141.

[94] Schechner, *The Future of Ritual*, 228.

[95] See, for example, Bell: although she retains its usage in the titles of her books.

Current scholarship in ritual studies goes beyond 'ritual' in several ways. For a start, it no longer looks for a single theory to explain the nature of ritual, acknowledging that it is no longer appropriate to compare it to an innate, universal phenomenon such as language-formation because of diversity of practice and diversity of understanding.

In subsequently finding similarities in patterns of practice (such as with rites of passage) scholars are careful to remain focused on the rites in their historical contexts rather than to draw from them conclusions about the nature of *all* rites. This marks a significant departure from the field to which these scholars were heir, wherein ritual was understood to be a pan-cultural way of acting that 'achieved' a particular result in all locations, whether it was conjuring the myths of a people's origins, establishing and maintaining a social order, or facilitating symbol-systems for mediating the gods or spirits. Although each of these interpretations has been discredited, the point is not what the interpretation supposed but the fact that scholars no longer look for a single, all-encompassing, one-theory-fits-all description of what ritual is or does because, as Grimes remarks, 'Ritual is not a single kind of action. Rather it is a convergence of several kinds we normally think of as distinct. It is an "impure" genre'.[96]

Several methodological criteria are emerging in its place. As mentioned above, Catherine Bell, concluding that 'ritual, as such, does not exist',[97] suggests that we look instead to 'ritualising' with the purpose of encouraging a scholarly focus on the *process* as a means to overcoming the ingrained notion of ritual as a complete package (that can be studied as such). Ritualisation, Bell proposes, is a 'strategic way of acting'[98] (distinct from other ways of acting), a constant interplay of mutual negotiation aimed, she suspects, at consent-formation. The critical difference in Bell's account is its awareness of the indefinite nature of ritualised practices: the suggestion that the 'consent' which is at play is neither pre-determined (as a mythic or psychic code, or a social order, nor a fixed symbol system) nor inevitable.

Fiona Bowie likewise starts with warning against the 'fundamental problem in seeking to define ritual in western societies... as a cross-cultural category with parallels elsewhere'[99] but proceeds to advance a view of ritual based on Van Gennep's three-fold structure of rites of passage, concluding that 'it is the potential of rituals to transform people and situations that lends them their power'.[100] In this Bowie reflects a remarkable amount of contemporary scholarship which, despite its anti-universalising sensitivity, nevertheless attributes 'transformative power' to ritual and then maintains, moreover, that this is what

---

[96] Grimes, *Ritual Criticism*, 192.

[97] Bell, *Ritual Theory, Ritual Practice*, 140.

[98] Ibid., 141.

[99] F. Bowie, *The Anthropology of Religion* (Oxford: Blackwell, 2000) 154.

[100] Ibid., 183.

Beyond Ritual

distinguishes it from other forms of activity.[101] This position owes much to the influence of performance theory, in particular Schechner's vision of a 'continuum' with ritual (efficacy) and theatre (entertainment) at either end.[102] Schechner's theory proposes that all theatre involves ritual and *vice versa*, but for ritual to be truly ritual it has to manifest results in the arena of efficacy, not entertainment: something has to have changed. To describe a performance that is efficacious, a ritual, Schechner coins the term 'a transformance', emphasising the transformative thrust of the performance.

Grimes is more ambivalent about ascribing transformation to ritual in a general way, differentiating rites of passage and other rituals: 'To enact any kind of rite is to *per*form, but to enact a rite of passage is also to *trans*form.'[103] Grimes draws a distinction between the transformative purpose and power of rites of passage and other non-passage types of ritual such as, 'Witnessing a moving play, attending weekly worship, or experiencing an orgasm' which he suggests, 'can transport us into reverie, but a few days later our commitment needs rekindling.'[104] While this raises an important note of caution amid a general consensus that 'ritual transforms', it nevertheless begs the question of where the boundaries are being drawn between rites of passage and other types. Roman Catholic theology would claim that every Sunday mass, far from being a 'mere moment in which participants get carried away emotionally'[105] is, of its very nature, holistically transformative. Far from needing a weekly 'top up' because the last dose has been spent, these worshippers are committed to an ongoing process of transformation, where every ritual builds on the work of the last. One alternative might be to suggest a continuum from and including rites of passage to other sorts, to avoid this polarisation; this would, however, attract the critique of attributing transformation to all types.

A further alternative may be to follow Staal and refuse any appropriation of the language of efficacy at all; however, such a stance undervalues the extraordinary volume of ethnography wherein participants (individuals and communities) in ritual have reported a transformation. It also ignores the key question hidden in that data, which is why we (western scholars) want ritual to be transformative? And it fails to address the other key question which Grimes has highlighted: why rituals sometimes do not work: 'Rites can not only fail to achieve what they purport to do, they can also become a means of oppression, so we cannot

---

[101] For example, see also Bobby Alexander: ritual 'effects a transition from everyday life to an alternative context within which the everyday is transformed'. *Televangelism*, 139.

[102] See: R. Schechner, *Essays on Performance Theory, 1970-1976* (New York: Drama Book Specialists, 1977) 75 - 80.

[103] R.L. Grimes, *Deeply Into the Bone: Re-inventing Rites of Passage* (Berkeley, CA: University of California Press, 2000) 7.

[104] Ibid., 7.

[105] Ibid., 7.

afford to view them through a fuzzy, romanticised lens.'[106] Ambivalence also surrounds even the very basic claim that ritual transforms insofar as it renders the ordinary extraordinary. Recent studies expose and dispute the assumptions on which this is based; Michael Aune, for example, describes these as 'mystifying and romanticizing' and reports that in his fieldwork 'it was precisely the affirmation (and not the transformation) of *ordinary* life that was at issue'.[107]

Transformation, it seems, is widely perceived by North Atlantic scholarship to happen often in ritual, but it is far from certain whether this is due to a peculiar power resident exclusively in ritual processes themselves or because ritual is of itself transformative or has the power to transform. Indeed there is a strong current in contemporary ethnography that, refusing to see ritual behaviour as necessarily distinct from other ways of acting, would suggest that any attribution of 'transformation' to a set of actions makes no sense unless understood in a far fuller cultural context.

This position takes what Tambiah first knew, that the relation between ritual and non-ritual is entirely relative (rather than generic or absolute, as previously assumed)[108] and seeks to develop a methodology to suit. Based on their studies of British Quakers and Swedish charismatic Protestants, Coleman and Collins propose that 'there is much to be gained from removing ritual activities from their analytically isolated position as special paradigmatic acts and restoring them to the context of social activity in general'.[109] However, when it comes to actually accessing this they conclude that, 'Religious practice in collective contexts provides a focus for the exercise of such a *habitus* in its most favourable habitat; away from the meeting house or church, such practice becomes more attenuated or implicit as it encounters differing... contexts of practice.'[110] For the moment, then, in this study, a focus is retained on ritual, but with an awareness that it is an artificial construction; the events witnessed in Chapters Four and Five are rooted not in their own codes but in those of a far more complex web of lived experience.

The question of ritual's boundaries is one that is only just beginning to attract serious scholarly attention. Where does ritualising begin and end? Where does ordinary life (with which it is frequently contrasted) begin and end? For example, those who speak about a rite are ordinarily understood to be talking about a past event; however, as Grimes has recently suggested, this 'narrative' is not so

---

[106] Ibid., 7.

[107] M.B. Aune, 'The Subject of Ritual: Ideology and Experience in Action' in M.B. Aune and V. DeMarinis eds., *Religious and Social Ritual: Interdisciplinary Explorations* (Albany, NY: State University of New York Press, 1996) 142.

[108] See the collection of his early essays: S.J. Tambiah, *Culture, Thought and Social Action: An Anthropological Perspective* (Cambridge, MA: Harvard Universtiy Press, 1985).

[109] S. Coleman and P. Collins, 'The "Plain" and the "Positive": Ritual, Experience and Aesthetics in Quakerism and Charismatic Christianity', *Journal of Contemporary Religion* 15:3 (October 2000) 317.

[110] Ibid., 326.

much *about* the rite as a continuation *of* it: 'Sometimes the telling and retelling become extensions of the rite itself, stretching it from the original performance in the past until it touches and transforms the present.'[111] Yet this does not necessarily mean that the 'work' of the rite is the 'work' of the narrative: 'On the one hand, narratives can render rites even more meaningful than they were in the actual moment of their performance. On the other, they can downplay a rite's original significance.'[112] This profoundly challenges the established understanding of rituals as (singular) events, returning the debate to a position quite close to Asad's, for whom rituals were not special singular occasions but multiple parts of a broad fabric of constantly becoming a social agent.

If scholarship is to develop these various insights beyond what was previously understood as 'ritual', the difficulty that persistently presents is *how*. The demands that it move beyond the text are well documented, in anthropology as much as in liturgiology, but in its place, what? As seen above, discourse on methodology is nowadays tightly woven into the formation of ritual theory and criticism: each reveals the other. At the turn of the twentieth-century, anthropological method favoured fieldwork as a replacement for the 'armchair' approach of its nineteenth century predecessor. The task of anthropology was description, to provide a record of people's ways. By the 1970's, however, it was noticed that this method presented a significant problem: as John Saliba puts it, 'The chief experience of ethnographers was that of "culture shock"... which was obviously not shared by the indigenous people.'[113] In a position very close to Bell's, Saliba concludes that instead of studying the cultures of other peoples, anthropologists were in fact only reflecting their own.

In response, Saliba and others developed a 'cognitive' anthropology which aimed to 'elicit that culture's own semantic categories',[114] the basis of which still relied on fieldwork but emphasised the ethnographer as listener, 'allowing' the subject 'to choose, as often as possible, the topics of conversation and to discuss the issues they have in mind'.[115] These developments ended up revealing far more about the latent patriarchalism and imperialism of the project of anthropology than they did about any indigenous culture, which was, in itself, a massive step although not the expected one.[116]

Today, anthropology is not as paralysed as was at first feared by its late twentieth century reformers[117] and, with a current emphasis on social anthropology,

---

[111] Grimes, *Deeply into the Bone*, 10.

[112] Ibid., 10.

[113] J.Saliba, 'The New Ethnography and the Study of Religion', *Journal for the Scientific Study of Religion* 13 (1974) 146.

[114] Ibid., 147.

[115] Ibid., 148.

[116] Bruce Lincoln has written convincingly on the latent gender bias in sociological and anthropological approaches to religion. See: *Emerging from the Chrysalis*.

[117] See: C. Geertz, *The Theater State in Nineteenth Century Bali* (Princeton: Princeton University Press, 1980).

retains a methodological basis in field observation, now understood as, 'talking to and interacting with people and ultimately attempting to understand their symbolic worlds and *social action*'.[118] Yet the question of how one person from one culture, through talking to those of another, arrives at the point of 'understanding' is far from clear and almost never addressed. Grimes has at the centre of his programme of ritual criticism the claim that 'ritual embodiment is a primary means through which societies remember and thus create tradition'[119] and in all his writings seeks to interpret the embodied features of the action. His work is ground-breaking in its acknowledgement of the body of the supposed 'observer' in this interaction, in his awareness of the ways in which the participants are critical during the rite (and express this bodily) and in his persistent anti-romantic reminders that rituals can cause (bodily) harm and fail. However, his reliance in his most recent work on ritual narratives (what people say about the rites they have been part of)[120] suggests that it is only by looking at what people themselves say about their own rites that we can actually form judgements about what it is they think they are doing in them. Again this raises the specific problem of power, highlighted in Hess's remark, that the narrators themselves may be as blind as the ethnologist to 'oppressive systems of imperialism, race, class and gender'.[121]

In the following chapter I turn to the philosophy of Jürgen Habermas. His magnum opus, *The Theory of Communicative Action*, has sought to address these two precise - and connected - issues: access and power. It may seem strange that this study should investigate a somewhat anti-religious theory with the expectation that it holds the potential to allow a greater understanding of religious ritual, but that is its wager.

Theology, like ritual theory, is at an impasse. Having exhausted its long-established *modum operandi* in textual analysis, it is determined to reframe its interpretations in the context of the body; but it does not know how to do so without falling into the old trap of *x* (the elite power) judges *y* (the strange Other). For liturgical theology, a nascent discipline constructed in dialogue with now-outdated theories of sociology and anthropology, this presents a truly radical problem: having set itself up as an interpreter of experience, it has produced some marvellous works of theology as the result of the honesty and courage of those who have sought to describe and critique their own experiences (Kavanagh, Ramshaw, Saliers, Walton) and yet fails in its desire to say something of the experiences of a

---

[118] D.J. Hess, 'The New Ethnography and the Anthropology of Science and Technology', *Knowledge and Society* 9 (1992) 4.

[119] Grimes, *Reading Writing and Ritualising*, 14.

[120] See: Grimes, *Deeply into the Bone*, 9 - 10: 'In this book I do not approach ritual by way of *ritual myths* but by calling upon *passage narratives*, accounts told by individuals who narrate their experiences of passage... They reveal the joys and disappointments of ritual with less artifice and more candour than either myths or how-to and theoretical literature.'

[121] D.J. Hess, 'The New Ethnography', 10 - 11.

wider community because there are as yet no established models for accessing the experiences of anyone other than oneself. This is not to pretend or desire that the voice of the observer could disappear. It is, rather, more a question of degree, an effort to get a little closer to what people themselves experience in ritual practices.

· This chapter has examined the main theories of the emerging discipline of ritual studies, in an attempt to understand both the nature of ritual as a supposed genre of human behaviour and the methodologies used for approaching the study of this type of activity. Far from supporting the straight-forward view of ritual in contemporary sacramental and liturgical theology, which claims that rituality secures a particular, embodied religious/symbolic effect, the investigation reported a significant degree of ambivalence on the part of ritual theorists when it came to ascribing special powers to ritual, or even to considering it a unique and discrete genre of behaviour. The outcome exposed a much more variegated understanding of human ritual that focused on its properties as ritualisation, as a 'strategic way of acting'. It also uncovered a gaping lack of attention to the fact that while current scholarship insists on studying ritual in its embodied and experiential forms, *how* this is to be accessed (for the purposes of scholarship) remains largely unexplored. It is in light of Staal's assertion that such experience is not beyond the scope of the human sciences that the following chapter considers Jürgen Habermas's contention that a careful analysis of speech acts can afford the type of access ritual studies require.

PART II

Chapter Three

Developing a Theological Model of Communicative Action

If I look to myself alone, I am right nought; but if I look to all together, I am in hope, in oneness of charity with all my even-Christians.[1]

I

Chapter One identified the inadequacies of traditional definitions of sacrament in a world that has outgrown ontology and to which such metaphysically-based theology makes little sense. In the light of liturgical theology, it proposed that the appropriate location for the study of sacrament is in ritual. Chapter Two proceeded to test the central claim made by Chauvet and others that *rituality* (and therefore liturgy) gives privileged access to the symbolic against the evidence of the emerging field of ritual studies. Concurrently, the investigation also questioned the popular 'turn to language' in sacramental theology (espoused by Power, Fink, Ross, et al.) querying the limitations imposed on their conclusions by the wider evidence of linguistic philosophy. Several questions emerged from this debate, some methodological: what are the limits on theology consulting the social sciences, and how can we access experience; others interpretative: is ritual a meaning-oriented activity, is sacrament only to be encountered ritually, what are the implications of a non-metaphysical conception of sacrament for our understanding of God?

From discussion of the first of these questions, reviewed toward the end of Chapter Two, it became apparent that there is an impasse in ritual studies that is similar to the one facing contemporary liturgical theology regarding the issue of access. The question of *how* scholarship accesses ritual experience gives rise to the more fundamental question of how one accesses any experience (and the assumptions about 'meaning' that are often related to it).[2] It is this question that the following discussion of linguistic philosophy seeks to address, in an effort to

---

1   Julian of Norwich, *A Revelation of Love* (Exeter: University of Exeter Press, 1986) 9.
2   The current impasse in the discipline is discussed in: R.T. McCutcheon, *The Outsider/Insider Problem in the Study of Religion: A Reader* (London: Cassell, 1999); yet McCutcheon does not mention Habermas.

identify methodological criteria for the more interpretative task in the remainder of the book.

This chapter examines the work of Jürgen Habermas, in particular his *The Theory of Communicative Action*, and suggests that his theory may enable theology to resolve the question of access. It holds this potential because, unlike most other socio-philosophical theories, it takes not action but interaction as its fundamental unit of social and linguistic analysis; this affords theology a methodological basis which is appropriate to its subject, i.e.: the relationship *between* humanity and God. Conventionally, God *acts*, humans *act* (by God's grace) and the sacraments are described as *acts*, or *actions* (or even events). The methodology that will be proposed asks what it would look like if this mediation were understood in terms not of actors and actions but of *interactions* between speakers and hearers. Chapters Four and Five adopt this question as their framework; for now what is required is careful analysis of Habermas's model of interaction itself.

II

In opposition to both Marxism itself and to early critical theory, Habermas aims 'to free historical materialism from its philosophy-of-history ballast.'[3]

Many, like Outhwaite, see the German philosopher Jürgen Habermas as heir to the Frankfurt School, birthplace of what is now known as Critical Theory. In common with many others of that school, his formative influences are interdisciplinary: from history, Marx through Adorno; from philosophy, Kant and Hegel through Heidegger; and from the central methodological tenet of the Frankfurt discourse itself, the necessity of an interdisciplinary epistemology. Habermas's primary ideological influences are, then, a typical mixture of the ethical and the existential: 'Critical theory is best understood as attempting a theoretical synthesis of Marx's and radical liberalism's concern for the problem of justice (and so domination and exploitation) with continental philosophy's concern for the problem of meaning (and so the problem of nihilism).'[4] However, while acknowledging his philosophical background, it should also be noted that Habermas is not always in agreement with the luminaries of the school with which he is so closely associated; as will be suggested below, his criticism of both Heidegger and post-structuralism results in a nuanced, if not ambivalent, view of modernism itself.[5]

---

[3] W. Outhwaite, ed., *The Habermas Reader* (Cambridge: Polity Press, 1996) 307.

[4] J.M. Bernstein, *Recovering Ethical Life: Jürgen Habermas and the Future of Critical Theory* (London, New York: Routledge, 1995) 2.

[5] David Ingram comments that, 'In general, Habermas does not think that his predecessors succeeded in either of these tasks[:] ...The first concerns the *grounding* of critical theory in normative expectations and values that necessarily govern human conduct. The second... is concerned with the problem of working out a *scientific method* that will

This reflects the fact that Habermas's mature influences, like his concerns, stretch far beyond the limits of the school to which he is said to belong. From America, he based his own work on that of George Herbert Mead and drew inspiration from his sparring partner, Richard Rorty; from England, he was affected by Austin, Searle and particularly Wittgenstein; and from France, the existentialists. His main concern in all these philosophical conversations is the impact of a global capitalist economy and ethic on the contemporary world, and how these influence human relationships at all levels from the personal and intimate to the corporate and technical. His ongoing project, which he understands as both an exposition of and a manifesto for resistance to this 'colonisation of the lifeworld',[6] is a comprehensive theory of society, based on a radical reconceptualisation of the subject.

The unique contribution Habermas has made to philosophy at large, according to his peers, has been to shift it from the 'work' model of activity to one based on communicative action. Prior to Habermas, the essence of the philosophy of the subject was that the subject was defined by his or her 'work'; after Habermas, philosophy is required to explore the ramifications of a theory of the subject wherein it is the subject-subject relation, not a subject-object relation, that gives the point of access to the subject. Moreover, following Habermas, the channel by which this access is mediated is (entirely) linguistic. One of his students and critics, Seyla Benhabbib gives a concise summary of Habermas's place in the tradition:

> The concept of communicative reason brings with it two major revisions in critical theory: first, the relation between self-reflection and autonomy is re-established in light of a theory of discourse. It is claimed that the cognitive capacity to engage in discourse justification of validity claims also implies a universalist ethical standpoint. Second, autonomy is understood in communicative terms. Autonomy no longer means self-legislation, as in Kant, self-actualization as with Hegel and Marx, or mimesis as with Adorno and Horkheimer, but the cognitive competence to adopt a universalist standpoint and the interactive competence to act on such a basis.[7]

In his conclusions to date, Habermas has been criticised for clinging to the goals and assumptions of modernism which, according to many post-modernist thinkers, are responsible for the perpetuation of much of the iniquity in contemporary society. Yet Habermas insists that he is not naïve to the problems

---

endow social critique with a high degree of objectivity and precision.' D. Ingram, *Critical Theory and Philosophy* (New York: Paragon House, 1990) 108.

6 This phrase is repeated many times in Habermas's work. See for example, J. Habermas, *The Theory of Communicative Action* Vol. 2. *Lifeworld and System: A Critique of Functionalist Reason* (Cambridge: Polity Press, 1987) 154 - 157, 332 - 342.

7 S. Benhabbib, *Critique, Norm and Utopia: A Study of the Foundations of Critical Theory* (New York: Columbia University Press, 1986) 282.

caused by modernism and believes that these occur precisely because it is incomplete as a project. He prefers, therefore, the twin goals of both criticism and reform. Outhwaite highlights the way in which Habermas thus breaks with modernism as a project while also espousing its continuation:

> To do philosophical justice to this project ... we must move away from what [Habermas] variously calls the philosophy of consciousness, the philosophy of the subject, or subject-centred reason, to an alternative model based on the communicative relations *between* human subjects. Only in this way can we recover and reanimate what he calls the normative content of modernity.[8]

It is this insight, to focus on the relations between people rather than examining (a network of) individuals' actions and motivations, that enables Habermas to straddle the old world of modernism and the new, post-modernist world of its critics.

Arguing against Parsons,[9] whose delineation of action as the basic unit of social analysis had been the dominant force in social theory for twenty years, Habermas maintained that *interaction*, not action, is that analytical unit. In this he was developing the work of George Herbert Mead, furthering his theory that our very selves, personally and culturally, are created through such units and so to access an understanding of particular actions, or to construct a theory of society, one must first have considered the interactive processes that created it. The result of this argument against the dominant epistemology of the social sciences was *The Theory of Communicative Action*. While it did not amount to the ambitious attempt to provide a linguistic foundation for the social sciences which he had originally attempted, it was nevertheless embedded in the context of his ongoing proposal of a (interactively-based) theory of society.[10]

In this theory of communicative action Habermas lays out the theoretical principles which he uses to model the essentially interactive conduct of individuals within a society. Initially, Habermas called these 'universal pragmatics', but in more recent work has changed this to 'formal pragmatics'. It is an important distinction in introducing his theory, as it sheds light on two aspects of the theory itself. By 'universal', he meant to signify that rather than being concerned with particular, identifiable situations, he wanted to create a model of those aspects of communication that were applicable to any context; by 'formal' he intended to overcome the negative associations with 'universal' in post-modern anti-Enlightenment critiques, while simultaneously showing his hand to be a formalist one.

---

8 Outhwaite, *The Habermas Reader*, 307.
9 T. Parsons, *The Social System* (New York: Free Press, 1951).
10 Reflecting this, according to Arie Brand, 'Habermas presents his views partly through a history of theory, which is interwoven with the account of his own ideas.' A. Brand, *The Force of Reason: An Introduction to Habermas's Theory of Communicative Action* (Sydney: Allen and Unwin, 1990) 67.

Maeve Cooke suggests that Habermas chose the phrase 'formal pragmatics' to remind readers of the relationship between his work and that of formal semantics;[11] but it can also be taken as a reminder of the wider world of Formalism, a cross-disciplinary deconstructive/reconstructive analytical hermeneutic that has flourished in the twentieth century. Formalists are the structural engineers of the twentieth century academic world. Habermas's principal concern is the spoken word (in dialogue) and a useful analogy for understanding the nature of its formal analysis is with the written word (in literature). Terry Eagleton argues that Formalism as a literary theory gained its description as 'formal' because it was:

> essentially the application of linguistics to the study of literature; and because the linguistics in questions were of a formal kind, concerned with the structures of language rather than with what one might actually say, the Formalists passed over the analysis of literary 'content' (where one might always be tempted into psychology or sociology) for the study of literary form.[12]

What literary formalism has done for literary criticism, Habermas proposes to do for language-use: apply linguistics to uncover not the text, not the context, but the *pretext* of communication: the 'pragmatic' elements that make it possible, that make it what it is. Habermas makes clear from the start that although these elements could include such things as the non-verbal and body language, he intends to focus only on the verbal language in play, the 'speech actions'[13] and, as the following passage from Cooke's introduction to his recent anthology suggests, analysing the 'pragmatics' of speech actions brings us into the realm of the intuitive:

> Habermas's starting point is that formal analysis of language should not be restricted to semantic analysis, for formal investigation of the pragmatic dimensions of language is equally possible and important... Formal pragmatics, then, aims at a systematic construction of the intuitive linguistic knowledge of competent subjects, the intuitive 'rule consciousness' that a competent speaker has of her own language.[14]

To dispel any preconception that intuition is synonymous with the inaccessible, deeply personal or obscure, Habermas argues that the intuitive in each person is

---

[11] M. Cooke, 'Introduction' in J. Habermas, *On the Pragmatics of Communication* (Cambridge, MA: MIT Press, 1998) 1.

[12] T. Eagleton, *Literary Theory: An Introduction* (Oxford: Blackwell, 1983) 3.

[13] '...as language is the specific medium of understanding at the sociocultural stage of evolution, I want to ... single out explicit speech actions from other forms of communicative action. I shall ignore non-verbalised actions and bodily expressions.' J. Habermas, *Communication and the Evolution of Society* (Boston: Beacon Press, 1979) 1.

[14] Cooke, 'Introduction', 2.

intrinsically related to the intuitive in the Other with whom she or he relates. His proposal is that the intuitive is culturally conditioned, semantically-formed and, therefore, available for analysis by study of the language-use of competent[15] speakers and hearers:

> The task of universal pragmatics is to identify and reconstruct universal conditions of possible understanding *[Verständigung]*. In other contexts one also speaks of 'general presuppositions of communication', but I prefer to speak of general presuppositions of communicative action because I take the type of action aimed at reaching understanding to be fundamental.[16]

The distinction Habermas makes here, between 'communication' and 'communicative action', will be crucial to the application of his social theory to case studies of ritual practices later in this book. It is important at this point to note the reasoning behind his choice of terminology: he proposes that the *fundamental* type of human social action is that geared to reaching understanding and this is not adequately conveyed in the word 'communication' (with its implication of a 'successful' exchange, one which has been brought to resolution); whereas the phrase 'communicative action' leaves open its possibility.[17] The nub of the matter, which will be examined toward the end this chapter, is seeing speech acts as *bringing about* an understanding (through 'communicative action') rather than presuming, or even necessarily arriving at the point of, understanding ('communication'). The vocabulary is important because the differentiation in words allows a comprehension of communicative action which does not assume that it is synonymous with agreement. Agreement may be the goal but it is not always the result.[18] Habermas clearly acknowledges that there do exist non-agreement-achieving forms of social action (such as 'conflict, competition, strategic action in general'[19]) but he maintains that these are 'derivatives' of the fundamental type of action, which is that oriented to reaching understanding. Not all communicative actions result in agreement, but they are born of an instinct or,

---

[15] By competent, Habermas refers to those who are fluent in both the grammar and idiom of the language they are speaking, conversant with the culture in which they are speaking it and capable of speech. His use of 'competent speaker' does not have the pejorative tones associated with its English translation which may connote erudition or eloquence.

[16] Habermas, *Communication and the Evolution of Society*, 1.

[17] See, for example, Outhwaite's comment, 'His initial focus on linguistic communication, which paralleled, as he notes, what Karl-Otto Apel had called the "transformation of philosophy" broadens out into a substantive theory of communicative action, action oriented to the attainment and reproduction of mutual understanding. This may be a conversation, a political debate, or a decision-making process', or, as I shall argue later, a worship service. Outhwaite, *Reader*, 115.

[18] And to make this clearer, Habermas distinguishes in later work between *Verständigung* (mutual understanding) and *Einverständis* (agreement).

[19] Habermas, *Communication and the Evolution of Society*, 1.

more accurately perhaps, a technique, that has the possibility of reaching agreement as its ultimate purpose.

Habermas reconstructs the universal patterns involved in reaching mutual understanding as a series of *validity claims*. 'Coming to an understanding,' he says, 'is the process of bringing about an agreement on the presupposed basis of validity claims that can be mutually recognized'.[20] In communicative action we both raise and respond to these claims which, seen in the light of the following quotation, can be characterised as claims to comprehensibility, truth, truthfulness and rightness. Thus, Habermas suggests, 'in accepting a validity claim raised by the speaker, the hearer acknowledges the validity of symbolic structures; that is, he acknowledges that a sentence is grammatical, a statement true, an intention expression truthful, or an utterance correct.'[21] These validity claims are 'universal' in the sense that they are all in play in every speech act and although ordinarily just one may be raised explicitly, the others are always implied.[22] In 'argumentations' (a self-conscious, or examined, form of dialogue), 'validity claims which previously remained implicit because they arose performatively are expressly thematized.'[23] Interpretation of them can, therefore, make explicit that which is otherwise implicit.

In most of his subsequent work, Habermas streamlines these four validity claims to three: claims to truth, normative rightness and truthfulness, which Nick Crossley presents in terms of their reference, respectively, to:

1. Their propositional content,
2. The social and moral right of the speaker to say what he or she has said, and
3. The sincerity of the speaker.[24]

---

[20] Ibid., 19.

[21] Ibid.

[22] They are also 'universal' in the sense that Habermas is pursuing the Enlightenment goal of uncovering those human values that are utterly shared (while simultaneously decrying the colonisations that resulted from the Enlightenment project). Holding out for this notion of universality has attracted considerable controversy. Rorty, for example, writes, 'The residual difference I have with Habermas is that his universalism makes him substitute such convergence (as occurs in undistorted communication) for ahistorical grounding, whereas my insistence on the contingency of language makes me suspicious of the very idea of the "universal validity" which such convergence is supposed to underwrite...I want to replace this with a story of increasing willingness to live with plurality and to stop asking for universal validity.' R. Rorty, *Contingency, Irony and Solidarity* (Cambridge: Cambridge University Press, 1989) 67.

[23] J. Habermas, 'Transcendence from Within, Transcendence in the World' in D. Browning and F. Schüssler Fiorenza, eds., *Habermas, Modernity and Public Theology* (New York: Crossroad, 1992) 240.

[24] N. Crossley, 'Emotion and Communicative Action: Habermas, Linguistic Philosophy and Existentialism' in G. Bendelow and S.J. Williams, eds., *Emotions in Social Life: Critical Themes and Contemporary Issues* (London: Routledge, 1998) 16.

Because only one is normally raised explicitly (the others nevertheless remaining in play implicitly), utterances between speaker and hearer can be classified according to the principal validity claim that they make explicit. A difference in emphasis in validity claim affects a difference in nature of speech act. For example, according to Cooke, 'constative speech acts are connected in the first instance with truth claims, regulative speech acts with claims to normative rightness, and expressive speech acts with claims to truthfulness.'[25]

Cooke's threefold typography of speech acts complements Habermas's proposition that language is the mediator of three worlds: the whole external world, our shared social world and the particular inner world of the speaker:

> We can examine every utterance to see whether it is true or untrue, justified or unjustified, truthful or untruthful, because in speech, no matter what the emphasis, grammatical sentences are embedded in relations to reality in such a way that in an acceptable speech action segments of external nature, society and internal nature always come into appearance together.[26]

This raises the question, why do speakers and hearers need to refer to all three? 'In order to negotiate common definitions of the situation.'[27] And why do people need to negotiate a common definition of a situation? Because reaching an understanding is dependent upon it. And why do people need to reach understanding? Because justice in the modern world depends on it.

Habermas's theory of communicative action can only be understood within this, its overall context as a part of an explicitly ethically-motivated project. Habermas perceives that the social sciences prior to his work have sliced the world up into actors and actions, interpreting each from the perspective of purposive-rational action and this has resulted in a 'power-over'-determined social structure. This very structure can, however, be undermined, he argues, by a more nuanced interpretation of the language-exchange used in constructing it, which reveals a sub-structure that holds the seeds of more equal communicative action and hence more equal social relations.

When, toward the end of *The Theory of Communicative Action* he writes, 'The aspects of the rationality of action that we found in communicative action should now permit us to grasp processes of societal rationalization across their whole breadth, and no longer solely from the selective viewpoint of purposive-rational action',[28] Habermas makes plain what has been implied all along: he is not proposing a new way of being in the world; rather he is exposing a (potential) way of being that has been masked by the way language has been interpreted, but which has always nevertheless indwelt our language-exchange. Toward the end of this

---

[25]   Cooke, 'Introduction', 3.

[26]   Habermas, *Communication and the Evolution of Society*, 68.

[27]   J. Habermas, *The Theory of Communicative Action* Vol. 1. *Reason and the Rationalization of Society* (Boston: Beacon Press, 1984) 95.

[28]   Habermas, *The Theory of Communicative Action* Vol. 1, 335.

book, I suggest a revision of Chauvet's sacramental theology as a result of interpreting ritual in light of Habermas's theory; such a conversation is made possible only by the parallel exposed here: what Chauvet knows is that indwelling the metaphysical conception of sacrament is a deeper knowledge of God's mediation than has hitherto been possible, just as Habermas knows that a desire for communicative action (understanding) inhabits even our power-laden language use.

So to return to the question - why do hearers and speakers need to refer to all three 'worlds' - because by doing so they ensure that they are not being deluded into a merely partial construction of the situation which they inhabit. The 'colonisation of the lifeworld' that has, in Habermas's view, been wreaked on contemporary society depends on the submission, unwitting or otherwise, of individuals to a delusion (the partial construction of the situation); by revealing the hermeneutics of its power, Habermas intends to enable both dissent and the construction of alternative (emancipatory) social forms.

Habermas developed a 'pragmatic' theory of meaning in response to his dissatisfaction with both speech-act theory and formal-semantic theories of meaning which, in his view, were responsible for perpetuating a one-sided interpretative model. In earlier work he had presented his theory of meaning as an extension of formal-semantic theories, but in his later work[29] he claims his own theory 'undercuts' these. It does so via its pragmatics, and the chief mechanism of his pragmatics is his epistemology: studying the raising and redeeming of validity claims in language usage. Unlike speech-act theory, he makes a connection between all communicative actions and validity claims that are potentially context-transcendent and, unlike formal semantics, he accounts for the communicative (instead of solely the non-communicative) use of language via the rational basis of its conditioning validity claims. Where semantics is concerned with sentences, Habermas is concerned with *utterances* (i.e.: the whole pragmatic context in which the sentence is located and which includes the sentence) which he defines as acts of raising validity claims.

The basic premise of this approach is that we can access meaning by looking at the pragmatics of speech acts, and the ground on which he makes his claim is that *communicative action has a rational basis*. The particular aspect of validity claims which offers the social scientist a break-through hermeneutic is not that they are raised in every speech act, but that they can be questioned and disputed. If I raise a validity claim, I must be prepared to defend my use of it; if challenged, I must be prepared to give reasons. If I hear a validity claim, I am entitled to question its use, to ask for reasons:

> Speaker and hearer can reciprocally motivate one another to recognize validity-claims because the context of the speaker's engagement is determined by a

---

29 See especially the discussion of his reply to Herb Schnädelbach's criticisms in: A. Honneth and H. Joas, eds., *Communicative Action: Essays on Jürgen Habermas's The Theory of Communicative Action* (Cambridge: Polity, 1991).

specific reference to a thematically stressed validity-claim, whereby the speaker, in a cognitively testable way, assumes,

a)   with a truth claim, obligations to provide grounds,
b)   with a rightness claim, obligations to provide justification, and
c)   with a truthfulness claim, obligations to prove trustworthy.[30]

The scholar can look at the validity claims raised and responded to (or 'redeemed') and analyse them, and by analysing them access the interaction that occurs between two (or more) communicatively acting agents.

In devising this methodology, Habermas is building on the work of Wittgenstein and his developers, Austin and Searle, for whom the *illocutionary* force of language is what bestows its effectiveness. Habermas extends the definition of 'illocutionary' in light of the *rational* foundations of his theory of meaning and argues that:

> The illocutionary force of a speech act consists in its capacity to move a hearer to act under the premises that the engagement signalled by the speaker is seriously meant:
>
> a)   in the case of institutionally bound speech acts, the speaker can borrow this force from the binding force of existing norms;
> b)   in the case of institutionally unbound speech acts, the speaker can develop this force by inducing the recognition of validity claims.[31]

In other words: by appealing to mutually recognisable articulations of the situation. In Habermas's hands, as Cooke points out, 'Illocutionary force is a rational force, for in performing a speech act, the speaker undertakes to support what she says with reasons, if necessary.'[32]

Underpinning his ability to use the term with this particular implication is what Habermas calls the 'epistemic turn' of Michael Dummett who shifted the focus on truth conditions to a focus on how one knows when a truth condition has been satisfied. No longer are we looking at the criteria, but at what it is to know what the criteria are. Habermas, however, in line with his pragmatic methodology, goes beyond Dummett by insisting that the validity of utterances is embedded in the utterances themselves rather than in an (external) ideal to which one can appeal (as is intrinsic to the idea of truth conditions). Habermas speaks of 'acceptability conditions' where Dummett speaks of 'assertability conditions', signalling his foundational pragmatic point: 'we understand the meaning of a speech act when we know what makes it acceptable. We know what makes a speech act acceptable when we know the *kinds* of reasons that a speaker can offer, if challenged, in order

---

[30]   Habermas, *Communication and the Evolution of Society*, 66.
[31]   Habermas, *Communication and the Evolution of Society*, 66.
[32]   Cooke, 'Introduction', 8.

to reach understanding with a hearer concerning the validity of the disputed claim.'[33]

But the main point that Habermas takes from Dummett remains: the appeals to truth that we make in any given situation are entirely conditioned by the context of that particular situation. The validity of the kinds of reasons that a speaker can offer only have relevance in a particular context: they are 'always in principle subject to revision in the light of new arguments based on new evidence and insights'[34] and this is one reason why Habermas's theory is 'pragmatic', because the validity of any claim is necessarily contingent on the concrete context of justification. However, and importantly for the use of his work by theologians, there is another reason why his theory is pragmatic: because he argues in his pragmatic theories of truth and justice that validity is itself pragmatic. 'Moral validity [is]... internally linked to the idea of discursively achieved consensus and hence to pragmatic contexts of justification.'[35]

Habermas is consequently distancing himself from those philosophers for whom truth is forever relative (e.g.: Rorty[36]) in an effort to maintain what he learnt from the heart of his theory of communicative action: 'the potential power of validity claims to explode actual contexts of justification.'[37] Validity claims can do this, he proposes, because of what he has established as their characteristic inherent unconditionality, their context-transcendent power. All forms of argumentation, and all arguments, are subsequently shown to be flawed. Are we then to settle for a permanently flawed idea of truth? The opposite, however, a Platonist ideal, had also been shown to be flawed. The middle path that Habermas proposes is one where we focus on the process of truth-making (rational discourse) rather than on the idea of truth as an outcome.

To do this he looks at the 'idealizing suppositions' or 'idealizations' of discourse, and it is 'from such idealizations, which guide the process of argumentation, that the idea of truth draws its power as a regulative idea'.[38] Truth *as a process*, and neither as an outcome nor as a presumed ideal or goal, is the 'universal' regulatory idea. And it is this revision that holds the key to the interpretative (rather than instrumental) sacramental theology that is proposed in Chapter Six.

---

[33] Ibid., 11.

[34] Ibid., 12.

[35] Ibid., 13.

[36] See R. Rorty, *Objectivity, Relativism and Truth* (Cambridge: Cambridge University Press, 1991). Cheetham characterises this insistence on ultimate relativity as the essence of '*post-modern* freedom... a breaking out of the Enlightenment straitjacket, a loosening of the bonds of reason and realism. There are facts no longer.' D. Cheetham, 'Postmodern Freedom and Religion', *Theology* 103:811 (Jan/Feb 2000) 29.

[37] Cooke, 'Introduction', 13.

[38] Ibid., 14.

III

To understand how the idealisations of argument give rise to a regulatory ethic of truth, it is necessary to return to certain aspects of Habermas's theory of communicative action. In particular, in light of this study's proposed application of the theory to (the 'data' of) Christian liturgy, four aspects of the theory are considered in more depth: the idea of communicative action *as a model,* its characterisation as both *co-operative* and *rational,* and the concept of the '*ideal speech situation*' which it sustains.

Highlighting the tendency of the theoretical social sciences to make 'ontological assumptions' about the actor who is their subject, Habermas argues that the actor has been (largely implicitly) assigned/allowed four basic ways of relating to the world. He demarcates these four methodologically-perceptible concepts of 'action' as teleological, normatively regulated, dramaturgical and communicative. According to Habermas, the first three of these models both serve and constrain the social sciences because the 'rationality problematic' (similar to the question of access outlined above) remains at the level of the social scientist, the observer; whereas in the fourth, the rationality problematic becomes part of the actor's own context. This is because, with the development of communicative action as a model, one is obliged to take into account *language,* the mediator of an actor's own relations to the world they inhabit. The actor's world is apparent in the linguistic interaction between herself and another in a way in which it is not in the other models of action. The differences between these various dynamics are illustrated in the following figure:[39]

Figure 1

Type of action	Location of actors	Central concept	Characteristics
Teleological	Solitary actor	Decision between possible courses of action	Actor calculates means to an end
Normatively regulated	Member of social group	Complying with a norm	Members expect certain behaviour
Dramaturgical (or 'Performative')	Participants become 'public' for one another	Presentation of self	Stylised display of oneself to an audience
Communicative	More than one actor	Interpretation	Subjects trying to reach understanding

---

[39] The diagram is my own construction based on the prose account of: Habermas, *The Theory of Communicative Action* Vol. 1, 82 - 90.

One could argue that a linguistic medium reflecting the actor's relations to the world is in fact present not just in communicative action but in all the models of action, in that each actor is revealed through his or her speech acts; however, the distinction Habermas perceives is that only the latter model makes this accessible to the academic observer *in the form in which the actor experiences it* (through the raising and redeeming of validity claims). Habermas describes the differences as follows:

> The teleological model of action takes language as one of several media through which speakers oriented to their own success can influence one another in order to bring opponents to form or to grasp beliefs and intentions that are in the speaker's own interest... The normative model presupposes a consensus that is merely reproduced with each additional act of understanding... The dramaturgical model of action presupposes language as a medium of self-presentation; the cognitive significance of the propositional components and the inter-personal significance of the illocutionary components are thereby played down in favour of the expressive functions of speech acts.[40]

Whereas the model of communicative action, by contrast, 'presupposes language as a medium of uncurtailed communication whereby speakers and hearers, out of the context of their pre-interpreted lifeworld, refer simultaneously to things in the objective, social and subjective worlds in order to negotiate common definitions of the situation.'[41] As a model, then, communicative action affords the social scientist the ability to differentiate different types of action from the perspective of its foundational premise which takes the type of action oriented to reaching understanding as fundamental.

To explore what this means in practice, it is helpful to examine Maeve Cooke's characterisation of the model as: a) co-operative and b) rational. By co-operative, Cooke is referring to the model's liberative achievement: 'In presenting social order as a network of co-operation involving commitment and responsibility, it opposes models of social order that take interactions between strategically acting subjects as fundamental, for example, models grounded in decision or game theory.'[42] If social order is understood as being reliant on co-operation, Habermas's model would seem also to contrast sharply with those current theories of competition that have resulted from the resurgence of Darwinian theories, particularly those arising from the field of genetics. Such has been the impact of these theories that the phrase 'survival of the fittest', or stories about male animals killing the offspring of their competitors for the females, are part of our everyday mythology. In human terms it would seem, therefore, that Habermas is behind the times, unaware of these supposed biological imperatives, when he chooses a model of animals working together to reach a consensus rather than catching one another

---

[40] Habermas, *The Theory of Communicative Action* Vol. 1, 95
[41] Ibid.
[42] Cooke, 'Introduction', 5.

out in a competitive elimination round. However, the co-operative element in Habermas's model is more radical than that: his suggestion is that conflict, competition, manipulation, etc., as 'strategic' ways of acting, are dependent on, indeed they are derived from, a more basic way of acting that is essentially co-operative because it requires communicative action. So it is co-operative in the sense that it does not take the competition as fundamental: it sees something else behind it, a first principle, which is a co-operative standard to which one can appeal.

Cooke also alerts us to the idea that the type of co-operation on which the model relies is one based on 'relationships of commitment and responsibility'.[43] Certainly the conclusions most commentators draw from Habermas's work support Cooke's characterisation, but it is suspect to have at the core of a sociological model a requirement for such a high *quality* of relationship between acting subjects, and there is little evidence that it is intrinsic to Habermas's theory itself. Does co-operation *require* relationships of commitment and responsibility? My own reading of Habermas leads to an understanding of this co-operative element more in terms of its 'reflexivity', an essential reflective dimension that is not essentially bound to the nature of the pre-existing relationship, that is open to more ambivalent participants.[44]

It could be argued that such an exchange requires a high degree of commitment and responsibility in order to take place at all; but again I would argue that the model is in no way diminished if one also applies it to more 'haphazard' situations in which a commitment to being anything other than present is by no means presupposed. These words convey a far higher level of pre-existing relationship (to or for particular causes) than Habermas seems to require. He frames the relationship more in terms of what we might call *co-ordination,* reflecting the fact that it is where the actors go with their exchange rather than where they are coming from individually which conditions the success of the communicative action. 'Concepts of social action are distinguished... according to how they specify co-ordination among the goal-directed actions of different participants.'[45] In order to co-ordinate co-operatively, does one require a certain quality of relationship?

'Speakers, in employing sentences with an orientation to reaching understanding,' he says, 'no longer relate *straightaway* to something in the

---

[43]   Cooke, 'Introduction', 4.

[44]   In the communicative model of action Habermas says, 'Speakers, in employing sentences with an orientation to reaching understanding, take up relations to the world, not only directly as in teleological, normatively regulated or dramaturgical action, but in a reflective way.' *The Theory of Communicative Action* Vol. 1, 95. See also, p. 82: 'The participants must thereby adopt a reflective attitude toward cultural patterns of interpretation that ordinarily make possible their interpretative accomplishments. This change in attitude means that the validity of the thematized interpretive pattern is suspended and the corresponding knowledge rendered problematic.'

[45]   Ibid., 101.

objective, social or subjective worlds; they relativize their utterances against the possibility that their validity will be contested by other actors.'[46] There is a 'relativity', a requirement to take into account one's position *relative to an other's* or to one's perception of an other's via the challenges that other poses to oneself, and this can happen between actors in hostile and accidental situations as well as intentionally communicative ones. Ambivalence about commitment or responsibility does not necessarily equal acting strategically. Either way, and regardless of the nuances of the words, it cannot be disputed that the model is, at its basic level, as Cooke asserted, a co-operative one because it is based on agents *operating together* as opposed to one in which agents operate over and/or against one another. As Habermas points out, 'The actors seek to reach an understanding about the action situation and their plans of action in order to co-ordinate their actions by way of agreement. The central concept of interpretation refers in the first instance to negotiating definitions of the situation which admit of consensus.'[47]

Cooke also characterises Habermas's model of communicative action as *rational,* and this is the model's most significant feature in terms of its usefulness to the question of access outlined in Chapter Two.[48] The thesis of three universal validity claims, according to Cooke, 'proposes that language has an inbuilt connection with validity claims, thereby giving rise to a particular conception of social order as reproduced through communicative action.'[49] In communicative action, the speakers undertake to give reasons for the claim they make and their hearer can either accept or reject these, giving alternative reasons in support of their rejection. Habermas calls the everyday practice of giving reasons for and against every claim made 'naïve' communicative action or 'argumentation' and it

---

[46] Ibid., 98 - 99.

[47] Ibid.

[48] It is essential to note the distance Habermas and scholars of his theory of communicative action here place between themselves and the post-modernist project, for which rationality has become something of a dirty word. As Herb Schnädelbach remarks, 'today our cultural climate tends to blame rationality for all evil in the world. Thus it seems we are obliged to search for normativity in nature, in emotions, in imagination or the like, but not by any means in reason.' Arguing that rationality can itself be normative, he insists that 'communication itself is only made possible on the basis of fundamental presumptions of rationality - or intelligibility - relating to the participants as well as to their utterances and actions... I cannot act at all without presuming, in principle, that I am rational, and we cannot act communicatively without presuming that we are reasonable.' H. Schnädelbach, 'Rationality and Normativity' in J. Kotkavirta, ed., *Problems of the Communicative Rationality: Proceedings of the Habermas Colloquium in Jyäskylä* (Jyäskylä yliopisto: Filosofian laitos, 1987) 3' 27.
Why rationality has become so benighted is the very motivation behind Habermas's *communicative* rationality: the 'reduction of rationality to technocratic and strategic reasoning.' See F. Schüssler Fiorenza, 'Introduction' in D. Browning and F. Schüssler Fiorenza, eds., *Habermas, Modernity and Public Theology* (New York: Crossroad, 1992).

[49] Cooke, 'Introduction', 3 - 4.

points to the more developed argumentation in 'discourse', which is the intentional, self-conscious, process of reaching mutual understanding.

Not only does argumentation 'point to' discourse, the validity claims raised within argumentation gain their context-transcendent power from their potential vindication in discourse and, as Cooke observes, 'This power is the rational potential built in to everyday processes of communication'.[50] The strength of this theory lies in the fact that reason, and its consequent appeals to truth and justice (or other norms), is situated permanently in everyday communicative action, in everyday life. As such it is a profoundly post-metaphysical conception. Habermas is saying that the idealisations we make as part of our daily rounds and conversations, transmitted and negotiated via our speech acts, afford us the rational grounds upon which we found our values because the validity claims transcend[51] their particular social location, not by appeal to an abstract, separate, ideal, but by virtue of their immersion in the rational world we inhabit and express through our raising and redeeming of them.

Another significant characteristic of his model is that the *kind of* rationality Habermas proposes, being formed dialogically, is one that is inherently dependent on a 'generalised other', one that is forever relative to an other; one which cannot, in other words, be created in a vacuum.[52] The radical feature of this conception of rationality from the perspective of the generalised other is, Allison Weir comments, 'The idea that through linguistic interactions a human child develops an understanding of social norms not simply as expressions of arbitrary

---

[50] Cooke, 'Introduction', 5.

[51] In terms of its applicability to theology, this aspect of Habermas's theory exhibits a major point of potential interest. Habermas had taken from Mead the opinion that children learned how to behave ('norm-regulated action') by taking the attitude of 'the generalised other'. But Habermas wanted to explain how this notion of 'the generalised other' arose in the first place and turned to Durkheim's work on the origins of the sense of the sacred. Although he disagrees with him on many points, Habermas basically agrees with Durkheim's account 'that the integrative function of religion was mainly exercised via a collective attachment of material symbols, the totems, and that it was via these material signs that the believers could communicate their collective feelings. Their use allowed for an intersubjectivity that went beyond and above the primitive force of mutual suggestion, which could be found in any expression of feeling.' Brand, *The Force of Reason*, 70. It is for this reason that Habermas understands that the core of the process of validity claim redemption is synonymous with a 'linguistification of the sacred'. *The Theory of Communicative Action* Vol. 2 (Cambridge: Polity Press, 1987) 85 - 86.

[52] As David Tracy has remarked, 'By his reformulations of Weber on 'rationalization processes' and of Luckacs and Adorno-Horkheimer on reification, Habermas has also managed to free both the early Frankfurt School and Weber from their own implicitly monological philosophy of consciousness categories. Thereby he retrieves the dialogical, interactive character of the Hegelian-Marxist tradition.' D. Tracy, 'Theology, Critical Social Theory and the Public Realm' in D. Browning and F. Schüssler Fiorenza, eds., *Habermas, Modernity and Public Theology* (New York: Crossroad, 1992) 29.

choice or self-interest, but subject to demands for and tests of validity'.[53] This is perhaps one of the ways in which we can see most directly Habermas's development of the project of modernity. The kind of rationality that Enlightenment figures presupposed was one based entirely in the mind of the individual; 'reason' was a high form of thought, it was not, as Habermas has it, a dialectic. For Habermas, we can do nothing - effectively there is no meaning - without an other, because it is only through language *exchange* (which requires an other, at its simplest level, to hear us), it is only through being 'subject to demands for and tests of validity', that our world, our identity, is created

It is in order to insist on this rational basis of speech that Habermas prefers a *'formal* pragmatics' to the more commonly used *empirical* versions: it accesses the intuitive content of action, and can thus reveal what is going on 'at the backs of' participants; because, as we saw earlier, 'the question of validity is tied to pragmatic contexts of justification'.[54] Without knowledge of this background lifeworld - made up of the tripartite social, external and personal worlds - there could be no meaning: it would be impossible. The power of everyday speech acts, derived from their illocutionary force, is only possible or meaningful if one can access the lifeworld from which they stem:

> Every process of understanding takes place against a background of culturally ingrained pre-understanding ... To the extent that definitions of situations are negotiated by participants *themselves*, this thematic segment of the lifeworld is at their disposal with the negotiation of each new definition of the situation' because, 'Communicative action designates a type of interaction that is *co-ordinated through* speech acts and does *not coincide* with them.[55]

In strategic forms of action, this is not possible, save that they can be recognised as parasitic on their communicative forms and principles. Any meaning derived from study of strategic actions alone would be a mirage.

The reciprocal bonds between hearer and speaker can be analysed because they have a rational basis. The following diagram from *Communication and The Evolution of Society* displays how Habermas envisages the relationships between different types of social action. In the note attached to the diagram he comments that the way that the different types of action can be distinguished is 'by virtue of their relations to the validity basis of speech', that is, rationally, via the reasoning of validity claims that are raised in the language-exchange of participants.[56]

---

[53] A. Weir, 'Toward a Model of Self-Identity' in J. Meehan, ed., *Feminists Read Habermas: Gendering the Subject of Discourse* (New York: Routledge, 1995) 269.

[54] Cooke, 'Introduction', 12.

[55] Habermas, *The Theory of Communicative Action* Vol. 1, 100.

[56] Habermas, *Communication and the Evolution of Society*, fig. 10.2.

Beyond Ritual

Figure 2

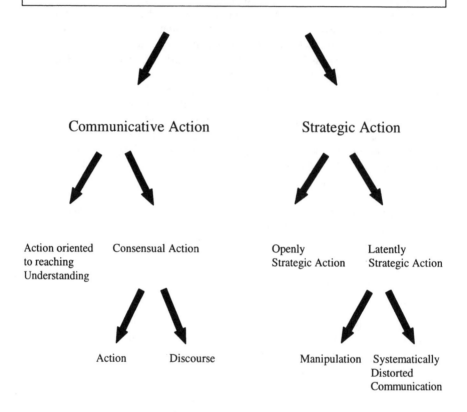

Strategic actions are actions oriented to achieving success (personally or as a corporation). Openly strategic actions are therefore easy to spot, as they are uncomplicated manifestations of the purposive-rational way of acting. Latently strategic action is, however, more wily. Its first form, manipulation, is where one party acts in a way oriented towards success but conceals this by pretending to be engaging in communicative action. Systematically distorted communication on the other hand, 'Can be conceived of' Habermas suggests, 'as the result of a confusion between actions oriented to reaching understanding and actions oriented to reaching success'[57] and it is difficult to identify from 'inside' a given situation.

All social life is dependent on language to constitute it, but language is in turn dependent on the social processes that create it and it can be just as easily an instrument of domination as one of freedom, being essentially ideologically-bound. The kind of hermeneutics Habermas hopes to counter is the mainstream form of social analysis which looks primarily to the given meaning complex (as in sociology). For Habermas this is inadequate because it cannot 'distinguish between a real and a deceptive consensus, between true communication and pseudo-communication' and so he proposes a 'depth-hermeneutic'. This is 'a hermeneutic which connects agents' self-interpretation to the "depth-grammar" of social relations which, operating like a natural force upon them (but behind their backs) distorts and mutilates their communicative actions.'[58]

It is interesting to note at this point Habermas's foundations in classical thought, particularly as the place from where he derives his fundamental idea of freedom. In the discussion above an easy parallel can be seen with Plato's archetypal story of the slaves and the shadows on the wall,[59] and it leads to the question with regard to what Habermas calls systematically distorted communication, *how* can we discern genuine freedom from the illusion of freedom?

Behind the rationality-dynamic of the model, lies a fundamental appeal to the imagination: we are required to imagine an alternative; we are required to think, in any given situation, what that situation would look like if it were free of systematically distorted communication. What Habermas proposes that we bring to mind is an '*ideal speech situation*', a situation where the conditions of discourse are such that genuine communicative action can occur. It is a philosophical and analytic device for gauging the extent to which genuine interaction is in evidence. Distorted communication only happens in contexts of broken intersubjectivity, and so by maintaining a common 'fiction',[60] referring to an ideal, an abstraction, one can retain a measure of the elements genuine communication would require.

---

[57]   Habermas, *The Theory of Communicative Action*, 332.

[58]   Bernstein, *Recovering Ethical Life*, 46.

[59]   Plato (422 - 347 BCE) wrote the *Myth of the Cave* (in which cave-dwellers believe they know the extent of the whole world because of the shadows of supreme beings cast on the wall) to illustrate the danger that the nature of freedom can be relative to perception. The cave-dweller who escapes the dark cave, realises that the world-beings are in fact just the shadows of cave-dwellers themselves, and rushes back to bring his companions to 'freedom', is killed by them because of the strength of their conviction in the limits of the world, and liberty, as they know it.

[60]   This is to borrow from terminology Maeve Cooke is developing for use in her forthcoming book. She writes: 'In contrast to his earlier writings, where truth is conceived as a regulative ideal that might some day be realized, it is now construed as a fiction that is unavoidably presupposed by participants in argumentation (Habermas himself does not refer to fictions – this is my suggestion).' Maeve Cooke, 'Habermas on

These elements basically reside in there being parity in the power-dynamic between participants. 'The ideal speech situation' Bernstein comments, 'models an ideal form of life because ideal communication requires the realisation of conditions which would underwrite the equality of effective chances for participants to enter into the dialogue.'[61] What this means in practice is that the participants have to be phenomenally self-aware. It draws attention to the fact that, as we saw above, the model of communicative action on which it is predicated has at its heart the central concept of *interpretation* and what the ideal speech situation makes clear is that this manifests itself not just in the need for interpretation of speaker by hearer, but in the self-interpretation of each. The ideal speech situation refers to the *conditions* which would allow speaker and hearer each to know their own selves, needs and interests. The parity of power-dynamic mentioned above is instituted through this mutual self-understanding (and is discussed in greater detail in the following chapter).

Unlike others who also recognise that we need to view social configurations in counterfactual terms, Habermas insists that we can do so only from the perspective of the speech acts of the participants in discourse themselves (rather than through, say, analysis of socio-economic indicators or other social scientific methodologies; or, again, through formal semantic linguistics which would concentrate exclusively on the presupposed meaning of the words spoken). Bernstein remarks that the distinguishing feature of Habermas's construction, its novelty, lies in this 'assumption that the privilege of knowing what is truly in our interests and what norms ought to be binding for us cannot be had by anyone other than us'.[62] Consequently, the ability to achieve genuine communication (and thus liberation) arises from the self-understanding of participants (which, as Habermas demonstrated above, can be acquired only via linguistic relationship with an other).

Bernstein continues: 'Without the ideal form of life which would bring into being an ideal speech situation, our liberty can be only partial.'[63] Habermas has been criticised for his use of an 'ideal' because of its metaphysical overtones, but, as discussed above, he is developing a notion of the ideal *as a process* and neither as an outcome nor as a pre-determined entity: 'Habermas... increasingly conceives of the constraints in the ideal speech situation as negative and critical in function rather than projecting an ideal future'.[64] So the ideal speech situation is not to be confused with the 'transcendence' that is embedded in communicative action; it is more a regulatory imaginative tool which, when expertly wielded, may

---

Truth, Justice and Democratic Legitimacy: the Weaknesses of Strong Intersubjectivism' (paper delivered at the Yale University Political Theory Workshop, 6 May 2003).
[61] Bernstein, *Recovering Ethical Life*, 51.
[62] Ibid., 54.
[63] Ibid,, 54.
[64] Ibid., 56.

manifest that transcendence by allowing it to be-come.[65] It is all about the process: Habermas writes that communicative action is different from strategic action because in the latter, 'competent speakers are casually exerting an influence *upon* others' whereas in communicative action 'they are coming to an understanding *with* them'.[66]

Habermas maintains that it is not enough to analyse sentences: analysts must look at the whole utterance of which the sentence is a part. This necessitates learning to examine the sentence in a different way, looking for its function in the interpersonal dynamic within which it occurs (is it strategic or communicative action?) and this is to be done by analysing the universal validity claims which it employs and to which it appeals. His theory alerts us that study of the discourse is not possible without study of the conditions of discourse; but it goes further then (arguing 'backwards' into this premise), to propose that for genuine discourse to occur at all, certain conditions have to pertain and participants in dialogue have to hold an ideal (of these conditions) in mind.

IV

Several sustained criticisms have been levelled at Habermas's theory of communicative action which have a bearing on the use I propose to make of it. The criticisms presented below are not intended to provide a survey of the reaction to Habermas's work: what is presented is an analysis of those critiques which alert the theologian to potential constraints in the applicability of the model to the theological questions in hand.

Perhaps the most significant of these comes from feminist theorists who argue that Habermas does not take the issue of gender into adequate account, even though there has been much acceptance of his theory among feminists because 'his discourse theory is one of the most persuasive current reflections on politics and moral and social norms'.[67] Given his location in the philosophical world of the late twentieth century, it is surprising that Habermas neglects to engage with the wide

---

[65] Habermas describes it thus: 'The ideal speech situation would be best compared with a transcendental illusion, if this illusion were not to owe its existence to an impermissable transgression (as in the use of categories that transcend experience) but would also be the constitutive condition of rational speech. The anticipation of the ideal speech situation has the significance of a constitutive illusion for every possible communication; it is simultaneously the anticipation of a life-form.' J. Habermas, 'Wahrheitstheorien', 256. Translation by S. Benhabbib, *Critique, Norm and Utopia: A Study of the Foundations of Critical Theory* (New York: Columbia University Press, 1986) 401 n.23.

[66] Habermas, *The Theory of Communicative Action* Vol. 1, 286.

[67] J. Meehan, ed., *Feminists Read Habermas: Gendering the Subject of Discourse* (New York: Routledge, 1995) 1.

body of feminist work within his field, particularly given his overarching concern with issues of equity, inclusion, parity and access.

Habermas recognises that one of the main problems with modernity is that it has differentiated public from private, system from life-world and so in his work seeks to cross public/private, personal/political boundaries. However, Nancy Fraser alerts us to the non-gender-critical nature of this analysis: 'While linking the relationships between the economic sphere and the family, for example, he does not recognise that this relationship is affected as much by gender as it is by money.'[68]

Interpersonal relationships are at the heart of Habermas's theory. So to neglect the role of gender in these relationships is to present a serious limitation on the conclusions one can draw from them. It is not that Habermas says that gender does not matter, or that it does not impinge on the formation that occurs as a result of our relationships and interactions. The criticism is rather that Habermas simply neglects it - he fails to address gender specifically - and not only is this a serious gap, given the overall purpose of his project, but his theory suffers for the lack of it.

The ramifications of an absence of gender analysis can perhaps be most clearly seen by comparing Habermas's communication theory to that of feminist linguistic philosopher Julia Kristeva.[69] The crucial difference in their work is Kristeva's acknowledgement of the particularity of one's social location, which includes, in large part, one's gender. In both their models, identity is constituted intersubjectively, through the medium of linguistic communication, but by allowing for the nuances of the socio-symbolic nature of language-formation, Kristeva presents a model that allows for an account of the gender-conditioning embedded within language itself.

Allison Weir comments, 'Habermas makes it clear that the self-identity of the adult involves becoming a communicative agent, but he does not explain how it is that we come to commit ourselves to the *particular* socially produced meaning, choices, or goals which guide our practices and justify our claims':[70]

> Like Habermas, Kristeva focuses on the need to take positions in everyday social interactions as central to the constitution of self-identity... But whereas for Habermas the need to take a position means the need to relate to norms in a critical and questioning manner, for Kristeva taking a position tends to mean taking a position of identity within the symbolic order, which will allow 'non-identity' or difference to emerge - to be realized or expressed - thereby producing a new position. ... The strength of Kristeva's account, for feminism, is her insistence that the affective relationship cannot serve... as a means of producing individual or particular meanings. Rather it serves as a means of investing in a world of shared meanings, of constituting and experiencing oneself as a

---

[68] Meehan, *Feminists Read Habermas*, 7.

[69] See, for example: J. Kristeva, *Language - The Unknown: An Initiation into Linguistics* (New York: Columbia Univeristy Press, 1989); also: K. Oliver, *Ethics, Politics and Difference in Julia Kristeva's Writing* (New York: Routledge, 1993).

[70] Meehan, *Feminists Read Habermas*, 19.

participant in that world and of making those meanings constantly open to diversity and change.[71]

A further feminist critique, that Habermas neglects the emotional in his pursuit of the cognitive,[72] has been taken up in the wider philosophical field. In his recent article, Nick Crossley argues that Habermas's failure to allow for the emotional (in a theory which could, he proposes, both easily accommodate and, indeed, be strengthened by it) hampers the success of his theory. Knowledge is what concerns Habermas, how one acquires it, how one accesses it; but, as Crossley demonstrates, knowledge comes in many forms and to understand its function in communication it is necessary to avoid restricting knowledge to its cognitive forms and to recognise emotional knowledge as well. This is in contrast to Habermas, who, he says, 'fails to consider that communication is (or at least can be) more than an exchange of symbols and ideas; that it is a process of mutual affecting in which interlocutors make emotional as well as cognitive appeals.'[73]

Starting from the same source as Habermas - linguistic philosophy - Crossley shows that 'emotion plays a constitutive role in social life'[74] by exposing the communicative rationality of the language we use to describe/express emotion. At the core of linguistic philosophy is the presupposition that the words we use in our everyday lives constitute the world we inhabit. We can only know or understand this world within the framework of the words we use to describe/express it and so to investigate anything (according to linguistic philosophy), even emotion, one has to start with the language we use to describe it. Thus, following Coulter's account of how emotional knowledge is observable via the language-game within which they are expressed, Crossley can propose that:

> Emotional expressions can be contested in terms of the same three validity claims that Habermas identifies with all other communicative actions: that is, in terms of the facts of the situation (do they warrant the emotion?), the sincerity of the agent (are they *really* sad/happy?) and the moral-social rights of the agent (is their relation to the situation such as to warrant their reaction to it?).[75]

However, such an account can only ever provide an understanding of our understanding of emotion, not an understanding of emotion itself as it is lived. To incorporate the 'lived emotion' into communicative rationality, Crossley turns to phenomenology, which was also a source for Habermas. But where Habermas looked to Husserl and Schutz, Crossley draws more on the work of existentialists

---

[71] Weir, 'Toward a Model of Self-Identity', 275, 279.

[72] See: J. Braaten, 'From Communicative Rationality to Communicative Thinking: A Basis for Feminist Theory and Practice' in J. Meehan, ed., *Feminists Read Habermas: Gendering the Subject of Discourse* (New York: Routledge, 1995).

[73] Crossley, 'Emotion and Communicative Action', 16 - 17.

[74] Ibid., 17.

[75] Ibid., 20.

such as Sartre and Merleau-Ponty. Seeing a parallel in the kind of split Sartre makes between instrumental and intersubjective contexts and that which Habermas makes between instrumental and communicative actions, Crossley suggests that the existentialists' claim that emotion is an intentional mode of being beneath our ordinary reflective awareness exposes a serious weakness in Habermas's model: 'Like any other human action they [emotional responses] open out into a shared inter-world, where they assume a significance and call for a response... the significance of any emotional response will not necessarily be reducible to the particularity of an individual's current situation (or role) but will also point backwards to that individual's personal history.'[76]

Habermas's lack of attention to the emotional precludes both the 'magical' (in the sense of transformatory) and the 'embodied', two features of both contemporary theology and ritual studies that emerged as pressing issues in the previous chapters. If the only knowledge we access is cognitive, there can be no magic. And what of the body? Arguing against those who would claim that 'bodily movements do not represent the substratum through which actions enter into the world but are themselves primitive actions,' Habermas suggests that:

> In a certain sense, actions are realized through movements of the body, but only in such a way as the actor, in following a technical or social rule, *concomitantly executes* these movements. Concomitant execution means that the actor intends an action but not the bodily movements with the help of which he realises it.[77]

In such a definition, while not quite relegating the body to little more than an unwitting puppet of the mind, Habermas nevertheless falls far short of the contemporary emphasis on embodiment reported in the preceding chapters. Central to that emphasis was a conceptualisation of speech as an intrinsically bodily act and the conclusion not merely that speech *is* a bodily action but that 'corporality is the body's very speech'.[78] While Habermas may not necessarily disagree (and certainly there are elements of similarity between Chauvet and Habermas's conclusions: the concrete illocutionary effects of speech, its bodily *effect* on the threefold world), there nevertheless arises a constraint in his theory in that its parameters are permanently cognitive. So the body acts, but as an 'execution' (albeit a concomitant one) of the mind. The mind is still in charge.

In the above I have highlighted certain constraints relating to Habermas's theory of communicative action: his lack of gender analysis; his stress on cognitive at the expense of emotional knowledge; and his lack of attention to the body, or speech as embodied. These criticisms signal some of the limitations within the theory itself, but of perhaps more immediate significance to this dissertation are the

---

[76] Ibid., 33.

[77] Habermas, *The Theory of Communicative Action* Vol. 1, 97.

[78] L.M. Chauvet, *Symbol and Sacrament: A Sacramental Reinterpretation of Christian Existence* (Collegeville, MN: Liturgical Press, 1995) 146.

limitations of the theory as a whole in terms of its usefulness to theology. Habermas's model was developed for application in the socio-political sphere and its imagined *modi operandi* are in legal rather than liturgical contexts. As a theory, the critique of communicative action is not designed with theology in mind; so any attempt to use it in relation to the discourse of the theological community is an intentional 'borrowing' and inevitably will not be an exact 'match'; adaptation and development of details will, therefore, be evident in the following chapters in employing his central epistemology.[79]

Moreover, Habermas tends to the anti-religious and the anti-theological, especially in his earlier work (in the later work he is more ambivalent). While this should alert the theologian to tread with caution, it does not invalidate the theological potential of the model he presents. The very reasons for which Habermas is sceptical about religion (the damage it has done in its institutional forms) can, with careful interpretation, enrich the self-critique of the Christian community. However, the institutionally powerful forms of the church are not its only forms and although much can be learned from his work, it is necessary also to criticise the doggedly one-dimensional view of religion he presents by looking only at institutionalised ecclesiastical authority and its role in the upholding of power-structures. By reducing religion in this way, Habermas preserves an ethic of justice that is supposedly attainable only through a thoroughly secular context. As Edmund Arens writes, 'Religion, as a denouncement of injustice and an announcement of liberation and redemption, is completely neglected by Habermas, who thus ignores its particular contribution to social critique and transformation.'[80]

While his view of religion may be historically lacking, it does not in actual fact affect the applicability to religion of his theory; indeed theologians cannot afford to ignore such a comprehensive theory of history and society, such a radical re-conceptualisation of the subject.[81] At the heart of Habermas's theory of communicative action is the idea of communicative rationality as both a goal and a criterion of discourse, and this 'standard' is a very helpful one for contemporary theology with its concern with negotiating the 'fundamental' in a post-metaphysical environment (as we saw in Chapter One). So it is helpful to theology as a whole; but it is of more specific help to a theology whose interpretative norms are located in liturgy as it is enacted (as opposed to being accessed through its written doctrinal texts). Habermas simultaneously presents a model of social action and a

---

[79] However, this fact alone cannot explain theologians' seeming reluctance to engage with Habermas. For example, in his recent work, *Theology and Contemporary Critical Theory* (London: Macmillan, 1996), Graham Ward ignores Habermas completely.

[80] E. Arens, *Theology after Habermas: An Introduction* (New York: Union Theological Seminary Library, 1992) 2.

[81] As David Tracy remarks, 'there is no lack of critical theory in most forms of public theology, but there is a real lack of critical *social* theory.' Tracy, 'Theology, Critical Theory and the Social Realm', 26.

methodology for deconstructing it; and because, as a methodology, it *is essentially reflexive*, it allows interpretative access to the subject of discourse.

In the remaining chapters I intend to show how this new form of access, by understanding liturgy as communicative action, might shed light on the nature of sacrament in Christian communities in the twenty-first century. While the factors raised by Habermas's critics are pertinent, none of them detract from the actual substance of his theory. They are nevertheless serious, and because they are designed with the intention of revising and reforming (rather than discrediting) his theory of communicative action, they will be taken into consideration in the following chapter's attempt to devise a theologically-appropriate tool for analysing ritual.

Chapter Four

A Liturgical Theology of Communicative Action

If Christianity be not altogether restless eschatology, there
remains in it no relation whatever with Christ.[1]

This chapter suggests how Habermas's theory of communicative action might be used to address the challenges presented in Chapters One and Two: respectively, the desire for a non-metaphysical foundation for a theology of sacrament and the difficulty of accessing ritual activity for the purposes of Christian theology. It takes Habermas's notion of an 'ideal speech situation' and applies it to the context of the celebration of the Eucharist, considering the suggestion that a parallel can be drawn between the ideal speech situation and the realm of God as envisaged in Christian eschatology.

In pursuing this analysis, however, the study continuously discerns a 'split' between theory and practice, between the doctrinal, written, scholarly appreciation of the Eucharist for all it 'should be' and reports of actual liturgical experience which suggest the 'is' of Eucharistic encounter may manifest itself quite differently. Consequently, there follows a discussion of the ecclesiological consequences of such a split for any projected 'definition' of sacrament, and an examination of the nature of the split via a presentation of the liturgical theology of an ordinary Sunday Eucharist.

This presentation takes the form of report and analysis of a case study of a typical Irish Roman Catholic Sunday Eucharist, conducted according to an adapted Habermasian model of communicative action. The conclusions do indeed provide evidence of a discrepancy between academic theology's writing about what Eucharist ought to be and a liturgical community's own practice of it, and yet, because of the nature of this particular ritual (which is shown *not* to be communicative action), there transpires little scope for theological interpretation. To answer the questions about the nature of sacrament that this thesis has highlighted (and the associated issues of eschatology, ecclesiology and ethics) the chapter concludes with a mandate to study the liturgical theology of ecclesially marginal communities, which is taken up in Chapter Five.

---

[1] K. Barth, *The Epistle to the Romans* (London: Oxford University Press, 1933) 314.

In his essay, 'Eucharist as Liberation from the Present',[2] Christopher Rowland argues that the Christian liturgy of the Eucharist is a manifestation of what Habermas calls the 'ideal speech situation', that is, it is not just communicative action, not just discourse, but is a living embodiment of the ultimate goal of discourse, the ideal of optimum openness and acceptance to which all interaction aspires. His argument is based in the first place on the work of three Latin American liberation theologians[3] and subsequently on an application of his own biblical scholarship to the themes he draws from their work. The themes he highlights are concerned with time and Eucharist and are situated in a wider body of work which he says, 'is typical of the compromises which are at the heart of so much of the liberation theology with which we are familiar; in which the conventional theological genre is infused with the reality of oppression and suffering of the majority, on whose behalf these theologians feel themselves called to articulate a case.'[4]

Rowland exhibits an awareness, firstly, that the liberation scholars are trained in the ways of the 'conventional theological genre', by which he refers to the biblical-doctrinal model of the North Atlantic universities and seminaries; and secondly, that this model shows its limitations when used in a different context. This alerts the reader from the outset to a significant question: is the 'conventional theological genre' adequate; not just adequate to the expressive needs of oppressed peoples, as Rowland implies, but adequate to the very task of theology itself, particularly when one is approaching subjects such as time or Eucharist. It raises in a concrete way one of the crucial questions of this study: if you want to say something about the Eucharist, or any sacrament, what is your point of access to that subject? For the liberation theologians with whom Rowland engages, it is the conventional biblical-doctrinal theological genre, albeit with 'compromises'.

Rowland, as far as his remit of interest goes, does not sit full square within the conventional tradition. He took seriously, studied and broadcast the theology of what Gutierrez called the 'underside of history' long before it was fashionable to do so; that is, at a time when the 'compromises' he speaks of were viewed not as compromises but as beyond the pale of the conventional genre. However, as far as his methodology is concerned, he, like the liberation theologians he writes about, is an expert in the conventional, particularly in the connection between New Testament studies and doctrine, and it is this expertise that he brings to bear on the subject of this study, arguing for an emancipatory reading of Hebrews in support of the arguments of the Latin American theologians he champions. Discerning in their writings an overarching concern with eschatology, Rowland uses his biblical 'examples' to back up 'the way in which future time presses upon the present to

---

[2] C. Rowland, 'Eucharist as Liberation from the Present' in D. Brown, and A. Loades, eds., *The Sense of the Sacramental: Movement and Measure in Art and Music, Place and Time* (London: SPCK, 1995).
[3] Leonardo Boff, Gustavo Gutiérrez and Jon Sobrino.
[4] Rowland, 'Eucharist as Liberation', 201.

create a fresh Eucharistic perspective on the sacrament as release from the limitations of the present social order',[5] the consequence of which, he argues with the Latin Americans, is solidarity with poor people.

'Liberation theologians ... make the Eucharist focus not merely on the reality of present human suffering but a future free of oppression and the distortions of the exercise of power and privilege'[6] and this, Rowland suggests, is tantamount to Habermas's ideal speech situation. Drawing on Nicholas Lash, who sees the Eucharist as the 'paradigm' of the realm of God, 'exhibiting criteria by which all *un*relationship, *un*brotherhood, all domination and division may be judged',[7] Rowland argues that it effects this paradigm not because it functions as a regulative tool, indicating precisely what does or does not qualify as 'kingdom behaviour' (indeed Rowland argues expressly it does not), but because it functions as what Habermas terms a 'constitutive illusion'. Lash is drawing on Habermas to say that in the Eucharist, 'Our true future in God... finds fictional appearance'; it is a sort of 'acted parable'[8] and due to the way in which it is told among the poor, Rowland argues, 'the Eucharist is shot through with anticipation of an ideal communication'.[9]

Several significant themes emerge from Rowland's essay. First of all is the basic premise that Habermas's theory of communicative action can be introduced in serious theological thought in such a way that it allows insights into theology that were previously obscure. However, *how* exactly scholars such as Rowland proceed to use Habermas, their particular reading of his theory, and the conclusions they subsequently draw, all demand careful analysis.

Second is the idea that theologians in their writing can 'make the Eucharist' have a particular focus, or more generally, make it 'do' something; or just make it, define it. This is an overt example of an idea implicit in the argument surveyed in Chapter One: that the formation of Eucharistic theology lies with trained writers rather than with the performance of the rite. This prompts questions of methodology because, as was reported in Chapter One, the central tenet of liturgical theology holds that the Eucharist is not something that biblical-doctrinal theologians can 'make' any more than they can 'make' the history to which it refers. What makes the Eucharist, according to liturgical theology, is the liturgy of the Eucharist as it is enacted by the assembly present in the ritual space; theologians cannot therefore make it focus on anything other than how it impacts, experientially, on the ritual body: the participants. Neither Rowland nor the

---

[5] Rowland, 'Eucharist as Liberation', 211.

[6] Rowland, 'Eucharist as Liberation', 213.

[7] N. Lash, 'Conversation in Gethsemane' in W. Jeanrond and J. Rike, eds., *Radical Pluralism and Truth: David Tracy and the Hermeneutics of Religion* (New York: Crossroad, 1991) 57.

[8] Ibid. For a strong exposition of the idea of Eucharist as acted parable, see: N. Mitchell, *Eucharist as Sacrament of Initiation* (Chicago: LTP, 1994).

[9] Rowland, 'Eucharist as Liberation', 214.

theologians who inspired his argument mention any Eucharistic *rite* or narrative of worship practice; their sources are entirely biblical-doctrinal.

Eschatology is the third theme Rowland introduces that requires attention. Rowland comments, 'One of the most intriguing themes in eucharistic theology... is the link between Eucharist and eschatology.'[10] It is one of the most 'intriguing' and also one of the most resurgent at this time in the mainstream of liturgical theology.[11] In feminist accounts however, direct reference to eschatology is almost completely absent, leading to a question of the degree to which the particular vision that the Christian community has of its eschaton is a gendered and/or patriarchal construction.

Fourth and finally, Rowland raises the theme of the ideal speech situation and its relevance to theology, and this is a potentially rich area for development in theology, particularly any theology which takes liturgy as its starting point. Each of these four themes will now be considered in greater detail.

The 'Ideal Speech Situation'

The central concept of Habermas's communicative ethics is that of 'dominance-free communication' (*herrschaftsfreie Kommunikation*). The ideal speech situation is part of the theory of communicative action that sets out the foundational premises of his ethical scheme. According to this theory, in speech acts, when the three validity claims (to truth, rightness and truthfulness) are challenged, we can begin an exchange of justifications, an 'argumentation', through which we examine the claims made.[12] The aim of this exchange is to find a 'rationally motivated consensus' which will resolve the challenge to the claim, and the concept of the ideal speech situation is introduced in this context. It is a conversational technique - although often a sub-conscious one - which allows speaker and hearer to ensure that their exchange is carried out in a fair way and that any agreement they reach has been achieved solely by the force of rationally-motivated argument (that is, not by any form of dominance, such as coercion or manipulation). As will become apparent, calling it a 'technique' barely does it justice, as it comes to represent the situation it seeks to describe: a situation free of any and all iniquity or limit; but it is necessary for the moment to remain with a description of its technical characteristics.

---

[10] Ibid., 212.

[11] Regarding its recent history in the wider theological world, however, Gunton remarks, 'So far as systematic theology is concerned, what is notable is this century's failure to decide what eschatology is, and how it relates to the other loci of the discipline.' C. Gunton, 'Editorial' in *International Journal of Systematic Theology* 2:1 (March 2000) 1.

[12] This was reported in the discussion in Chapter Three.

Habermas defines the ideal speech situation by its four conditions:

1. Each actor has to have an equal chance to initiate and continue communication.
2. Each has to have an equal chance to propose, explain and challenge justifications.
3. Each has to have an equal chance to express their wishes and feelings.
4. Each must act as if they each have an equal chance 'to order and resist orders, to promise and to refuse, to be accountable for one's conduct and to demand accountability from others'.[13]

What each of these conditions has in common is that they all require a sort of living fiction, an imaginative force, a 'suspension' of the normal perceptual reality of the situation in which one is conducting the discourse. In the first two (which are known as the 'symmetry conditions') one is required to suspend belief. In the second two (known as the 'reciprocity conditions') one is required to suspend the action context itself. The ideal speech situation, then, is a semi-fiction, what Benhabbib calls a 'normative justification procedure', designed 'to illustrate the consensus principle of legitimacy.'[14] She points out that:

> 'The ideal speech situation' describes a set of rules which participants in a discourse would have to follow (the symmetry conditions), and a set of relations (the reciprocity conditions) which would have to obtain between them, if we were to say of the agreement they reach that it was rationally motivated, dependent on the force of the better argument alone.[15]

And this is the key point: any consensus, if it is truly to be a consensus, has to be *dependent on the force of the better argument alone*. Two crucial points are summarised in Benhabbib's last sentence: a) consensus is dependent on argument (as we saw in the preceding chapter, Habermas's concept of reason is a *communicative* one, that is: reason only exists, is only created, through communicative action, that is: through argumentation); and b) only by the sheer force of argument *alone* can consensus arise (that is: neither by coercion, manipulation, bullying nor any other form of power-play). Consensus is entirely contingent on the uncurtailed interaction of equal parties.

Closely allied to this point is another: the ideal speech situation is not a normative entity, a pre-ordained 'given', standard or truth. It is the direct result of the argument itself; indeed it can only be created by that argumentation. The

---

[13] J. Habermas, 'Wahrheitstheorien' in H. Fahrenbach, ed., *Wirklichkeit und Reflexion* (Pfüllingen: Neske, 1973) 256. Translation by S. Benhabbib, *Critique, Norm and Utopia: A Study of the Foundations of Critical Theory* (New York: Columbia University Press, 1986) 285.
[14] Benhabbib, *Critique, Norm and Utopia*, 289.
[15] Ibid., 285.

principle of the ideal speech situation is a universal function of language, like the notion of syntax or grammar; but its content (i.e.: what the ideal speech situation involves or depicts) is in each and every case unique. By thinking of its Utopian content or possibilities, there may be a tendency to align the ideal speech situation with previously encountered Utopian imagery, so it is salient to be reminded that, 'Habermas intends discourse or communicative ethics to be interpreted as... providing a critical test for uncovering non-generalizable interests rather than for generating a universal one'.[16]

Because Habermas's theory of communicative action has its foundations in the norms of rational speech, the normative conditions that comprise the ideal speech situation (first) need to be argued for. Or, as Benhabbib succinctly puts it, 'One extracts from the ideal speech situation what one has already put into it.'[17] This serves to indicate the radical nature of the model Habermas is proposing: it is essentially reflexive. Unlike Kant who: 'thought that through solitary reflection, a single rational self could come to define a standpoint which would be acceptable to all *qua* rational agents... [Habermas's] communicative ethics defend a *dialogical* model of moral reasoning, according to which *real* actors engage in *actual* processes of deliberation on moral questions.'[18] The purpose of the ideal speech situation, then, is to safeguard the basis of any interactive consensus by safeguarding the *participation* of all concerned in reaching it.

Due to the changes he brings to the philosophy of the subject, combined with this emphasis on the necessity of participation for the formation of basic norms, Habermas's theory expresses an essentially *emancipatory* ethic. As Benhabbib comments, 'It is no longer assumed that there is a privileged standpoint in the social structure which bestows upon its occupiers a special vision of the social totality... [and] the experience of difference that cannot be co-opted in imposed identity is liberative.'[19] This is the bottom line of Habermas's purpose in articulating an ideal speech situation: liberty. In order to understand it, it is essential to note that it forms part of his theory of communicative action, the end goal of which is not better language theory but a better world: it is justice, it is ethics.

The liberative quality of his intent is present on both micro and macro levels. On the personal level, as Bernstein here comments, the process of self-reflection that is required in order to participate (in the formation of an ideal speech situation) demands (and simultaneously enables) a form of self-emancipation: a responsibility-taking, a co-creatorship:

---

[16] Ibid., 312.

[17] Ibid., 293. The concomitant of which, as Bernstein notes, is 'that the privilege of knowing what is tuly in our interests and what norms ought to be binding for us cannot be had by anyone other than us.' J.M. Bernstein, *Recovering Ethical Life: Jürgen Habermas and the Future of Critical Theory* (London and New York: Routledge, 1995) 54.

[18] Bernstein, *Recovering Ethical Life*, 299 - 300.

[19] Benhabbib, *Critique, Norm and Utopia*, 352.

One of the most striking features of Habermas's thought is the way in which the problems of self-knowledge and self-understanding form the centre of his account of normative practical discourse. Not only does the ideal speech situation itself depend upon agents not being self-deceived, but positively, agents can attain a true understanding of themselves, of their needs, wants and interests, only in the context of an ideal communication.[20]

On a societal level, the ideal speech situation provides a vision, the creating of which is itself liberative but which also simultaneously permits that society to define for itself the kind of society it would like to be(come). Habermas writes:

> Only in an emancipated society, whose members' autonomy and responsibility have been realised would communication have developed into the non-authoritarian and universally practised dialogue from which both our model of reciprocally-constituted ego-identity and our idea of true consensus are always implicitly derived. To this extent the truth of statements is based on anticipating the realization of the good life.[21]

If one phrase could sum up the goal of Christianity, it is perhaps that one: the realisation of the good life. The vexed question for all, philosopher and theologian alike, is what does the good life look like?

For Habermas the concept of emancipation goes hand in hand with that of social justice and this distinguishes his work from that of others among his contemporaries, notably Rorty. It can be argued that it is a concern he inherited from the critical theory of the Frankfurt school, with its extraordinary philosophical prioritisation of the problems presented by injustice and nihilism; and it is easy to see why this makes it uniquely attractive to today's Christian theology, concerned as it is, too, with those exact problems.[22] There is an ethic of equality at the heart

---

[20] Bernstein, *Recovering Ethical Life*, 53.

[21] Ibid., 51.

[22] However the *kind* of freedom Habermas envisages has been strongly criticised by one of the few Christian scholars to engage seriously with his theory. J.B. Metz challenges Habermas's modernist concept of emancipation with a reconstructed presentation of the Christian concept of redemption. As parent of 'political theology' Metz is keen to expose the 'emancipation' that philosophy speaks of as a 'false ideology' (arguing that it pales in comparison to the sort of emancipation that Christianity has as its centre). According to Metz, Habermas's conception of social evolution 'dissolves the possibility of liberation in the constant homogenous process of evolutionary progression' (J. Bohmann, 'On Political Theology' in H. Peukert, *Science, Action and Fundamental Theology: Toward a Theology of Communicative Action* (Cambridge, MA: MIT Press, 1986) x); whereas the liberation that Christianity espouses implodes an ideal *but also real* future in the present moment. It is not just a possibility or a fiction, but a presence.
Metz may, however, be underestimating the extent to which the processes of ideal-formation that constitute a major regulative part of this process of evolutionary progression not only prevent it from being 'homogenous' but actually touch on, *make apparent*, the transcendent possibilities inherent within any speech situation.

of Habermas's vision of society, and a perception that equality is the route to liberty, which echoes Christian teaching, although Bernstein sees it, like Christianity, as having roots in classical philosophy: 'Habermas agrees with Hannah Arendt that the classical political conception of liberty is best understood as a structure of unimpaired intersubjectivity brought about through unconstrained communicative action, where the purpose of unconstrained communication is just the forming and maintaining of an intersubjective space where reciprocal speech is possible.'[23]

What does this 'intersubjective space' look like, what are its characteristics? It seems that the process of communicative action that Habermas outlines results in a desire to answer such a question, in that the conditions he lays out for defining the ideal speech situation encourage a 'vision' or a 'form' of how things could be: the necessity of imagining/envisioning an alternative, more equable situation in any given context results in the projection of a 'life' onto the one in question. Bernstein explains how this works: 'The ideal speech situation models an ideal form of life because ideal communication ... itself presupposes freedom from all forms of coercion and constraint which might in any way engender less than full discursive reciprocity.'[24] 'Without the ideal form of life which would bring into being an ideal speech situation, our liberty can be only partial.'[25] Unlike his classical influences, however, Habermas's desire for an ideal is not for any sort of authoritative or external or other-timely ideal, but is, rather, embedded in the emancipative tendency of every single verbal utterance.

Habermas himself describes the product of this intuitive imaginative process as tending to a particular 'form', which he calls a 'life form': 'The anticipation of the ideal speech situation has the significance of a constitutive illusion for every possible communication; it is simultaneously the anticipation of a life form.'[26] In speaking of this 'life form' or 'ideal form of life' is he speaking about a Utopia? Habermas, answering interpreters who have detected a parallel between the ideal speech situation and Utopia replies that, 'communicative ethics does indeed have a Utopian content, but it does not sketch out a Utopia.'[27] This is a contentious line, because it is hard to deny that a proposal of a specific imaginary life form is not a Utopian image. It is perhaps best understood to propose that the nature of discourse necessarily involves the imagination of a Utopian situation but, because every single speech act is so utterly conditioned by the context of its utterance, it would be impossible to describe what that Utopia were in any sort of a

---

[23] Bernstein, *Recovering Ethical Life*, 36.

[24] Ibid., 51.

[25] Ibid., 54.

[26] Habermas, 'Wahrheitstheorien', 256. Translation by Benhabbib, *Critique, Norm and Utopia*, 401 n.23.

[27] J. Habermas, 'Reply to My Critics' in *The Theory of Communicative Action*, Vol. 2: *Lifeworld and System: A Critique of Functionalist Reason* (Cambridge: Polity Press, 1992) 251.

fixed or universal way. While the truth conditions which underlie the argument may be thought of as seeking universality, the ideal speech situation, according to Habermas, is not. Language is a meta-institution of society which affects all social life and while its conditioning elements may have universal themes, and while we might be able to say that it requires a suspension of belief so as to grasp the transcendent possibilities within it that ultimately allow it to function, the imaginations of those involved are endlessly various and their products cannot be prescribed.

Given the above, it could be concluded that the ideal speech situation is, as Bernstein puts it, 'critical in function rather than projecting an ideal future'.[28] However, as soon as Habermas's theory is applied to any concrete situation, we glimpse that while we may not be able to sketch it out precisely, an ideal is (to some degree) precisely what we are projecting. Indeed the 'critical function' that the ideal speech situation can play is dependent on such a projection. It is not, however, being projected in any way that suggests it as a possibility for future enactment; rather the imagined idea of an ideal is being projected onto a given present situation as a monitory counter-image.[29]

The problematic word is 'future'. The ideal speech situation is undeniably projecting an ideal, but that does not mean it has to be a *future* ideal. However, the two words are so frequently understood in tandem that it is important to draw out their distinctions. Why should imagining the good life (a new life form) make it a 'future'? It is an impossible future: the conditions which exist now, in which this monitory counter-image has arisen, which have borne it, will not be conditions in the future and therefore the 'Utopia' will have changed by the time the (needs of) the future are reached. To think of imagining something is, ordinarily, to think of imagining how it could be in the future, perhaps because the imagination's power to reconstruct the present has been undervalued by modernism's overly-rationalist demands. Yet the kind of modernist attitude Habermas advocates depends totally on such an ability to imagine the present. According to his very particular type of critique, the imagination is the tool of the present moment and it works not by dreaming up a future and reading it into the now, but by reading the now and transforming the now with the differences it identifies there. The ideal speech situation then is neither a backward- nor a forward-looking Utopia, but a means of critically engaging the present via its own Utopian imagination.

---

[28]　Bernstein, *Recovering Ethical Life*, 56.

[29]　See: J. Habermas, 'Transcendence from Within, Transcendence in this World' in D.S. Browning and F. Schüssler Fiorenza, eds., *Habermas, Modernity and Public Theology* (New York: Crossroad Press, 1992) 226 - 250. Responding to Peukert's warning 'to take into account the temporal diversions of action that is oriented toward reaching understanding', Habermas explains, 'Karl-Otto Apel and I have, up to now, appropriated only the fundamental insight of [Pierce's] theory of truth, that a transcending power dwells within validity claims which assures a relation to the future for every speech act.' 241.

Benhabbib qualifies the effects of this theoretical, imaginative, critical tool in concrete social terms as:

> In late capitalist societies, emancipation does not mean alone 'the democratization of administrative decision-making processes', but the formation of communities of need and solidarity in the interstices of our societies. Such Utopia is no longer Utopian, for it is not a mere beyond. It is the negation of the existent in the name of a future that bursts open the possibilities of the present. Such Utopia is not antagonistic to norm, it complements it.[30]

Such talk of a 'future bursting open on the present' is reminiscent of much that is written about the nature the realm of God in Christian eschatology. It is, in Benhabbib's interpretation, a significant departure from Habermas's notion of the future as a 'constitutive illusion', yet it retains Habermas's emphasis on the present (not any supposed future) as normative. Two aspects of her interpretation are particularly pertinent for theology. Firstly, the manifestation of the ideal speech situation is located not merely within the overthrow of prevailing bureaucratic systems, but with 'the formation of communities of need and solidarity at the interstices of our societies'. This issues an imperative, in seeking to elucidate the expression of the Christian ideal speech situation, to look (as Rowland did) not to the bureaucratically-acceptable communities but to those at the margins of this particular 'norm'.

Secondly, it engenders a revised type of Utopia that is 'participatory' rather than 'bureaucratic'. Habermas scholar and theologian Jens Glebe-Möller, advocating the revival of the idea of a Christian Utopia, writes 'a conversation that takes place under the influence of any form of restraint is not a genuine conversation.'[31] A Utopia that is someone else's idea is not, therefore, a genuine Utopia. How this translates in a theological context, he argues, is that a notion of the realm of God which one has not had a stake in creating is probably functioning to limit communicative action, to oppress rather than, as it may seem, to liberate. And if this all sounds very worthy but laboured, Benhabbib asks: '[Whether] the goal of realizing bourgeois universalism, of making good the unfulfilled promise of justice and freedom, ... must exhaust itself in a "joyless reformism", or whether,

---

[30] Benhabbib, *Critique, Norm and Utopia*, 352 - 353. Benhabbib is effectively arguing that the actual understanding we have of Utopia has changed, been redefined, by critical theory: 'The demise of the philosophy of the subject changes the meaning of Utopia in our societies' because, 'a common shared perspective is one that we create insofar as in acting with others we discover our identity and difference, our distinctiveness from, and unity with, others. The emergence of such unity-in-difference comes through a process of self-transformation and collective action. It cannot be pre-empted either by a discourse that defines the identity of struggling subjects for them [e.g.: Marxism] or by methods of organizing which eliminate normative processes of consensus formation and self-transformation [e.g.: late capitalist societies].' Ibid., 348.

[31] J. Glebe-Möller, *A Political Dogmatic* (Philadelphia: Fortress Press, 1987) 17.

speaking with Benjamin, one cannot see a *Jetztzeit*, a moment of transfiguration in this very process?'[32] In the parallel with the realm of God, is there a theology which might restore to this Utopia the magical quality (if not the authoritative nature) of its previous, more conventional uses?

Eschatology

Helmut Peukert in his study of Habermas and Apel finds the groundwork for positing a return to a 'transcendental' (i.e.: Utopian) understanding of fundamental theology.[33] It is in his Germanic theological world that the idea of a Utopia formed by communicative action has been most urgently examined, perhaps because of the radical challenges to Christian theology in Germany in the aftermath of the holocaust (or perhaps because it has taken so long for the central works to be translated into English). The result of Peukert's research is an affirmation of the *dialectical* over and against the power of any single individual or ideology. Inevitably, such a conclusion involves serious criticism of German theology from the period prior to and during the Second World War. Bultmann, for example, while often praised as the first to take the question of methodology seriously, and as originator of theological hermeneutics, is criticised in equal part for the auto-actor conception of God and Christians that his theology fosters. For Glebe-Möller (a Dane), as for Moltmann, Metz and Peukert, the issue of overcoming ideology comes to a head around the subject of eschatology. The fundamentally non-dialectical conception of the realm of God that late twentieth-century theology inherited from Barth, Bultmann and their generation exhibited a presupposition 'that there exists an absolute chasm between earthly existence and the Kingdom of God - that 'lordship' of God - which Jesus talks about.' In common to all these authors is a desire to address the crisis to which they are heir: the sense that contemporary Christianity has not merely created, but fallen into this 'chasm' and thus cut itself off from both earthly and sacred existence.

The problem, the source of the chasm, as discerned by Glebe-Möller is that, 'Christian eschatology [has] lost... its most essential context, namely, the Utopian element.'[34] Metz likewise, heavily influenced by Jewish mysticism and the writings of Ernst Bloch (sources to which he turns for their specific articulation of alternative eschatological paradigms), perceives a pressing need for the revival of

---

[32] Benhabbib, *Critique, Norm and Utopia*, 329.

[33] However, he insists that this cannot work if theology is something to be stuck on to communicative theory as an after-thought; the theory itself has to have a theological foundation for it to be useful to theology because, he argues, 'the interdependence of theology and society belongs to the methodological consciousness of theology.' Hodgson disagrees with this position; see: P. Hodgson, *God in History: Shapes of Freedom* (Nashville: Abingdon Press, 1989) 224 - 228.

[34] Glebe-Möller, *A Political Dogmatic*, 116.

Utopias. The kind of Utopia Metz summons finds its conditioning criteria in apocalyptic imagery, and this is in contrast to Glebe-Möller, whose Utopia fights shy of the violence attending biblical imagery of apocalypse.[35] Nevertheless, the purpose intended by both is to use the notion of Utopia to accent eschatology in such a way that it fosters firstly a sense of *urgency* in Christian praxis of solidarity with poor and oppressed people, and secondly a direct connection between the world God wants us to live in and the one we make for ourselves.

Both Metz and Glebe-Möller pursue such a focus in opposition to a prevailing mood in theology, according to which Utopias are seen as entirely profane creations,[36] of no use to and as threat to what is presumed to be the far richer vein of thinking in Christian notions of the realm of God. Their argument is that the very idea of the realm of God cannot function without doing so at a profoundly Utopian level: remove the Utopian content of the realm of God and you are left either with 'middle class' values choosing only the 'safe' apocalyptic images and the comforting community-building virtues (Metz) or with the militaristic tendencies of those who seek to preserve a supposedly Christian social order (Glebe-Möller). So both insist on the manufacture of Utopia for its disturbing, subverting presence, while at the same time demarcating and amplifying the central difference between secular and Christian Utopias: hope. Eschatology, they argue with Moltmann, restores to Christian theology its fundamental character as a theology of hope.

Problematic to both accounts is the question of how.[37] How can Christianity precipitate a connection between solidarity and Utopia, bridging the damaging 'now' and 'then' associations respectively, in the context of contemporary society? Both propose communicative action, but have difficulty finding a home for it in ordinary Christian experience. Metz suggests narrative: through the narrative-memories of suffering one confronts the apocalyptic mandate for 'practical solidarity'; but how are such narratives to be presented or accessed? As Morrill observes, 'When one begins ... to press Metz with the question of *how* apocalyptic-eschatological narratives actually (practically) motivate solidarity with the living and the dead, Metz's program becomes somewhat less clear.'[38]

In contrast, Glebe-Möller draws a parallel between Peukert's 'remembering solidarity' with those who have been destroyed and the traditional

---

[35] See: G. Aichele and T. Pippin, eds., *Violence, Utopia and the Kingdom of God: Fantasy and Ideology in the Bible* (London: Routledge, 1998).

[36] For example, see: Rowland: 'Liberation theology's realism, however, does not allow such talk to degenerate into Utopianism'; Rowland, 'Eucharist as Liberation', 213.

[37] Charles Davis's suggestion that 'Habermas provides theologians with a framework in which to explore the rational underpinnings of the distinctive validity claims of religious hope' has remained largely undeveloped. D.S. Browning, 'Introduction' in D.S. Browning and F. Schüssler Fiorenza, eds., *Habermas, Modernity and Public Theology* (New York: Crossroad Press, 1992) 6.

[38] B.T. Morrill, *Anamnesis as Dangerous Memory: Political and Liturgical Theology in Dialogue* (Collegeville, MN: Liturgical Press, 2000) 44.

definition of the church as the 'communion of saints': 'When the church - despite its organization - confesses itself a communion of saints, it enters into remembering solidarity with all those who like Jesus lived and died under oppression.'[39] And, Glebe-Möller notes, the main way the church instigates this is through its worship, not in his view because worship is itself potentially a form of communicative action (as will later be contended in this study), but because of the peculiarity of 'time' in that setting, the way he believes worship can serve to undermine the norm of capitalism's technical-productionist conception of time. However, his assertion that 'The church offers through its liturgy a clear alternative to the quantitative, abstract conception of time, and to the orientation to futurity that has saturated modernity'[40] underestimates the extent to which the liturgical year has itself become commodified (by the hierarchical institutions, by state governments, by culture itself). Furthermore, it neglects the fact that many of the oppressed peoples he witnesses as the 'communion of saints' are excluded from or oppressed by the very worship of the church; and, moreover, he proceeds in his argument without further reference to the liturgy or any of its content, choosing instead biblical and doctrinal sources. So it remains unclear exactly *how* Christian eschatology's forgotten Utopia may be envisaged or created.

Moltmann insists that, 'Eschatology can not really be only a part of Christian doctrine. Rather the eschatological outlook is characteristic of all Christian proclamation, of every Christian existence and of the whole church.'[41] According to Dermot Lane, the precise location therefore for eschatological critique is neither narrative nor worship in general but the liturgy of the Eucharist in particular. Lane argues that the reason eschatology prior to Moltmann has been so underdeveloped is because, 'Over the centuries... the emphasis has fallen on a treatment of the individual *eschata* [death, judgement, heaven and hell] to the detriment of the *Eschaton* in Christ.'[42] This has undermined the Christian understanding of hope, Lane suggests, because the focus of the eschata is the future, whereas the focus of the Eschaton is the present and the future combined. Lane locates this coming-to-consciousness specifically in the Eucharistic worship of the church, seeing it as the pivotal point of the various identities to which Moltmann refers.

Arguing that the historical narratives of Christian eschatology are present in the liturgy of the Eucharist in such a way that they unite past, present and future, Lane claims that, 'It is in and through the liberating power of memory that the Eucharist embodies the Eschaton in the world today',[43] prompting his naming it the

---

[39] Glebe-Möller, *A Political Dogmatic*, 73.

[40] Ibid., 77.

[41] J. Moltmann, *Theology of Hope: On the Ground and Implications of a Christian Theology* (New York: Harper Collins, 1991) 16.

[42] D.A. Lane, *Keeping Hope Alive: Stirrings in Christian Theology* (Dublin: Gill & Macmillan, 1996) 2.

[43] Ibid., 194.

'Sacrament of the Eschaton'. But *how* is memory 'liberating'? Lane's conclusion derives from his interpretation of Jewish biblical hermeneutics and the philosophy of the Frankfurt School, particularly that of Walter Benjamin, both of which he sees as in different ways presenting memory as an emancipatory force: 'If divine memory is about making the past active in the present [Jewish exegesis] and if human memory is about being faithful to the agreement of solidarity that exists between past and present generations [Benjamin], then the celebration of the Eucharist becomes that event which makes the eschatological work of Christ available in the present.'[44] For Lane this is liberating because 'Christ in the past and present stands out prophetically against all dominating forms of oppression, suffering and death'[45] and this represents 'an anticipation of the future and a prefiguration of what is to come'.[46]

By positing the Eucharist as the conduit *par excellence* of Christian eschatology, Lane reflects a growing concern among scholars to restore to the sacraments an eschatological dimension which, as Alexander Schmemann first lamented, was neglected for centuries by the church in both East and West. In Schmemann's work, however, the purpose of this eschatological dimension is not liberation, but conversion: a constant process of coming-to-faith. The manner in which this is achieved is the same as it was for Lane: memory - 'the whole liturgy is a *remembrance* of Christ'[47] - but what is being remembered by Schmemann is not suffering, but joy; and as such it instills not solidarity of praxis but gratitude in the affections of worshippers. Indeed Schmemann vilifies the notion that solidarity of praxis, a concentration on social justice, has any kind of priority in Christian faith practice. Early in his career he wrote that, 'to save the world from social injustices, the need first of all is not so much to go down to its miseries, as to have a few witnesses in this world to the possible ascension [our going up in Christ's].'[48] This conviction was strengthened in the course of his life, until, in his last and major work, he sees a burgeoning low Christology typified in 'one or another "theology of liberation" as more "spiritually dangerous and frightening" than any 'social "hatred, division and bloodshed."'[49] He continues:

> Issues relating to economics, politics and psychology have replaced a Christian vision of the world at the service of God. Theologians, clergy and other professional 'religious' run busily around the world defending - from God? - this or that 'right', however perverse, and all this in the name of peace, unity and

---

[44]   Ibid., 205.
[45]   Ibid., 205.
[46]   Ibid., 207.
[47]   A. Schmemann, *The Eucharist: Sacrament of the Kingdom of God* (Crestwood, NY: St. Vladimir's Seminary Press, 1987) 129.
[48]   A. Schmemann, 'Sacrifice and Worship' in T. Fisch ed., *Liturgy and Tradition: Theological Reflections of Alexander Schmemann* (Crestwood, NY: St. Vladimir's Press, 1990) 135.
[49]   Schmemann, *The Eucharist*, 9.

brotherhood. Yet in fact, the peace, unity and brotherhood that they invoke are not the peace, unity and brotherhood that has been brought to us by our Lord Jesus Christ.[50]

Lane's would be the type of theology Schmemann has in mind and yet despite their differences they hold two problematic central themes in common: first, by locating the core eschatological dimension of Christian faith only in the liturgy of the Eucharist they undermine the signs of the realm of God in the whole of (the rest of) life, be they in the political sphere that seems so dangerous to Schmemann or the 'fatalism and cynicism' of the culture that Lane sees the Eucharist as countering.[51] It is an example of the problem identified in Chapter One, whereby the sacraments are taken as given, privileged as normative, and set up *in opposition to* the world. Secondly, both see these signs as representing a vision of the realm of God which is particular and known (in advance) and claim for this vision the power to induce liberation and/or conversion. This is in contrast to the Habermas-influenced accounts given by their German contemporaries, for whom no ideal scenario, Utopia or realm can be imagined except dialectically. Part of this problem is due to a prevailing metaphysical view of 'signs' in Anglo-American theology, but more of it is due to a lack of attention to the question of *how* memory, the act of 'remembrancing', achieves what they claim for it.

In what follows I will suggest that the liberative or convertative effect of memory is, contrary to Lane or Schmemann's arguments, by no means a guaranteed function of memory itself, that (following Habermas) it is entirely dependent on the interactions by which it is formed. *(The corollary being that the vision we have of the realm of God is likewise entirely contingent on the interactions by which we form it.)* Memory may serve to liberate; it may equally serve to oppress. This includes the memory of Christ: there is a naïveté in much theology that presumes that because the memory is of Christ the effect of remembering will foster Christ-likeness. If that were the case, of course, there would be no 'chasm' and no sectarianism. We are confronted with evidence that how the remembering is done is crucial to the effect that the remembering has (my Habermasian interpretation of Eucharist will suggest that memory is only liberative if ushered by a discourse that is liberative: communicative action).

So it needs to be asked how memory works for others who relate Eucharist and eschatology, first by returning to Chauvet. For Chauvet, 'The sacraments speak of the eschatological "in-between-time"' because, 'they are the bearers of the joy of the already and the distress of the not yet.'[52] They do this, he argues, because they engage our bodies: 'the resurrection of Jesus Christ and the gift of the Holy Spirit specify *corporality* as the eschatological place of God. God wants to assume flesh,

---

[50] Ibid., 10.

[51] Lane, *Keeping Hope Alive*, 200.

[52] L.M. Chauvet, *Symbol and Sacrament: A Sacramental Reinterpretation of Christian Existence* (Collegeville, MN: Liturgical Press, 1995) 555.

the flesh of Christ, by the Spirit',[53] and thus we have the (body-demanding) ritual
of the Eucharist: 'the ritual memory [of Jesus's death and resurrection] sends us to
the existential memory.'[54] Chauvet indicates that 'two conditions are required to
make it theologically tenable that God takes on the eschatological body the
sacraments symbolize... 1) *God must be thought of according to corporality*
[and]... 2) such an embodiment must be conceived in the order of grace',[55] and he
emphasises that this 'eschatological body' cannot be conceived as anything other
than the *ecclesial* community.

Chauvet's comments reflect the triangular relationship between
eschatology, ethics and ecclesiology that has dominated Roman Catholic
commentary on the Eucharist since Rahner. Like Bultmann, Rahner recognised that
the way the eschatological dimension of Jesus's proclamation of the realm of God
was perceived in post-Vatican II theology depended on a notion of divine
intervention at the end of time which was totally alien to modernity's worldview. In
subsequent 'existentialist' interpretations of biblical and historical texts,
'"eschatological" became another term for the immediate demand, the claim, the
decision or choice between authentic and inauthentic existence, with which the
kerygma, the proclamation of the gospel [in the liturgy], confronts the hearer
now.'[56]   As a result, Rahner could argue for a definition of eschatology that
stemmed primarily from how the Christian community was instituted a) by its
Christian acts in response to the kerygma (ethics) and b) by its Eucharistic
identification as the sacrament of Christ's presence on earth (ecclesiology).

The novelty in Chauvet's approach is his emphasis on the body. This
addresses part of the problem articulated above: on the question of how memory
works in the celebration of the Eucharist, Chauvet argues that the very peculiar type
of activity that is ritual summons memory as an embodied rather than an
intellectual remembrance. He sees God as taking on the eschatological body that
the sacraments symbolize and, thus, divine and human memory, being of one body,
merge. However, the problem of the pre-ordained assumptions of the nature of
God's realm remains and is joined by an additional problem: if the eschatological
body is the ecclesial body, where does that leave those people who are excluded or
alienated from the sacraments; have they no part in the memory of God? This
problem will be addressed in the following section; for the moment the discussion
remains with the question of how memory works.

As discussed in Chapter One, the emphasis one finds in Chauvet's work
on the body has a parallel in contemporary feminist liturgical accounts of the
embodied nature of liturgy. Both would agree that memory is embodied, and yet

---

53   Ibid., 264.
54   Ibid., 260.
55   Ibid., 536 - 537.
56   Glebe-Möller, *A Political Dogmatic*, 115 - 116.

feminist theology makes scant mention of eschatology. Memory is accented[57] but memory of the eschata or eschaton is played down.[58] In writing about Eucharist women have emphasised its intrinsic connection with ethics rather than with something called eschatology, arguing that as a meal of freedom the Eucharist presages the liberation that Christians should seek in their lives and in the world at large, social and ecological.[59] One of the earliest tenets of feminist theology was that male-authored theology had the threat of mortality as its starting point, whereas women experienced the immanence of life, birth-giving and living as the primary sources of their models of God.[60] Because it is not seeking to first answer the question of what happens after death, the key issues emerging from feminist reflection on the Eucharist concern not individual salvation but the salvation of the

---

[57] Much of the work of feminist theology has been to remember forgotten histories. The biblical scholarship of Schussler-Fiorenza and Phyllis Trible were early influential studies; see: E. Schüssler Fiorenza, *In Memory of Her* (New York: Crossroad, 1983) and P. Trible, *Texts of Terror: Literary-Feminist Readings of Biblical Narratives* (Philadelphia: Fortress Press, 1984). Regarding liturgy, Marjorie Procter Smith writes of the missing histories of Christian women: 'Without them as part of our living memory and of our liturgical memorials, we have no measure against which to judge who we are or who we might be.' *In Her Own Rite: Constructing Feminist Liturgical Tradition* (Nashville: Abingdon Press, 1990) 36. See also: Miriam Therese Winter's prolific body of liturgical resources based on a creative interpretation of previously forgotten women in the church, e.g.: *WomanWord: A Feminist Lectionary and Psalter* (New York: Crossroad, 1992).

[58] Peter Phan comments, 'while feminist theology has rearticualted almost all fundamental Christian doctrines, from hermeneutics and theological method to the doctrines of God and the Trinity, christology, ecclesiology, anthropology, ethics and spirituality, it has not given a systematic treatment to what Ernst Käsemann called "the mother of all Christian theology". Even recent comprehensive expositions of feminist theology have ignored eschatology as a special theme altogether'. P.C. Phan, 'Woman and the Last Things: A Feminist Eschatology' in A. O'Hara Graff, ed., *In the Embrace of God: Feminist Approaches to Theological Anthropology* (Maryknoll: Orbis, 1995) 206.

[59] For theoretical discussions of eschatology in terms of ethics see: R. Radford Ruether, 'Eschatology and Feminism', *Sexism and God-Talk: Toward a Feminist Theology* (Boston: Beacon Press, 1983) 235 - 258; S. McFague, 'Eschatology: A New Shape for Humanity' in *The Body of God: An Ecological Theology* (Minneapolis: Fortress Press, 1993) 197 - 212. For feminist liturgical theology's interpretation of Eucharistic eschatology as ethics see: M. Hellwig, *The Eucharist and the Hunger of the World* (Chicago: Theological Book Service, 1992) and J.R. Walton, *Feminist Liturgy: A Matter of Justice* (Collegeville, MN: Liturgical Press, 2000).

[60] This view has, however, become more nuanced in later developments, incorporating an awareness that while the theological starting-point for many women may lie in the way their sexuality is differentiated culturally from men's, this does not necessarily involve a focus on birthing-ability. See for example: S. Ross, 'Extravagant Affections: Women's Sexuality and Theological Anthropology' in A. O'Hara Graff, ed., *In The Embrace of God: Feminist Approaches to Theological Anthropology* (Maryknoll: Orbis Books, 1995) 105 - 121.

world as envisioned in social justice (the good of the community) and ecology (the good of the earth).

What is being witnessed in women's liturgical theology is not a rejection of eschatology, nor an ignorance of it, but a redefinition of it *as* ethics. A notion of eschatology is emerging which rejects the idea that everything will be made aright in the future (the *Eschaton* as second coming) in favour of a vision of God's engagement in the world which has the power to make it aright now. It rejects any vestiges of the other-worldy God of metaphysics who reserves judgement on our efforts (the God of the *eschata*) in favour of a God who seeks to work with us, without reservation, in living as God's followers. And any sense in which mortality may be transcended in this scheme is relativised by insisting that it is a) unknown and unknowable[61] and b) only possible to imagine alongside an affirmation of the goodness of creation, including our bodies.

Feminist theology includes many elements that can be identified as eschatological: memory of past and imagination of future bound together in a rendering of the present. However, while it acknowledges the need to theologically frame the issues implicit in these elements, such as time or the nature of community, it deliberately eschews conventional descriptions in doing so. For example, God's engagement in the world is described not as Kingdom or even realm but as vision, commonwealth or communion of saints.[62] This choice of alternative metaphors exposes the androcentrism of the vocabulary of classically construed eschatology (in its disdain for the female body, in its dualistic splitting of body and soul, in its fear of death) while fostering a definition that provides imagery which significantly furthers the debate. Yet there remains in these alternative metaphors the sense that the reality described is part of a pre-ordained plan or inevitable destiny, rather than something wholly, contingently, dependent on present actions.

Most importantly, however, by maintaining a focus on Eucharist, and interpreting it in the context of experience rather than making it fit the parameters of a pre-existing doctrine of either the eschata or the Eschaton (i.e.: a hermeneutical framework glued to a patriarchal institution), feminist theology throws new light on the fullness of the Eucharist as well as its relationship to the realm of God and the church. It does not, as Rowland sees the liberation theologians doing, 'make the Eucharist focus' on a particular idea: it focuses on the interaction of the Eucharist itself and reflects on what it reveals.[63]

---

[61] What Ruether calls 'agnostic': *Sexism and God-Talk,* 235.

[62] See for example: E.A. Johnson, *Friends of God and Prophets: A Feminist Theological Reading of the Communion of Saints* (New York: Continuum, 1999).

[63] See, for example, the way Mary Collins draws her challenges from certain specific 'symbolic ritual transactions "erupting" in eucharistic assemblies', such as the restriction of cup-sharing or the prohibition of female lectors in: 'Liturgy for a Laity Called and Sent', *Chicago Studies* 39:1 (Spring 2000) 71. See also: M. Procter-Smith, 'Christian

While an identification between Eucharist and eschatology (redefined in terms of ethics) is thus central to feminist liturgical theology, what is more ambiguous is any identification between the Eucharistic communion and the body that calls itself 'church'. Although some authors make a strong identification between Eucharist and the body of Christ, between Eucharist and the realm of God, between Eucharist and the assembly that gathers in the name of that realm, where they speak of church, feminist Christians expose as problematic any alignment of Eucharist and church. Some differentiate between the church as it is on the ground with its patriarchal hierarchies, rules and institutions and the idea of 'church' as a broad category for the community of the faithful on earth who eat together. Others, like Mary Collins, see this latter distinction as 'confused' pointing out that, 'Theologically, ...bishops and church bureaucrats, like all the baptized and ordained, express and draw their identity and mission most fully in the ecclesial community that is the liturgical assembly.'[64]

Collins nevertheless notes alongside those she sees as 'confused' that the way things are is a far cry from how they could or should be; her subsequent comment that, 'Deep faith and great courage will be needed by mature adult Catholics to stay connected with a passive, narcissistic ecclesial body that is scarcely credible as the Body of Christ'[65] demonstrates that she too recognises a discrepancy between the body of the individual assembly, the group who gather to worship God and reflect on their Eucharistic meal, and a specific 'ecclesial body' who do down the very notion of 'body' in relation to Eucharist. And so we ask:

What Constitutes the Eucharist's Focus?

The route by which Chauvet links eschatology and ecclesiology is typical of Roman Catholic orthodoxy in the wake of Vatican II, insofar as it expresses a 'communion ecclesiology': the notion that the church is constituted primarily by the celebration of the Eucharist[66] allied to the tenet that the church is itself a sacrament.[67] The doctrinal argument on which this is based can be summarised as:

Feminist Eucharistic Praying' in *Praying with Our Eyes Open: Engendering Feminist Liturgical Prayer* (Nashville: Abingdon Press, 1995) 115 - 142.

[64] Ibid., 60.

[65] Ibid., 78.

[66] Vatican II described the Eucharist as, 'the chief means through which believers are expressing in their lives and demonstrating to others the mystery which is Christ, and the sort of entity that the true Church really is.' *Sacrosanctumn concilium*, 2.

[67] The opening paragraph of *Lumen gentium* calls the church a sacrament. However, the idea of church as sacrament is not confined to the Roman Catholic denomination. Gareth Jones, surveying Christian theology from a non-denominational perspective writes: 'To speak of Church as the image of Jesus, in terms of the Sacrament of hope, is to speak of the way in which Church understands itself. It is to speak liturgically of the church's self-definition, and what it is to be part of a community which celebrates something

Christ, as the incarnation, represents the point in history where human and divine merge and thus, as the first true mediator between humanity and God, he is the 'primordial' sacrament. Through his memory in the Eucharist as bread, Christ's body becomes the body of the assembly. The Church is, because of the Eucharist, the body of Christ; it is thus also the 'basic' sacrament, the body that mediates and makes possible any and all other sacraments.[68] Within this general framework, however, significant differences in emphasis are apparent. Dennis Doyle, through his comparative study of twentieth-century Catholic authors, discerns six different choices of emphasis and comments that, 'Any ecclesiological approach that would systematically exclude one of these versions would be less than Catholic':[69]

1.   A CDF [Congregation for the Doctrine of the Faith] version, notable for its emphasis on the priority of the Church universal and the importance of certain visible church structures.
2.   A Rahnerian version, notable for its emphasis on the sacramentality of the world and on the communion with God that exists within all of humankind.
3.   A Balthasarian version, notable for its emphasis on the uniqueness of Christian revelation and its aesthetic character.
4.   A liberation version, notable for its emphasis on the option for the poor and on the political implications of communion.
5.   A contextual version, notable for its emphasis on gender, ethnicity, and social location as the context for appreciating relationality.
6.   A reforming version, notable for its emphasis on the need for Roman Catholics to challenge radically their own ecclesiological presuppositions in the interests of ecumenical progress.

The beauty of Doyle's synthesis is its inclusivity, its determination to foster a conversation about church that embraces diversity while enjoying unity (which he sees as being authored or symbolised by the episcopacy as well as by the Eucharist) in a climate in which discussions of ecclesiology have often proved divisive. There is, however, a constraint in his analysis in that it ignores the voices of those who have been excluded from or abused by the very sacramental worship that communion ecclesiology posits as constitutive. With a 'communion ecclesiology', if you take away communion, you take away ecclesiology, such that those who are not part of the communion ritual are deemed not part of church.

Doyle's analysis underestimates the degree to which those represented in number five, the contextual version, acknowledge the possibility that a) if the context is destructive, communion may not be possible and b) an alternative

---

which, fundamentally, is still to come.' G. Jones, *Critical Theology: Questions of Truth and Method* (Cambridge: Polity Press, 1995) 222.

[68]   Such a theology owes much to pre-conciliar theologians, particularly de Lubac's pin-pointing of the Eucharist as the sacramental manifestation of the church. See: P. McPartlan, *The Eucharist Makes the Church: Henri de Lubac and John Zizioulas in Dialogue* (Edinburgh: T. and T. Clark, 1993).

[69]   D.M. Doyle, *Communion Ecclesiology* (Maryknoll: Orbis, 2000) 19.

context, beyond the bounds of the episcopacy to which Doyle attaches the celebration of the Eucharist, may be sought. Thus there is, for example, in the emergence of women's Eucharist groups or in the Basic Christian Communities, the celebration of the Eucharist without an ordained priest. There are also openly gay Christians meeting to celebrate the Eucharist together and ecumenical Christians doing the same. By naming themselves 'church' these assemblies are including themselves in the family that 'communion ecclesiology' posits as church, although many of the church's mainstream ecclesiologists would dispute their right to name themselves thus.

There are also many thousands of Christians who have no 'alternative' community with which to worship: those non-Catholic parents who cannot be in communion with their Catholic children; divorced and remarried Christians who cannot be in communion with their communities; gay Christians who have the choice of either receiving communion and denying their sexuality or of living as an openly gay person and being excluded from the sacraments; women who want to be part of the church but who cannot take communion because they recognise the sexism of Christian worship, in its structures and language and leadership, as abusive to women. There are theologians who have been excommunicated because their church hierarchy deemed their teachings false. None of Doyle's six categories include the 'communion ecclesiology' of these Christians. For them, the idea of church as sacrament may be extremely problematic: how can this church which seeks to destroy their personal identities simultaneously claim that it is acting as a mediator of the same God who, in Christ, sat and broke bread with those whom society despised?

It is with the assessment that Jesus was killed 'because of the way he ate' that Nathan Mitchell begins his book *Eucharist as Sacrament of Initiation*. Reading the biblical accounts of Jesus's table-manners (scruffy attire, eating with tax-collectors and sinners, letting a woman anoint his feet with her hair, etc.) as an 'acted parable' (as Lash did also),[70] Mitchell argues that in the society of his day Jesus's vagabond looks and disgraceful company-keeping were profoundly contrary to acceptable norms of behaviour. Every aspect of his etiquette was, Mitchell argues, designed as a challenge to the social status quo, the purpose of which, like the analogy with the verbal parable, was to prompt conversion. So in his last supper, in instituting the meal that Christians continue to celebrate as the Eucharist, Jesus modelled 'not just a rite but a way of life';[71] a way of life that demands eating with the socially-unacceptable as the actual point of initiation into the community called church and its subject, the realm of God. The Eucharist initiates the individual into the church because, Mitchell argues, it institutes the church itself: 'because it celebrates not the past but the present coming-to-be of this

---

[70] N.D. Mitchell, *Eucharist as Sacrament of Initiation* (Chicago: Liturgy Training Publications, 1994) 30.

[71] Ibid., 48.

assembly as church, because it announces not so much who we are as who we are to become in the full and final presence of God's reign.'[72]

Mitchell, unlike Rowland, construes Christian eschatology from reflection on the meal of the Eucharist rather than the other way around, and from this he construes his ecclesiology: the Eucharist makes the church, the church makes the Eucharist.[73] He is not alone in this liturgical theological methodology. It was by the same route that Lathrop came to propose that, 'The meeting for worship is the church becoming church'[74] and Kelleher that, 'the church gives birth to the church.'[75] In most respects, Mitchell's conclusions vary little from Rowland's; but one difference apparent at the heart of Mitchell's way of thinking is an emphasis on the activity that comprises the whole meal, on *how* we eat rather than *what* we eat: on the relationships between participants rather than on bread or wine or words as objects or symbols.

Drawing on Mary Douglas's claim that meals are more about social relations than they are about nutrition, Mitchell proposes that: 'All meals - including those of Jesus - commit participants to a particular vision of culture and society, while at the same time engaging them in the symbolic embodiment of what relations among diners are, can and should be. To participate in the meal is to enact that vision, to surrender oneself to its value, meaning and truth.'[76] Following Mitchell, the importance of the issue of ecclesiology is increased, because the ability of the individual to be part of the realm of God - their participation in Christian eschatology - is conditional on their participation in the meal. In light of the barriers to participation outlined above, Mitchell's view seems to offer a profoundly inclusive theology, by means of which no one can be considered too untableworthy to be initiated into the vision of God's realm and thus God's church on earth: 'The only thing we need to bring to God's table is the ability to die (as Jesus did, surrounded by doubts and questions, by suffering and sorrow - and finally by surrender and self-forgetting). Dying we arrive at the table of dreams, where all humanity is gathered and the world's transfiguration is begun.'[77] However, Mitchell is a Roman Catholic and the fact that he fails to address the likelihood that at his church on Sunday there will be many people who are able to die yet are absent from, indeed unwelcome at, the 'table of dreams' renders his position idealistic.

---

[72] Ibid., 48.
[73] On 'the Eucharist Makes the Church' see also: J. Vellian, 'Theological Dimensions of Liturgy', *Studia Liturgica* 1:13 (2000) 11.
[74] G.W. Lathrop, *Holy People: A Liturgical Ecclesiology* (Minneapolis: Augsburg/Fortress Press, 1999) 9.
[75] M.M. Kelleher, 'Sacraments and the Ecclesial Mediation of Grace', *Louvain Studies* 23 (1998) 197.
[76] Mitchell, *Eucharist as Sacrament of Initiation*, 77.
[77] Ibid., 43.

Nevertheless, it is crucial that theology heed Mitchell's proposition that it look at the whole meal and the relations between diners rather than at what are usually seen as 'the symbols'. This change in perspective breaks through the wall of a single given image of God's realm to one that involves a more complex coalition of actuality, possibility and imagination: 'what diners are, can and should be.'[78]

However, apparent within this argument is the problem of a largely unacknowledged difference between the 'is', the 'can', and the 'should be' of the assembly gathered at Eucharist (and, by extension, of the church as a whole) in nearly all mainstream writing about Eucharist. Although feminist theological methodology is founded on a more interactive unit of analysis than conventional theology in its evaluation of or theological reflection on liturgy,[79] even it, like its patriarchal counterparts, tends to focus on what ought to have happened (from the point of view of the planners) rather than on what did happen. In doing so it reports liturgies either via isolated fragments (a piece of music or a text and why it was chosen; a scenario or vignette from within a much longer liturgy) or as 'Orders of Service', rather than via the specific experiences of the actual interactions between all the people and things present.

This subject is addressed, regarding conventional Roman Catholic worship, by Kathleen Hughes. Hughes argues that while the forthcoming *Sacramentary* corrects many of the mistakes of the first English language one which was hastily complied after Vatican II, these corrected words will not make worship any more 'memorable' (her criteria for effective worship) unless the understanding of how words work is similarly reformed. The way words work, according to Hughes, has more in common with poetry than with our traditional understanding of liturgy (cause and effect). So, as with poetry, even good words will be cancelled out if read badly or heard inattentively: 'after thirty years of liturgical reform, new texts and well-trained presiders won't make the slightest bit of difference unless we, hearers of the word spoken in our name, recognise that we are the third party in the speech act of prayer.'[80]

Hughes raises two interesting points: firstly, her application to worship of a very Habermasian linguistic analysis which posits three parties in any liturgical act (speaker, word spoken and hearer) and demands that for worship to work, 'the

---

[78] Mitchell writes, 'all meals - including those of Jesus - commit participants to a particular vision of culture and society, while at the same time engaging them in the symbolic embodiment of what relations between diners are, can and should be. To participate in the meal is to enact that vision, to surrender oneself to its value, meaning and truth.' Ibid., 77.

[79] According to Janet Walton this exhibits a threefold pattern: to remember especially what has been lost, to honour and tell stories as community, and to imagine how things could be. Walton, *Feminist Liturgy*, 31 - 47.

[80] K. Hughes, 'Some Musings on the Poetry of Prayer' in *Finding Voice to Give God Praise: Essays in the Many Languages of the Liturgy* (Collegeville, MN: Liturgical Press, 1998) 114.

word has a certain truth and gravity; the speaker is credible; and the hearer is receptive.'[81] This represents a call for greater attention to the composite of speech acts rather than simply the words spoken and the individual who is speaking them; it demands a 'poetic' analysis which recognises that, 'The poetry of prayer is not something we hear nor something we observe, but something we create each time we gather for liturgy.'[82] In this, Hughes has presented an interesting model for liturgical theology: in every liturgical action, we must consider as one:

[speaker = presider] + [word spoken] + [hearer = congregation].

Quite *how* she intends us to proceed with interpretation based on this model remains unclear, but that cannot detract from the significance of her point: theology has to cease looking at liturgy's component parts and look at it instead in terms of interactions.

Yet if liturgy is to be seen as a co-created prayer, Hughes's particular model is doubtful because, despite her desire that this way of viewing liturgical action should 'invite us again and again into a new way of being in relationship with God', it seems to forget God. If the speaker is the presider, if the word is spoken (by her or him) in our name and if we are the hearer, is God reduced to an eavesdropper on this interaction? If the word is being 'spoken in our name' then we are already speaking with the speaker and the hearer is therefore not us but God. This would mean that:

[speaker = whole assembly (including presider)] + [word spoken] + [Hearer = God]

and given the experience of many people that God speaks in liturgy then, unlike her model above in which speaker never becomes hearer, with God the roles are mutual, so also:

[speaker = God] + [word spoken] + [Hearer = whole assembly (including presider)]

---

[81] Ibid., 110. On pages 108 - 109 Hughes outlines the rationale behind this point and her remarks seem to have been very influenced by Habermas although she makes no mention of him or of any other scholars of communicative action. She even mounts an original criticism of what would be Habermas's appeal to the trustworthiness of the speaker as one of the universal validity claims: 'it is not enough that a speaker be credible and trustworthy. The word itself has to be of a certain quality', 109.
Moreover, in anticipation of the criticisms that will be levelled at Hughes's model below, it should be noted at the outset that few literary critics would agree that the hearer or reader of a poem is the passive vessel Hughes describes in this analogy between prayer and poetry.

[82] Ibid., 115.

Two problems remain. The first is argumentative: the objection may be raised that the speaker is not speaking on anyone's 'behalf', because this is open to abuses of power; that in worship, the congregation is conceived as much as speaker as it is as hearer. Secondly, and perhaps more significantly, quite often in liturgy the nature of the sentence uttered is not one of 'behalf' anyway; quite often the words of the presider are a direct address to the congregation: on a small level as, for example, 'The Lord be with you' or on a more prolonged level, in the sermon. Even the Eucharistic Prayer, which might be seen as the main word spoken on the congregation's behalf, requires in actual fact a high degree of *dialogue between presider and congregation* ('Lift up your hearts'; 'We lift them up'...). These objections can be incorporated into Hughes's original model, with its recognition that the co-creatorship of liturgy is dependent on a dialogue between presider and congregation, via the amendments that a) the roles of speaker and hearer have to be mutual/exchangeable, and b) the words spoken are not done so vicariously but in effect.

However, the problem of God's creatorship in this process remains. What Hughes's model might seem to imply is that God, the logos, is present at the centre of each and every interaction as 'word'; but this is not her conclusion. Far more implicit in Hughes's model is the notion that each and every human interaction, because of its creative facility, says something of God; that the only way we can find 'new ways of being in relationship with God' is by finding new ways of interacting with one another. God is neither speaker nor word spoken nor hearer in the interaction of the liturgy; God is the whole interaction. So, can it be suggested:

[speaker] + [word spoken] + [hearer] = God?

Is it possible, effectively, to return to Mitchell but propose that God *is* 'the symbolic embodiment of what relations among diners are, can and should be'? What would make the Eucharist, then, would be the embodiment of God in and through the interactions of its participants. This theoretical approach to the discourse of Christian Eucharist (a methodology that has been shown to be flawed in terms of theological praxis) must now be tested against the liturgical theology of an actual Christian community, in order to access better the understanding of God embodied therein. The difficulties of accessing such knowledge were outlined in the first two chapters; the third chapter suggested a possible approach via Habermas's communicative ethics, and the following section develops a Habermasian methodology appropriate to the study of religious ritual in general. The final section of the chapter examines the liturgy of the Eucharist in particular and adapts these Habermasian hermeneutics to a case study of a community's worship.

Application of Habermas to Theology

The discussion so far in this chapter has resulted in some unresolved issues. Contemporary theology, whether systematic or liturgical, feminist or otherwise, in seeing Eucharistic liturgy as some sort of 'ideal speech situation' posits it as the best vantage point for expressing Christian ethics, eschatology and ecclesiology, and seems in its conclusions to have merged the boundaries of these aspects of faith. The Eucharist has become the realm of God, and the realm of God has become the church: 'In the Eucharist the church becomes what it celebrates: the visible, tangible, permanent presence of God's saving grace poured out in and for the world through the death and resurrection of Jesus.'[83] The assembly at Eucharist has become the ethical body of Christian witnessing and confessing, and even itself the embodiment of God. The Eucharist has become all things to all people.

Perhaps this is as it should be. However, it leads to the question whether what the relations between diners at ordinary Sunday Eucharist 'are, can and should be' always measure up to the theory written about them. It is difficult for theologians to consider the Eucharist with the liturgy of the Eucharist as a starting point: because so much is written about what it 'should be' it can blinker the interpretation of what 'is'. Habermas is helpful in this regard, promoting an attitude of study that concentrates not on extrapolating the meaning of phenomena but on uncovering the conditions upon which interaction depends (and seeing these as themselves disclosive). As has already been reported, however, Habermas did not have the application of his theory to worship in mind when he wrote it, so in order to learn from his theory it will be necessary to adapt it to this particular subject.

Some commentators have generalised Habermas's theory in order to apply it to theology, noticing how the concepts of, for example, conditions of discourse or the ideal speech situation find parallels with theological concepts; this is the method by which Lash and Rowland proceeded. Yet Habermas has articulated a very specific sociological model of linguistic analysis with the intention that it be applied to specific human interactive situations. His whole theory advocates an analysis not of general themes (because these are, he proposes, invariably the themes dictated only by the dominant cultural actor) but of what was actually said in any given situation. This is under-explored in theology, and, as such, the attempt to apply his theory literally rather than idea-logically (as Rowland did) is an improvisation.

Five criteria for the study of liturgy have emerged from the various analyses of this lacuna in the preceding chapters. First of all, in the light of the methodological criteria of ritual studies reported in Chapter Two, and in order to move from the general to the specific, the choice of 'specific human interactive situation' has to be explained. Secondly, with a nod to Grimes, an awareness that the observer in this situation is not 'detached' from it has to be acknowledged. This has two consequences: a) the analysis itself must self-consciously reflect the

---

[83]   Mitchell, *Eucharist as Sacrament of Initiation*, 108.

presence of the 'observer' and b) the exchanges studied cannot be represented as a script with stage directions because our familiarity with this format means we are used to presuming that text dictates practice. So, for example, in a liturgical scenario, it cannot be assumed that what is designed to be said (for example on a service sheet) is what was actually said, and to avoid this assumption-making, it is necessary to develop a means of report other than an 'Order of Service'.

Thirdly, the liturgy must be reported in a way that reflects what it is: a narrative of a dialogue, not a script thereof. Fourthly, in light of Habermas, it has to find a way of articulating the speakers' and hearers' *own* understanding of what was said. To this end, this study will develop a method of analysing dialogue by means of exposing the validity claims raised and redeemed, allowing these to expose the (implicit, mutual) conditions of possible understanding. And fifthly, the emergent analysis will have to give weight to poetic interpretations to complement literal/analytic interpretations in order to relate the findings to those of the broader field of theology, and in order to suit theology's discourse as interpretation.

In developing this model it is necessary to try to compensate for some of the constraints of Habermas's work as reported in Chapter Three. Thus, the limitations of Habermas's neglect of gender will be offset by: recognising in every case the gender of the speaker and hearer in dialogue; attentiveness to any and all gender-specific vocabulary; and an acknowledgement of the unavoidable context of this study in a culture which conditions language and, therefore, gender-formation according to values that privilege male over female. Regarding Habermas's allied neglect of the emotional, this study will, following Crossley, seek to apply the analysis of validity claims to emotional as well as cognitive verbal expressions, if and when they occur.

A use of Habermas in a theological context, therefore, suggests an analysis of Christian liturgy which:

1)   Seeing interaction rather than action as the basic unit of analysis, concentrates on audible instances of linguistic interaction.

The subject of the scholar's enquiry is dialogue. In this context, dialogue within liturgy is privileged over the more conventional points of access for liturgical interpretation: particular symbols, such as bread; the text-form of liturgically prescribed words, such as the creed; a doctrinal tenet or teaching enacted in the liturgy; historical information about the liturgy; analysis of what participants said about worship after the event[84] or the feelings discerned by the observer.

---

[84]   As, for example, in one of the few collaborative studies of liturgy between theologians and social scientists: L.J. Madden, *The Awakening Church: Twenty-five Years of Liturgical Renewal* (Collegeville, MN: Liturgical Press, 1992).

2)   Looks at the pragmatics of speech acts via the raising and redeeming of Habermas's three validity claims.

The method concentrates on discerning which validity claim (to truth, rightness and trustworthiness) is being explicitly raised and the result of any ensuing challenge.

3)   Moves to represent the possible universal conditions of understanding constructed between speaker and hearer via reportage of the claims raised and redeemed.

In the process of reporting the dialogue, the study identifies possible conditions of understanding uncovered by the speaker and hearer in the dialogue itself. The implicit question governing this hermeneutic is: for there to be understanding, what rules need to be in play?

Using Habermas as a guide in interpreting this liturgy demands a focus solely on the verbal interactions. Habermas recognises that the non-verbal is an extremely important component in communication, yet insists that this is currently beyond the scope of the methodology of the human sciences. This is, initially at least, frustrating. Reading the case study account below, most theologians would note that the non-verbal expressions reported are probably more expressive of the faith of the participants and of their personal and corporate understanding of what this ritual entails than the verbal which, at first glance, seem to be lacking on their part. For example, while only 5% of the congregation greeted the gospel with the words, 'Praise to you Lord Jesus Christ', 90% of them simultaneously traced a series of three small cross marks on their upper body with their right hand thumb. Surely there is a strong challenge here: if one wants to interpret what participants are doing in this ritual one should emphasise this gesture which was apparently the most participated-in action of the mass.

In the interpretation below, however, while seeing it as important to record the gesture as part of the narrative, there will be no analysis of it as a gesture at all. This is for two reasons: first, on what grounds would this gesture be accessed? There has been, as reported in Chapter Two, a wealth of criticism of liturgical theologians and other ritual critics who ascribe meaning to ritual gestures without addressing the problem of how gesture-makers themselves understand their action. This study has no critical precedent or model on which to base an interpretation of bodily gesture. Furthermore, I might personally think that I understand this gesture, as a member of a community whose members made it, or as a scholar who has witnessed many such acts and can see a pattern between them; but, in seeking to elucidate the understanding a community has of the acts it performs (which is what all theology, but liturgical theology specifically, claims as its intention), any application of my own experience to theirs would constitute not just conjecture but a small act of imperialism. Finally, a 'positive' reason for concentrating on the verbal exchanges in the liturgy is Mitchell's suggestion (based on Douglas, noted above) that Eucharistic theology needs to focus on the relations between diners as these are symbolically composed, and the dialogue between diners seems the most accessible avenue for such a study.

As for the constraint of Habermas's negative account of religion, in offering an attempted application of his theory to theology, this study aims to show that the 'embodied' and 'liberative' aspects of religion that he eschews are nevertheless evidenced, and even privileged, as a result of a Habermasian account of the dialogue that comprises liturgy.

Case Study: A Roman Catholic Eucharist in Ireland

The subject chosen is the liturgy of the Eucharist, as celebrated at noon in a Roman Catholic church in the west of Ireland. The expectation is that a Habermasian analysis will expose how people in this assembly themselves understand the actions they perform, and that the subsequent commentary will highlight the ways in which these understandings relate to traditional theological categories such as ethics, eschatology and ecclesiology. It was necessary to develop a methodology for calculating the level of verbal participation in this liturgy in this large assembly, and this is outlined in detail in the Appendix.

Each member of the congregation entered the church through either the front or side door, most of them picking up a newsletter from a stand in the narthex. They silently found a place in the pews which all face the altar at the front of the church and some knelt while others sat until a male voice coming through the amplification system said, 'Please stand for the first hymn, number eight'. It is not known who said this or from where. The people stood and the organ at the back of church started to play. About 5% of the congregation picked up the hymn sheets and sang 'Christ Be beside Me'.

The presider walked from a door at the side of the sacristy past the tabernacle, up several steps to the raised dais on which stood the altar, several large chairs and the lectern. The organ stopped and the presider said, 'In the Name of the Father [the majority of the assembly made the sign of the cross with their hand, but did not speak] and of the Son and of the Holy Spirit. Amen. I want to welcome today Fr.X as concelebrant of this mass. Fr.X is originally from Ballyglass and I know you would want me to welcome him on your behalf. He is stationed on the missions in Nigeria and he's here visiting for two weeks and we're delighted he will concelebrate mass with me today, so, you are very welcome Fr.X. Today we hear the story of Jesus' forgiveness of Peter; let us keep this in mind as we pray to God our Father, I confess to almighty God...' About 10% of the congregation joined him in saying this prayer of confession, at the end of which, without pausing he continued, 'May almighty God have mercy on us, forgive, us our sins and bring us to everlasting life. Glory be to the Father...' and again the congregation joined him in saying the Gloria. About 20% of people seemed to be speaking, but none could be heard because the priest said the prayer loudly through the microphone.

At the end of the Gloria, the priest continued 'Let us pray. God our Father, may we look forward with hope to our resurrection, for you have made us your sons and daughters, and restored the joy of our youth. Today's reading is from Acts. Please sit down.'   The congregation sat. A woman came from the congregation to the lectern and read the first reading, finishing with 'This is the word of the Lord', to which half of the congregation replied 'Thanks be to God'. She told us the words of the response to the psalm, began reading the first verse of the psalm and said 'response' to which about 25% of the congregation replied with the words she had told us, 'I will praise you, Lord, you have rescued me'. She said the words too, through the microphone. At the end of the last 'response', the woman said 'The...' but the presider stood up in his place and interrupted with, 'The second reading is from the book of the Apocalypse.' The woman then read it, ending as before with 'This is the word of the Lord'. The congregation did not reply this time; instead the priest said 'Please stand. Alleluia, Alleluia. Lord Jesus, explain the scriptures to us. Make our hearts burn within us as you talk to us. Alleluia. A Reading from the holy Gospel according to Luke.'   About 5% of the congregation said, 'Praise to you Lord Jesus Christ'; simultaneously about 90% of them made three small cross marks with their right hand on their head, lips and breast. People were still arriving and walking up and down the side aisles of the church as the priest read the long version of the gospel appointed for the day, which he ended by saying, 'This is the Gospel of the Lord.'   Less than two percent of the congregation joined in as the priest said 'Praise to you Lord Jesus Christ.'

The congregation sat down and the presider started the homily straight away. 'In the name of the Father and of the Son and of the Holy Spirit. Amen. It's a terrible feeling to know you have let someone down. In today's gospel reading, the one who denied him, the one who thought he could never be forgiven, was the one who was chosen by Christ. This is a message for all of you and for me. We all at times deny Christ. To be true to the gospel makes demands of us in these times. We can all recall times we've rejected Christ in one way or another. The message of today's gospel is consoling. The past is the past. Our task is to move on with the past firmly behind us, to follow Christ. Let us pray today, asking the Lord to help us take up his challenge to 'follow me'. May the Lord help us as we try to follow him in word and action this week. Amen. Please stand up for the Creed.'   There was a lot of background noise: rustling of papers, coughs, children crying, brief conversations at the back all the time the priest was speaking. About 40% of the congregation said the Creed, but one could mostly hear the jangling of coins all round the church and the priest saying it loudly through the microphone.

The woman returned to the lectern and said four bidding prayers, all of which concerned local issues and to which 60% of the congregation responded each time with, 'Lord graciously hear us.'   The priest said a further bidding prayer for the dead, giving details of those who had died that week and when their funerals would be as part of the prayer. Most of the congregation again said 'Lord graciously hear us' and the presider said, 'Let us pause for a moment and bring to Mass any intentions we may have as individuals or as families'. He left two seconds then said a concluding prayer to which 1% of people responded, 'Amen'.

Everyone sat down and a team of men passed small baskets among the congregation to collect money. There was a low hum of chatter and the sound of coins chinking together. On the altar, the altar boys had taken the items for communion from a table a yard away from the altar and handed them to the priest. He lifted first the bread, then the cup, bowing each time as he put them back on the altar. He said, 'Pray, brethren, that our sacrifice may be acceptable to God the almighty Father.' No one said the response, nor 'Amen' to the brief prayer that followed. The presider said 'The Lord be with you' and, even though about 10% of the congregation were saying 'And also with you', he followed immediately with 'Lift up your hearts' and again 'Let us give thanks to the Lord our God', each time coming in with his next line while the congregation were still saying the previous one. After he said the Preface about 20% of the people said the 'Hosanna' antiphon and all the congregation knelt down.

The priest said the Eucharistic Prayer and the memorial acclamation; the concelebrant said the prayers for the dead and for sinners and about 70% of the congregation, who had had their heads bowed for the whole prayer, even when bells rang at certain points, joined the presider as he said, 'Through him, with him, in him, in the unity of the Holy Spirit, all glory and honour is yours, almighty Father, for ever and ever, Amen'. The people stood and over 70% said the 'Our Father' and, after the priest had continued alone with the subsequent prayer, 'For the kingdom, the power, and the glory are yours, now and forever.' This responsiveness dropped to about 5%, however, when the presider next offered, 'The peace of the Lord be always with you' and few said 'And also with you.' The priest then said the 'Lamb of God' and again about 5% of the congregation accompanied him. Two people in front of me offered a quiet handshake to one another.

Two more priests had come into the sanctuary from the sacristy and while the two celebrants each ate a large host and drank wine, these others were walking across the sanctuary from tabernacle to altar, ferrying a total of ten stacking silver bowls full of hosts. These were distributed from ten points around the church. The presider said, 'Please go to the station nearest to you for the distribution of communion.' At the point where a host was offered to each congregant, the minister said 'The body of Christ' and about 20% of recipients said 'Amen' (only a host, and not the cup, was offered). The priest, after cleaning up, stood at the microphone by the big chair behind the altar and read a long list of announcements: asking people to help the work of the missions by supporting a display in the townhall; telling everyone to take a newsletter home with them, as there were more announcements in there; thanking the schoolteachers for preparing children for the sacraments; asking people to move the hymn sheets to the end of the pews for easier collection afterwards; and ending by saying 'If you are a visitor at Mass today you are very welcome, whether you are visiting family or over on holidays, all visitors are welcome. Let us pray.' The congregation stood and most of them replied 'Amen' to the blessing and 'Thanks be to God' to 'The mass is ended. Go in peace.' The priest said, 'The final hymn is number 26', the organ sounded and perhaps as few as two people out of five hundred tried to sing, 'I Watched the Sunrise'. The organ only played two verses and before the second was finished, the congregation poured out of the church, greeting and talking to one another in the aisles, in the narthex and on the front plaza.

Analysis as Communicative Action

A woman came from the congregation to the lectern and read the first reading, finishing with, 'This is the word of the Lord', to which half of the congregation replied, 'Thanks be to God'.

This brief exchange seems to be the first occasion in the liturgy where there is direct dialogue between a speaker and a hearer. The woman makes a *truth* claim, but she is not challenged to provide grounds. Instead, the congregation reply with an emotional truth claim: a statement which serves to express gratitude (and which is not challenged either) and which, because it is given in direct response to the woman's claim, also acts as implicit affirmation of the *truth* and *rightness* of her claim and her *trustworthiness* in making it.

But only half of them gave such an expression of gratitude. By remaining silent the other half reserved comment and not only refused an emotional claim, but also thus reserved verbal assent to the woman's claim.

> *For half the assembly: the evidence of God being heard is feeling grateful. For the other half, no dialogue: impossible to tell.*

The above Conditions of Possible Understanding (CPU) extract may seem the first instance of dialogue, but it is not the first instance of people speaking and it must be asked if the utterances made prior to this point were not dialogue, what were they?

'Please stand and sing the first hymn, number eight'. ... About 5% of the congregation picked up the hymn sheets and sang 'Christ Be Beside Me'.

This does not at first seem to be dialogue: a disembodied voice comes over the p.a., and requests something of the assembly. Some respond in the manner requested, many do not. Would they have stood and sung without being asked to do so? They would have stood, that being the custom when the Mass begins, but they would not have sung because they would not have known what to sing. So the nub of this strange voice's sentence is to impart information. This does not, however, make it neutral, unconcerned with communicative action. Seeing it as the opening utterance of an argumentation, rather than as a (somehow incontestable) announcement, it is transparently power-laden: it was a male voice, it was very loud, much louder than any other voice in the room could be; it did not come from a visible body (or visible microphone); it alone had information that was needed by all. Suddenly it does not seem quite so benign. And this is - perhaps - reflected in the response of 95% of the congregation who, having been told to do something they know to do anyway (stand) and given the information necessary to respond, nevertheless refrain from doing so. The hymn was a prayer, an address to God in Christ. 95% of the congregation thus began Mass by refusing to pray.

CPU: *This is not communicative action and therefore no conditions of possible understanding are exposed in this exchange.*

'In the Name of the Father [the majority of the assembly made the 'sign of the cross' with their hand, but did not speak] and of the Son and of the Holy Spirit. Amen. I want to welcome today Fr.X as concelebrant of this Mass. Fr.X is originally from Ballyglass and I know you would want me to welcome him on your behalf. He is stationed on the missions in Nigeria and he's here visiting for two weeks and we're delighted he will concelebrate mass with me today, so, you are very welcome Fr.X. Today we hear the story of Jesus' forgiveness of Peter; let us keep this in mind as we pray to God our Father, I confess to almighty God...' Less than 10% of the congregation joined him in saying this prayer.

Several things are going on here that merit attention in terms of analysing worship as communicative action: firstly, the presider does not greet the congregation, as the Roman Catholic missal says he should (in the text prescribed to be followed as, at a minimum, 'The Lord be with you': 'And also with you'). This establishes the priest as the sole speaker rather than the priest and congregation as partners in conversation. Secondly, this is confirmed in the subsequent monologue. He makes the opening trinitarian sign of the cross and immediately says 'Amen' without pausing, or lowering his voice which is booming through the p.a., to allow the congregation to say it with him. By so doing he raises a *truth* claim (that we gather in the name of...) but denies the congregation the opportunity to (challenge or) give their assent to this. (If they were allowed such an opportunity, would any of them challenge the two explicitly male nouns - Father and Son - and the lack of female ones used to name God?) Thirdly then, the presider immediately moves into a lengthy welcome of the concelebrant 'on your behalf'. The priest has not yet established any dialogue with the people on whose behalf he is claiming to speak and they get no opportunity to either challenge his speaking on their behalf or his offering a welcome to this single individual because he moves swiftly on. Fourthly, instead of saying 'let us pray' he instructs the congregation to keep his interpretation of a theme for the day in mind 'as we pray'. But, fifthly, 'we' do not pray. 90% of the congregation again refuse to respond verbally and those whose mouths can be seen to be moving can nevertheless not be heard because the presider's voice is so loudly amplified. More people joined in as the presider said the Gloria (he did not invite people to pray this time, just started into it) but again they could not be heard.

A validity claim is thus raised but not redeemed. The fact that people were listening and that some did speak means this cannot be dismissed as non-dialogical. However, it was not communicative action because the congregation's opportunity to speak was inhibited or denied by the priest's actions.

At the end of the last 'response', the woman said 'The...' but the presider stood up in his place and interrupted with, 'The second reading is from the book of the Apocalypse.'

This is a *truthfulness* claim. The presider interrupts the woman because he - presumably - does not think it appropriate for her to introduce the scriptures. It was not that the sentence itself was inappropriate (that would be a rightness claim), it was that the woman was not thought (trust)worthy to say it. The woman neither objected, nor insisted on continuing with her introductory line. (Nor did the congregation raise any objection.) She accepted the priest's interjection and when she next spoke it was to start directly into reading the scripture aloud.

CPU: *Only ordained people (and therefore only men) can introduce scripture.*

The woman then read it, ending as before with 'This is the word of the Lord'. The congregation did not reply this time; instead the priest said 'Please stand. Alleluia, Alleluia. Lord Jesus, explain the scriptures to us. Make our hearts burn within us as you talk to us. Alleluia. A reading from the holy Gospel according to Luke.' About 5% of the congregation said, 'Praise to you Lord Jesus Christ'; simultaneously about 90% of them made three small cross marks with their right hand on their head, lips and breast.

This exposes an important example of the different perspective provided by approaching a ritual as communicative action. Ordinarily, liturgical scholars would look to the texts prescribed to be followed and elucidate the theology contained in them. What the above account demonstrates is a) that in some cases the text may not be exactly followed, but also b) something quite different in communicative terms may replace that envisioned by the liturgical scholars who wrote those texts.

The congregation is supposed to reply 'Thanks be to God' but they do not. At the point in time they are meant to be saying this, the presider speaks instead. He again asks them to do something they are already doing (standing) and proceeds to say alone another prayer that ought, according to the text, to be said by all. It is a mixed address: the first sentence is a direct address to the congregation; the second is an acclamation. The third is a prayer to Christ. The fourth is an indirect address to the congregation. Had the priest followed the text, he would just have said 'a reading from the holy gospel according to Luke'; the indirect address to the congregation, and the congregation would have said all else that was required. Instead, the priest says all and the congregation are muted. This is perhaps why, at the end of the gospel, when given a chance to speak, only 5% say the prescribed response: 'Praise to you Lord Jesus Christ'. 95% of the assembly said nothing.

CPU: *Hearing the gospel gives rise to praise (for 5%); but, if there has*
                been no interaction, there has been no gospel and there is no
                reason to give praise. Being muted militates against praise-
                giving.

There was a lot of background noise: rustling of papers, coughs, children crying, brief conversations at the back all the time the priest was speaking.

This report of so much audible activity among the congregation while the priest was delivering his homily does not amount to 'dialogue': while it is audible sound, it is not audible language. This is not to say sermons in general are not potentially dialogical; on the contrary, the speaker needs the hearer and the hearer needs the speaker. However, in this instance there is no dialogue because although the speaker is speaking, most of the hearers are not listening. If they were, there would not be so much noise. (The noise in the body of the church was louder than it was during most congregational prayers.)

Is there anything in the dialogue itself that would indicate *why* the priest wanted to speak but the congregation did not want to listen? There seems to be a discrepancy between actions from the outset when the priest makes the sign of the cross but says the 'Amen' himself. Thus he denies the congregation their opportunity to give assent to the ritual action, establishing it as a monologue not a dialogue. The content of the sermon itself is anodyne and vague, reducing a multifaceted gospel reading to a 'message of consolation'. It has nothing in it designed to elicit any sort of response in the hearer, be it interest or agitation. The priest consents to his own words again at the end, saying 'Amen'. Then he leaves no time for the congregation to reflect on the sermon, the effect of which is to further the sense in which his is the only voice and to diminish further opportunity for listening. The presider is speaking on the dais: he is not attempting to engage in dialogue with the congregation; he is not seeking a response by the words he chooses for his sermon; he does not need the congregation's assent to prayers he leads or interpretations he offers; he does not even need them to listen or reflect on the sermon. Moreover, the fact he said the creed so loudly through the amplification system implies that he did not want the congregation to speak either, at least not to be heard at all.

The congregation are muted, denied the opportunity for dialogue, denied the opportunity to negotiate or express consent. This is not done blatantly but subtly. This is manipulation, it is not communicative action. 60% of the congregation seemed to know this and kept their mouths shut when subsequently asked to affirm their faith in the Creed.

The woman returned to the lectern and said four bidding prayers, all of which concerned local issues and to which 60% of the congregation responded each time with, 'Lord graciously hear us.'

Firstly, these bidding prayers act as *rightness* claims. The woman speaks prayers, each concerning concrete situations recognisable to the gathered community (those affected by foot and mouth disease, those suffering from loneliness, children heading into exams, the elderly and ill) and ends each one with 'Lord Hear us' to which the congregation respond 'Lord graciously hear us'. By including 'graciously' in their response, the congregation modify the leader's prayer, signalling that the appropriateness of the prayer is conditional upon the need to utter prayer with an awareness that it is grace that will answer it.

CPU: *It is the graciousness of God which makes prayer effective.*

Secondly, these bidding prayers overthrow the idea of presider and congregation as dialogue partners replacing it with that of congregation as speaker and God explicitly named as Hearer: 'Lord, hear us'

CPU 1:   *God is the dialogue partner in prayer.*
CPU 2:   *It is not enough to utter prayer; God must hear it.*

The presider said, 'Let us pause for a moment and bring to Mass any intentions we may have as individuals or as families.' He left two seconds then said a concluding prayer, to which 1% of people responded, 'Amen'.

Two seconds is not long enough to speak, hence the lack of assent. The prayer to which we were being asked to assent simply had not been said.

He said, 'Pray, brethren, that our sacrifice may be acceptable to God the almighty Father.' No one said the response or 'Amen' to the brief prayer that followed.

The fact that no one spoke the prescribed response or gave their assent might be interpreted in several ways, none of them accidental. The priest prays 'that our sacrifice may be acceptable', to which the people by their silence may be indicating that they do not recognise that a sacrifice has been offered. The money they offered was not placed on the altar, the bread and wine cannot be seen, they do not necessarily know what the priest was doing when he silently lifted them up and down a few minutes ago. So, what sacrifice? Or, by their silence they are perhaps indicating that this is not an acceptable sacrifice (i.e.: not enough or not appropriate) or that it is not a 'sacrifice' at all. Or, perhaps they objected to being called 'brethren' when more than 70% of them were female. Or the silence may be a form of dissent on another matter.

The problem with silence is that it is impossible to interpret accurately: one can register that the congregation was meant to say something and declined to do so, one can note that the interaction that was expected ('Pray brethren...') did not occur, but beyond that it is mere conjecture to suppose what the silence 'said'. It said, literally, nothing. All we can deduce, again, is that this was not communicative action. One half of the party of interaction did not act.

About 70% of the congregation, who had had their heads bowed for the whole prayer, even when bells rang at certain points, joined the presider as he said, 'Through him, with him, in him, in the unity of the Holy Spirit, all glory and honour is yours, almighty Father, for ever and ever, Amen'.

Given the lack of congregational verbal participation up to this point, the fact that so many spoke these words is doubly significant. It is significant in the first place because the words are prescribed for the priest alone to say, the congregation being required to utter their consent just with 'Amen'. So their speaking this prayer with the presider is a *trustworthiness* claim: it is literally claiming the right to speak, claiming that the truth of these words and their rightness at this time make it compelling that it is the whole assembly and not just one person who speaks them. For these words to be truthful, the speaker must be the assembly as a whole, not the presider alone.

CPU: *Certain prayers cannot be spoken on the congregation's behalf (even if they are scripted to be so).*

Furthermore, the number of people who participated in this speech act is significant. No other verbal expression in the Mass so far had been said by so many of those present. This directs us to consider the words of the doxology itself which, as said in this context, constitute a *truth* claim: 'Through him, with him, in him, in the unity of the Holy Spirit, all glory and honour is yours, almighty Father, for ever and ever. Amen.' The claim being so widely made is that it is through Christ, by the Holy Spirit that the people worship God. It is a trinitarian truth claim. It is also a truth claim about eternity ('for ever and ever') and about the congregation's relationship with God (God is almighty and Father). It is a truth claim which is followed with the word of assent, Amen. However, the assent in this case comes not merely from the fact that this word was said but from the number of people who said the whole thing: it was considered that a single word of assent was inadequate: the whole utterance had to be said.

CPU 1:	*For this congregation to worship God, they must do so consciously through Christ by the power of the Holy Spirit.*
CPU 2:	*Sometimes it is not enough to assent to what has been said with a single prescribed word; that is, sometimes it is necessary to speak the truth in full oneself.*
CPU 3:	*To say something in unison is to extend the idea of dialogue: it redeems whatever claim is being made because by the very act of making a claim together in unison, a congregation expresses its consensus on that claim.*

A similar condition of possible understanding emerges from the way the 'Our Father' was said. 70% of the congregation said this prayer in unison. Some of the imagery in the prayer, expressed as a truth claim, was also identical to that in the doxology: the primary image of God as Father and the contextualisation in eternity of the glory given to God ('... glory are yours, now and forever') these elements (God as Father, promise of eternity) are revealed as most important to this congregation, so:

CPU 1:	*God is Father*
CPU 2:	*Worship links us to eternity*
CPU 3:	*Assent is expressed by speaking in unison*

There are differences, too, however. For a start, the congregation is supposed to say this prayer, so the utterance is not in and of itself a truthfulness claim. What is interesting in this case is that it begins (and continues) as a direct address to God. Here again I am tempted to suggest that the only real dialogue in this liturgy is that which occurs between the assembly as a whole and God (i.e.: rather than between presider and congregation, or between individual members of the congregation - there was no sign of peace, except for the two individuals who alone quietly shook hands, but the whole congregation should have had the opportunity to greet their neighbour). When the opportunity arises in the ritual to address God directly, rather than to respond to the priest or talk to one another, a significant number do so. (Gloria, bidding prayers, doxology, Our Father).

As a speech act with God, the 'Our Father' is a *truthfulness* claim: a challenge to God to prove trustworthy, to do what we have been given reason to believe God can do. The subsequent prayer 'For the kingdom...' gives grounds which answer the trustworthiness claim; they give reasons why the congregation feel they can request things of God. The Amen is a consensus, a consensus to two things: to the call for God to do what we have asked and to the claim made that 'the kingdom the power and the glory' are God's; proof that God is trustworthy.

CPU: *The congregation know certain truths about God (the kingdom, the power and the glory are His) but need to test these in their relationship with God. God must continue to prove worthy of the trust placed in Him by them.*

I write 'His' and 'Him' because these prayers refer to God only as male: a *Father*, who has a *King*dom. It is important at this point to register that 30% of the congregation said neither the doxology nor the Our Father. Is this because people (consciously or sub-consciously) objected to the patriarchal connotations of this exclusively male naming? It is impossible to tell from the data. The conditions of possible understanding do not, therefore, apply to the 30% who did not speak, but there is insufficient evidence to warrant a suggestion that for them God is not imaged as Father, worship is not contextualised as eternity, or they have no desire to test God. As evinced above, silence expresses nothing verbally in terms of actual rationality (i.e.: 'reasons' that would answer the question 'why'), although as a simple refusal to say what one has been asked to say, or as a refusal to participate in unison speech acts, it can be seen as dissent. Non-participation is never accidental: it is born of a decision, no matter how unconscious, not to speak, and not to speak is to dissent.

The congregation stood and most of them replied 'Amen' to the blessing and 'Thanks be to God' to 'The Mass is ended. Go in peace.'

Interestingly, after communion, the majority of the congregation for the first time responded to the priest when he addressed them (with the blessing). Did the act of saying 'Amen' to the 'body of Christ' change their perspective, allowing them to speak where they were not previously able to do so? Did the priest say it in such a way that the congregation was given more space to reply (i.e.: he did not say the 'Amen' on their behalf as before, but fell silent so they could say it and be heard saying it.) Was it such a lengthy and specific account of events going on in their local town that made people feel that this blessing was quite specially for them, here and now, no longer an impersonal address? It seems fair to suggest that all three of these factors (consenting to the body of Christ, hearing local information, being allowed time to speak) which preceded the blessing were a factor in the new dialogue it created between presider and assembly. The congregation formed a consensus on the blessing and proceeded to give thanks to God when told, 'The Mass is ended. Go in peace.'

CPU 1:   *A blessing can only be formed interactively: without consent it does not happen.*

CPU 2:   *When the Mass is ended the people feel grateful.*

Are the people grateful that the mass is over (because it was such an ordeal) and they are free to go, or are they grateful for what they have received during the Mass? Perhaps this is best considered in relation to what happened next: the 'ordeal' scenario seems at first to be supported by the fact that:

Perhaps as few as two people out of five hundred [who] tried to sing, 'I watched the sunrise'

It is a melancholic hymn, often sung at funerals in this part of the world and it was metered at a slow tempo. Virtually no one sang it and many congregants started to leave long before it was curtailed and then ended. At first glance, all seems miserable; but in actual fact, by refusing to sing, the congregation were dissenting from misery, refusing to participate in an ordeal. Instead they left as fast as they could and in good spirits too:

The congregation poured out of the church, greeting and talking to one another in the aisles, in the narthex and on the front plaza.

Something radical had changed: people who had come into the space in dribs and drabs, not greeting one another at all, left *en masse* chatting away to everyone they met, lingering with their conversations outside the doors for a full five minutes. People who have just suffered an ordeal do not behave this way.

Something, no single exchange, just something in the course of this liturgy of the Eucharist made this congregation leave in brighter spirits and in more developed relation to one another than when they had come in. This was due to no single discernible verbal exchange, rather it seems to be the product of all the small moments of engaging in dialogue with God, testing God, and refusing to say things which are not true - taken as a whole. A more difficult scenario is raised, however, if one considers that for the bulk of their time in church, they were engaged in dialogue with neither God nor one another; rather they were muted - an audience rather than a congregation. It is not to be presumed that this would make one feel 'bad'; rather, given a certain pathology, fulfilling a role in an oppressive power-play may itself be the source of their spritely departure. Most of what happened in this church on this day was systematically distorted communication.

This chapter has moved from studying the type of theology that focuses on what the Eucharist ought to be, to attempting a type (informed by liturgical theology) that examines what the actual celebration of the Eucharist is and what it says of a Christian community's relations to one another and to God. Habermas's communicative ethics in general, and his notion of the ideal speech situation in particular, formed the backbone of this epistemological development. The study, in its desire to access the 'symbolic embodiment of what relations among diners are, can and should be' (in a manner that avoids the pitfalls of the established metaphysical symbolic critique) formed a specific hermeneutic tool on the basis of Habermas's theory of communicative action and applied this to a (ritual-studies type) case-study of a liturgy of the Eucharist in a Roman Catholic parish in Ireland. The outcome of this Habermasian analysis (of the 'is' of worship) was a perception of systematically distorted communication, a perception that stands in some contrast to the existing theology (of the 'could be' and 'should be') of Eucharistic worship.

A constant feature of the discussion prior to the report of the case study was an identification of the partiality of current accounts of Eucharist (and specifically their associated theories of eschatology, ecclesiology and ethics), not just in terms of the 'split' between the 'should be' and the 'is', but in terms of the absence of the voices and experiences of those people who are in various ways marginal to the Eucharist of the church. Both Rowland (from theology) and Benhabbib (from the social sciences) issued a warning that any cultural conclusions based on consideration of the dominant group alone are incomplete. It is necessary to look at feminist and other forms of marginal Christian worship in much greater depth if a fuller understanding of the nature of the symbolic relations among Christians (whether as eschatology, ethics or ecclesiology) is to be garnered. This is the subject of the following chapter.

PART III

Chapter Five

The Theology of Marginal Christian Communities

Underlying all rituals is an ultimate danger, lurking beneath the smallest and largest of them - the possibility that we will encounter ourselves making up our conceptions of the world, society, our very selves. We may slip into that fatal perspective of recognising culture as our construct, arbitrary, conventional, invented by mortals.[1]

The 'centre' of liturgical theology has been established by those, the majority of authors, who reflect on the implications of 'faithfully following the ordo.'[2] Several among them acknowledge a 'growing awareness'[3] of worship that is marginal to this centre, but there has not yet been a serious attempt to include the theologies emerging from marginal Christian communities in a general work of liturgical theology. Furthermore, the argument from the centre suggests that the internal theology of these marginal acts is not accessible to study, because the means of liturgical reflection that the centre has established as normative - participation in the texts of the *ordo* and the *ecclesia* it is held to establish - may be absent. Arguing that the theology of marginal Christian liturgies is both accessible to study (via the adapted Habermasian epistemology developed above) and vital as a component of contemporary theology, this chapter presents the results of fieldwork in a selection of marginal Christian communities.

Each of the previous chapters has highlighted the need for greater attention to 'marginal' Christian ritual experiences in scholarship, albeit in different ways. This chapter begins with a review of these scholarly foundations and a discussion of the ways in which each presents a mandate for this study to incorporate marginal worship. Prior to the presentation of the fieldwork data is a brief discussion of two issues arising in the review: clarification of the term 'marginal' and the methodology employed. Each case study of marginal liturgy is then followed with an application of Habermasian communicative ethics to the data

---

[1]   B.Myerhoff, 'A Death in Due Time' in J.J. McAloon, ed., *Rite, Drama, Festival, Spectacle* (Philadelphia: Institute for the Study of Human Issues, 1984) 152.

[2]   G. Lathrop, *Holy Things: A Liturgical Theology* (Minneapolis: Fortress Press, 1993) 212.

[3]   D.N. Power, *Sacrament: The Language of God's Giving* (New York: Crossroad, 1999) 32.

presented, and after the fifth and final analysis the preliminary outcomes of the case studies are drawn together.

It can be argued that the reason that sacramental theology has not, in general, interested itself with the voices of marginal Christians derives from the fact that conventional sacramental theology is specifically designed to hold all believers to a centre: marginality or varying degrees of participation are not an option. Where the sacraments of the institutional church are concerned, there are rules that apply and sacramental theology can only include those who abide by those rules, not those who do not. For example, regarding the Roman Catholic Church, if you divorce and wish to remarry, you knew the rules before you entered the second relationship; if you want your gay or lesbian marriage blessed, you knew the rules before you entered an openly homosexual relationship; if you are a non-Catholic who is married to a Catholic and you want to receive communion with your family, you knew the rules before you married; if you are female and want to preside at the celebration of the sacraments, you knew the rules before you came along; and if you live in a remote location and are left without an ordained priest for months on end you still cannot celebrate the Eucharist. If you teach that women should be priests or challenge any other of the church's teaching, you may be denied the sacraments. It is the 'club' argument: if you do not abide by the rules of the club, you cannot be a member. Or, to avoid the possibly inappropriate club metaphor, as Lathrop argues, *lex orandi lex credendi* as it impacts on ecclesiology means that those who do right worship are thought to be the right church; those who do not are not.[4]

In recent times, however, there has been a small but growing critique of the centre from the centre, a critique that is open to the activities of those at the margins as at least of interest if not as prophecy. In his work entitled 'Conversion and Critique', David Power sets out a manifesto for the reconstruction of liturgical sacramental appreciation and he cites attention to the marginal as the primary task:

> [First] we need to examine the use of space and ritual for the ways in which they may include and exclude, or set one thing or one person in opposition to another ... what is marginal to the symbolic code needs to be heard and integrated, especially in what has to do with women's experience and expression. How this surfaces may be learned from greater attention to feminist ritualization or womanist ritualization.[5]

This represents a key step in contemporary writing on sacrament. However, Power does not explore what is 'marginal to the symbolic code' other than in the case of women, leaving the door open for others to do this work vis-à-vis homosexual people, non-Catholics, dissidents, divorcees and all other sacrament-excluded

---

[4]   G. Lathrop, *Holy People: A Liturgical Ecclesiology* (Minneapolis: Augsburg/Fortress Press, 1999).
[5]   Power, *Sacrament*, 264.

groups. In embarking on a limited attempt at such work, this study is cautious of Power's assumption that the symbolic code of marginal groups can be 'integrated'; their very location as marginal implies that there is a problem integrating their worship with that of the mainstream in the first place.

It is important to note that when Power turns his attention to hearing the voices of women regarding sacramental experience, he moves beyond the categories in which he usually discusses sacramental 'events'. Making a case for the value of theological conversation with the social sciences, Power earlier drew on Kristeva, interpreting her 'claim that there is an underlying fund of feeling and expression that does not find its place within the prevailing Western symbol systems' as a pointer to the ways in which it does appear in 'religious' events marginal to those systems, particularly, he suggests, women's sacramental experience.[6] So instead of academic theological reflection on enacted rites, he turns to a prose piece by the poet Seamus Heaney where he reflects on the central role the Mass played in his mother's life. Power is trying to go broader, to learn more than can be learned from doctrinal theology alone, conveying an implicit recognition that if it is women's voices you want to hear, then the doctrinal tradition alone will not deliver them. It is for this reason that this chapter proceeds through attention to the liturgies (rather than the doctrinal reflection) of marginal groups of Christians, working from the epistemological tenets (of liturgy as *primary* theology, of narrative as valid discourse, of attention to Christian feminists' and others' theology via attention to their rituals) established by liturgical theology and reported in Chapter One.

Power is concerned with articulating a contemporary sacramental theology, one which can give credence to actual sacramental experience against the discursive background of post-modern vocabularies such as the rejection of metaphysics in favour of hermeneutics, the concomitant return to the subject and the commitment to pluralism and otherness. Crucial to the formation of this proposed contemporary sacramental theology, argues Power, must therefore be, 'a new awareness of those who have been excluded or marginalized' - in liturgy, in society and 'as earth.'[7] While Power has done more than any other sacramental theologian at the supposed centre to raise the standard of the ecclesiologically marginal, particularly in his respect for the work of his female colleagues, he nevertheless fails to follow the manifesto at the start of his study through to the conclusions at the end. In the main body of his argument and in the development of his central metaphor of gift, there is scant mention of those excluded voices which he initially deemed 'crucial' to the debate, neither from their writings nor from reports of their adapted liturgical forms and experiences. It is with Power's insistence on the necessity of considering the excluded and marginal at the very crux of any renewed theology of sacrament that this study proceeds, in the hope that it will be able to follow-through where he could not.

---

[6]   Ibid., 32.
[7]   Power, *Sacrament*, 16.

One of the serious criticisms of Chauvet was that he paid no attention to issues of gender nor to the voices of those excluded by the church's liturgical practice, and this too presents a mandate for this research. Chauvet's theology is concerned with the other, the 'concrete other', and insistence on 'openness to the other'. Coining Metz's phrase, he views it as a 'dangerous other' and yet makes it a very safe other by keeping it abstract or economic. He does not register the other who has been made other by the way the church celebrates the sacraments, by the way it has constructed the idea of sacrament. He does not heed the reports of his colleagues (Segundo, Balasurya and many feminist authors discussed in Chapter One) that the oppression they experience in society is reinforced rather than challenged by the church's celebration of the sacraments. It is by exclusion from the sacraments that a church signals to a believer that they are no longer entitled to belong to the community. It is not by a letter, nor by inadmission to church meetings; it is not by refusing their monetary contributions or preventing their charitable works on the church's behalf: it is by the sacraments, they are made the vehicle by which exclusion is enacted.

Perhaps a large part of the reason that the marginal liturgy fostered by this exclusion has received so little attention is that it is perceived to be a relatively new phenomenon. According to this impression, gays knew they could not get married in church and did not try to do so; women knew they couldn't be sacramental ministers and generally accepted that; communities knew that if they did not have an ordained priest, celebrating the Eucharist was simply not an option. Such a view has, however, been challenged by recent historical research which suggests that women, gays and isolated communities in many instances found creative liturgical ways of dealing with their situation which scholars simply ignored. Texts are coming to light that point to the existence, prior to modern times, of blessings of gay unions, women claiming sacramental authority and priestless communities developing liturgies to suit their needs.[8]

Moreover, scholarship into the nature of the evolution of rites has recently given much attention to the theory that it is (only) through the critical, creative and developmental forms of ritual in these marginal groups that the ritual of the wider community is reformed. This view is supported by scholars of the liturgical movement in the late nineteenth and early twentieth centuries, with their conclusions that the pioneering liturgical work of the movement (which seemed quite disparate at the time) had a profound effect on the church at large and a direct influence on both the occurrence of, and subsequent reforms approved by, Vatican II.[9]

---

[8]   On women's liturgies and ministries see: T. Berger, *Women's Ways of Worship: Gender Analysis and Liturgical History* (Collegeville, MN: Liturgical Press, 1999); on gay ceremonies see: J. Boswell, *Marriage and Likeness: Same Sex Unions in Pre-modern Europe* (New York: HarperCollins, 1994).

[9]   See Berger, *Women's Ways*, 69 - 106.

In the arena of religious studies, Ron Grimes credits Victor Turner with having shifted the way we understand the evolution of rites, changing the course of studies of ritual from one that approached it as a fixed thing to one that saw it as forever changing: 'Before Turner ritual was static, structural, conservative. After Turner it is imagined as flowing, processual, subversive.'[10] The consequence of this, Grimes suggests, is the exposure of the *invented* quality of all ritual. Turner unmasked the presumption that the format of ritual just is, always has been, always will be, unchanged, beyond critique.[11] An approach to the study of rituals that takes as a given the necessity of internal evolution has subsequently dominated ritual studies,[12] and hand-in-hand with it goes an awareness of the influence of context on practice, on issues of inculturation. It is, as was reported in Chapter Two, the new orthodoxy: rituals, like the human beings who perform them, evolve. The accepted corollary is that if they do not, like the human beings who perform them, they will die.

But *how* do they evolve? Grimes suggests that it is through 'ritualizing', which he defines as 'the activity of incubating ritual; it is the act of constructing ritual either self-consciously or deliberately or incrementally and editorially, as it were.'[13] Different ritual critics use the term 'ritualising' in different ways and it is important to note the discrete way in which Grimes uses it here (particularly compared to the way in which Bell was seen to employs it in Chapter Two). Grimes, in his use of the term 'ritualisation', is challenging the pre-figuring effects of the way the subject of ritual has been approached in anthropology. Instead, he employs the term 'ritualising' to 'denote emergent or newly constructed ritual.' By calling emerging ritual 'ritualisation' Grimes aims 'to call attention to the activity of deliberately cultivating rites.'[14] This activity typically 'happens on the margins;

---

[10] R.L. Grimes, *Reading, Writing, and Ritualizing: Ritual in Fictive, Liturgical and Public Places* (Washington, DC: The Pastoral Press 1993) 6.

[11] Although as Grimes also notes, Turner preferred the conservative view in his own personal convictions: 'If he had kept to his own definition, he would never have noticed most of what was distinctive about ritual.' R.L. Grimes, *Beginnings in Ritual Studies* (Washington, DC: University Press of America, 1982) 7.

[12] Although not exclusively, see: Staal and Asad, discussed in Chapter Two. See above: 69 - 75.

[13] Grimes, *Reading, Writing*, 53.

[14] Ibid., 24. Tom F. Driver also proposes a usage of 'ritualisation' to convey this sense of creative adaptation or experimentation (however, he does not associate it principally with 'emerging' social locations, as Grimes does). Perceiving ritual and ritualisation as two facts of a single continuum, he suggests that ritualisation is something one does on the way to producing ritual: 'Without its ritualising (new-making) component, ritual would be entirely repetitive and static. Without aiming at the condition of ritual, ritualising would lack purpose and avoid form; it would fall back into that realm of informal, non-communicative behaviour from which it arose.' *The Magic of Ritual: Our Need for Liberating Rites that Transform Our Lives and Our Communities* (San Francisco: Harper Collins, 1991) 30.

so it is alternatively stigmatized and eulogized',[15] both of which have their liabilities; however, he identifies the alternative to either and both - the appeal to tradition, to 'it's just the way it's done' - as a foil for criticism, an attempt to 'deflect explanation'.[16]

While an appreciation of the evolutionary character of rites may be the new orthodoxy, Grimes points out that nevertheless, 'With almost no exceptions, scholarly theories of ritual do not take into account this emergent ritualizing.'[17] They stick to either abstractions (Bell) or ethnographic studies of established rites (Geertz, Rappaport). This lack of attention to the emergent, in ritual as well as in social terms, coupled with the widespread conclusion that the emergent is crucial to our understanding of rites, issues a further mandate for this study.

The choice of Habermas's theory of communicative action was made because it was written specifically with the marginal in mind, as a way of accessing knowledge that was previously deemed inaccesible by its very marginality. The whole basis of Habermas's theory is to give strategies to the under-powered, while simultaneously limiting the power-use of the over-powered. The decision to pursue a theology that takes into account communities considered marginal to ordinary theological reflection is one that, according to a Habermasian epistemology, must be consciously entered into against the explicit concern of an ethic of justice because the solidarity ethics Habermas and others of the Frankfurt School espouse is solidarity with the poor of history, not the vanquished. Habermas's methodological project is devised with the stated intention of making explicit the very (linguistically constructed) forces that make some people marginal and others central; that include and exclude. He claims that previous philosophical/ sociological methods, while capable of highlighting the effects of power, have not been able to expose (make explicit) the implicit structures by which this power has been (and continues to be) created. But he gives the clue as to how to this can be accomplished: 'For Habermas the problems of morality are always problems of intersubjectivity. Moral doctrine must concern itself with the forms of broken intersubjectivity and its reinstatement. Kant's ethics [by contrast] is an ethics of intention; according to it, agents can be moral all alone.'[18]

Theology cannot afford to ignore Habermas's work, including his strong imperative to take issues of human injustice into account, because he is attempting to develop a methodology which suits exactly the primary way in which theology is created: liturgy. Christian worship is a discourse composed of many communicative actions and, because it is performed in the public realm (and not, say, at the bar of a pub, around a domestic table, or on the stands of a football terrace), it is available

---

[15]   Grimes, *Reading, Writing*, 24.

[16]   Ibid., 7.

[17]   Ibid., 6.

[18]   J. M. Bernstein, *Recovering Ethical Life: Jürgen Habermas and the Future of Critical Theory* (London and New York: Routledge, 1995) 55.

to the critic in a way that more private scenarios of faith construction/expression are not. Theology has, however, largely ignored the challenges Habermas presents and has not attempted to apply or adapt his methodologies to its subject, possibly because theology conventionally seeks its validity from the centre and this tends to militate against giving serious attention to the margins.[19]

The characteristics of the Utopia we see emerging, sketchily, from a Habermasian analysis of communicative action is 'the formation of communities of need and solidarity in the interstices of our societies.'[20] For theology this was shown to be no less the case (in Chapter Four) and as such it ushers a mandate to discern and pay theological attention to these communities. It was provisionally suggested that the interstices of this particular 'society' we call church were to be discerned at its margins, whether they be marginal by virtue of economy or geography (such as Basic Christian Communities in Latin America) or because of political differences with church leaders and/or teaching (such as feminist Eucharist groups).

Whilst accepting the necessity to examine these interstices or margins from a theological perspective, it is also important to heed Benhabbib's warning not to allow any one marginal group to claim the centre as normative. This is to relinquish the idea that an answer can be had in feminist, ecological, black, liberationist, gay, poor or ecumenical gatherings that will alone magically solve the problems of Christian liturgy or theology, or instantaneously provide a formula which allows privileged insight into any of the questions raised in this study. Benhabbib diagnoses this type of illusion, and it is a popular illusion, to be the product of the subjectivist/objectivist impasse: 'The philosophy of the subject always searches for a particular group - be it the proletariat, women, the avant-garde, Third World revolutionaries, or the Party - whose particularity represents universality as such.'[21] By contrast, Habermas's staunch ethic of intersubjectivity envisages a politics of empowerment which 'proceeds from the assumption that there is no single spot in the social structure that privileges those who occupy it with a vision of the social totality'.[22] In an attempt to avoid the aforementioned illusion, this study examines several different case studies from groups which, though marginal, were marginal in very different ways.

Whether and how these communities of solidarity and need at the interstices of the church are still 'church' emerged as a significant question in the discussion of Chapter Four and it is important to address this issue before proceeding to considerations of interpretation. Regarding feminist Christian

---

[19]   See, for example, where Ramshaw dismisses a student interested in a synthesis of religious belief as 'a girl [that] has no religion': G. Ramshaw, *Under the Tree of Life: The Religion of a Christian Feminist* (New York: Continuum, 1998) xi.

[20]   S. Benhabbib, *Critique, Norm and Utopia: A Study of the Foundations of Critical Theory* (New York: Columbia University Press, 1986) 352.

[21]   Benhabbib, *Critique, Norm and Utopia*, 352.

[22]   Ibid.

liturgies, as Mary Collins reports, 'many classical liturgical authorities' object not merely to the notion that these women are, by virtue of their faith practices, members of the same church as themselves, but also to the feminists' use of the word 'liturgy' to describe what they do.[23] Many also object to 'separatist' rites for gay and lesbian Christians, the celebration of the Eucharist with deacon or lay presiders in priestless parishes or the validity of the liturgies of denominations different to their own. Behind such an objection in all cases lies a concern with validity, and behind concerns about validity lie arguments about authority.

Ron Grimes frames the debate as being between tradition and invention,[24] and argues that ritualisation involves a synthesis of the two rather than a choice between them. Tradition is its own authority, but not because it has 'the aura of invariance' or because 'it boasts the sanction of perpetuity', as Hobsbawm's influential essay maintains.[25] Rather, 'the authority... of ritual is dependent on - in fact ought to grow organically out of - those who participate in it.' Grimes warns that, 'This view is not without its difficulties, but it is a cogent option.'[26] Amongst these difficulties is the danger of cultural misappropriation, which, more often than not, is a form of cultural imperialism: the practice of 'transplanting' fragments of an established rite from another culture into one's own liturgies. One example (and there are many thousands more) would be a group of Christian English businessmen themselves enacting a Native American sweat lodge ritual in a park in London. Not only would these men be 'stealing' a ritual practice that they do not understand (because they are not part of the culture to which such practices are authentic), but they have dismissed their own ritual rootedness in established Christian practices.

---

[23]   M. Collins, 'Principles of Feminist Liturgy' in M. Procter-Smith and J.R. Walton, eds., *Women at Worship: Interpretations of North-American Diversity* (Louisville: Westminster John Knox, 1993) 18 - 21.

[24]   For a survey of current writing on the issue of tradition versus invention across the spectrum of ritual studies, see: C. Bell, *Ritual Perspectives and Dimensions* (New York: Oxford University Press, 1997) 223 - 242. On the question of authority she writes: 'There is increased pressure for the invented rite to show that it "works"; this is what legitimates the rite since there is no tradition to do this. Of course, the expectations of what it means to work are also not the same as for traditional rituals, for which no one asked whether the rite worked, just whether it was done correctly.' (241). The evidence presented in the remainder of this chapter suggests that, in a Christian context at least, Bell's polarisation of tradition and invention is not sustainable; a sense of rootedness in tradition is indeed one of the criteria used by those who 'invent' their rites, and, as was seen in Chapter Four, people in traditional situations have more concerns than merely enacting a rite correctly (indeed they *refused* to enact it correctly - maybe because it was not 'working' in Bell's 'invented' sense).

[25]   E. Hobsbawm and T. Ranger, eds., *The Invention of Tradition* (Cambridge: Cambridge University Press, 1983).

[26]   Grimes, *Reading, Writing,* 46.

Yet the Christians reported in the last chapter who, excluded from the sacraments of the institutional church, meet to worship together do not, in the cases studied below, suffer from this difficulty. Considering their situation, Grimes's suggested alternative view of ritual authority seems indeed to be a 'cogent option'. Grimes does not, however, develop his argument in depth by asking *how* authority 'grows organically out of' those who participate in a ritual, except to say, 'Ritual has (or ought to have) authority only insofar as it is rooted in, generated by, and answerable to its infrastructures - bodily, cultural, ecological and spiritual'.[27]

This, like Mitchell's injunction to look at the relations between diners in the last chapter, supports the framework for interpreting the liturgy that has been developed in this study: looking at its infrastructures. Christian liturgy is a public practice, and because of this participants (and thus observers) can themselves analyse the dynamics conditioning the society in which they are immersed according to an ethic of justice. As Diann Neu comments, 'In liturgy we get in touch with fundamental experiences of justice or the lack of them.'[28]

Habermas's theory of communicative action is concerned precisely with affording access to this type of analysis. Communicative ethics, in Habermas's scheme, is rational and linguistically mediated and thus, as Don Browning remarks, 'Since communication brings about rationally motivated agreement, it serves not simply to transmit traditions or agreements, but to bring about agreement and thereby to constitute community.'[29] Accordingly, when applied to a theological context, Habermas's theory of communicative action can be seen to demonstrate not so much the tensions between (as theologians usually view it) tradition and invention but their essential *relatedness*: tradition is inevitably transmitted if a community is speaking its own language; invention is inevitably used in this (ongoing) construction of tradition because every speech act is new and unique.

Liturgically, this is to agree with Rowena Hill that, 'The church is the whole company of the baptised'.[30] The worship of those Christians discussed in the following case studies who are marginalised from mainstream Christian worship is as rooted in their baptism as that of high-church conservative Catholics. In Christianity no one has the monopoly on practice. Thus, to use Janet Walton's metaphor, the worship of feminist and other marginalised Christians, far from being an abuse of traditional worship is in fact 'widening the circles of tradition'.[31] Such

---

27 Ibid., 56.

28 D. Neu, 'Women-Church Transforming Liturgy' in M. Procter-Smith and J.R. Walton, eds., *Women at Worship: Interpretations of North-American Diversity* (Louisville: Westminster John Knox, 1993) 176.

29 D.S. Browning and F. Schüssler Fiorenza, eds., *Habermas, Modernity and Public Theology* (New York: Crossroad Press, 1992) 6.

30 R. Hill, 'Poured Out for You: Liturgy and Justice in the Life of Archbishop Romero', *Worship* 74:5 (Sept. 2000) 419.

31 J.R. Walton, *Feminist Liturgy: A Matter of Justice* (Collegeville, MN: Liturgical Press, 2000) 81. Walton is of course not naïve to the reasons why, contrary to her inclusive perception, others view feminist liturgies as having no authority: as Mary Collins

a perception is in line with the accepted view of ritual studies since Turner, that 'Tradition must be understood... as a mode of active construction'.[32]

It would seem that the idea of the marginal has gained a particularly strong currency in general discourse since the mid-1990s.[33] Moreover, it carries a certain weight, a certain esteem, as the result of what Grimes has called the 'eulogising' tendency among those who refer to it. In aiming to present a more balanced assessment, it is important to clarify the scope of the term as it impacts on this research as well as the hermeneutic that this study designs in order to avoid either a eulogising or stigmatising interpretation.

To say that something is marginal or at the margins is to use a metaphor based on reading and writing: the body of text appears at the centre of the page, small notes associated with or supplementary to the text are written in the margins. The analogy used to work well in certain circumstances. So at the annual conferences of major political parties, the key speeches were given to the whole assembly in the main hall while those with single-issue campaigns were allotted small stalls around the perimeter of the venue. They operated at the margins and although occasionally a lobbyist would 'hijack' the proceedings of the main hall, the vast majority were content that their proper place of operation - the place where they were held in balance with the centre - was at the margins.

However, the terminology of such events changed over the course of the past thirty years and where the lobbyists' work was once referred to as 'marginal campaigns' it is now more often called 'fringe'. This change in terminology is due to the notion of marginality becoming increasingly associated with the idea of being marginalised. With a growing awareness of the politics of marginalisation, one is no longer marginal simply by virtue of promoting a compatible but less popular position; one must have been marginalised in order to be so; i.e., a person or group in a dominant position has limited the access of the other to the centre, has pushed it to the sidelines. People now, therefore, reject the word because of the 'willing-victim' connotations that a consciousness of marginalisation brings with it. It is important to record that some of the women at the feminist liturgy I attended in Washington, DC were adamant that the word marginal was not for them. The host said, 'I just don't know how marginalised we are, not much I think; and it's certainly not part of why we get together.' Another participant in that evening's liturgy, a theologian, said she wanted to challenge my use of the word 'marginal' in a theological context because, 'It implies we have given the centre over to

---

reports, such liturgies are felt as a threat because 'Feminist liturgies within the Jewish and Christian traditions locate women where women never were: at the center... or at the head of things.' Collins, 'Principles of Feminist Liturgy' 21.

[32] Grimes, *Reading, Writing*, 9.

[33] For example, the Irish journal founded in 1998: *Ceide: A Review from the Margins*. Its editor, Kevin Hegarty, reports that when it first came out he constantly had to explain what was meant by 'the margins', and why they warranted a journal, whereas now, introducing it to new people, no one asks either question.

someone, somewhere, else and that is absolutely not the case. This is church, we are church; we are that centre, not at the margins of it. Women need to claim the centre.'[34]

Given her objection, how can I persist in calling their activities 'marginal'? The answer to this question is firmly conditioned by the remit of this study alone, not an internationalist or universalist approach to the issue. Writing in Ireland at the start of the twenty-first century it is, on the face of it, quite easy to discern a 'centre'. Ours is not yet a pluralist society; in terms of race it is overwhelmingly Caucasian, in terms of language it is overwhelmingly English-speaking and in terms of religious practice it is overwhelmingly organised by a single Christian denomination: Roman Catholic.[35] Anything that diverges from this apparent homogeneity is automatically 'marginal' by virtue simply of difference. But is it fair to say that because something constitutes a majority it should therefore be considered 'centre'?

Perhaps one way the anomaly can best be seen in this context is with the example of language: Irish speakers may be a minority, but the fact that many of the indicators of a socio-political 'centre' confirm Irish-speaking as normative suggests that they are not 'marginal': the constitution of the nation is written in Irish (with an English translation), road signs are all in Irish (with an English translation), Irish is a non-negotiable required subject in school: every English-speaking Irish child has to learn how to speak, read and write it. However, native Irish speakers have been shown to be 'not-central' in a host of ways that those grand gestures may serve to mask: they are far less likely to complete the leaving certificate, far less likely to graduate third level education, their earnings fall well below the national average, their access to information is likewise well below the national average, they suffer increased risk of disease and have a lower life expectancy than their English-speaking compatriots.[36] Consequently a persuasive argument is apparent that numerical minority status does indeed contribute to their being made marginal by a more powerful centre.

These examples of common usage of marginal and marginalised serve to contextualise the use of these terms in a study of liturgical practice. As reported above, the vast majority of Irish people living in Ireland identify themselves as Roman Catholic. Moreover, unlike in other European countries, such as France, in Ireland the majority of people actually attend Sunday worship every week.

---

[34] Mary E. Hunt. This profound sense of ownership of the church, of refusal to agree to the centre being aligned with patriarchal manifestations of organised Christian religion, is a very significant part of emerging feminist theology.

[35] Ron Grimes, Professor of Religious Studies at Wilfred Laurier University, Canada, commented that only one other nation in the developed world would be so extraordinarily homogenous in religious practice and that was Quebec. Launch of Ritual Studies Programme, Irish Centre for World Music and Dance, University of Limerick, February 25, 2000.

[36] See: The United Nations Social and Economic Council, 'Discrimination and Economic, Social and Cultural Rights' in *United Nations Initial Reports* (Ireland 20th June 1997) 5 - 56.

Furthermore, unlike in England, where within the Roman Catholic denomination there are greatly differing styles of worship within single geographic locations (from 'high' Latin to 'low' charismatic) the style of Roman Catholic practice in Ireland is generally similar (to borrow from the Anglican tradition, it is a 'broad church'). So the fact that over eighty per cent of a single nation attend the same type of liturgy every week establishes an unusually uniform pattern of practice, a pattern which accords with that established by Lathrop and others as an *ordo* of Christian faith practice and which, for the purposes of this study, is described as a centre. What is marginal to this centre is considered according to the two characteristics that emerged in the discussion above: people whose activities are marginal in the sense that they are in minority positions in relation to the majority that constitutes the centre; and those who are marginal because they have been deliberately marginalised.

Women are marginal to the centre that I have established for the purposes of this essay because the Roman Catholic liturgies that most people in Ireland attend only ever have a man and never a woman as presider. This church does not permit women to participate as fully as it permits men to. Men can be ordained as deacons and priests, as the (liturgical and administrative) leaders of the church; women cannot. Because only men can be ordained as priests and only priests can preside at the celebration of the sacraments, women are not allowed any of the key ministerial roles in the church. This is felt most keenly in relation to the Eucharist because it is the liturgy for which people gather every single week: women cannot ever lead this celebration.[37]

However, the teachings of the Roman Catholic church insist that women are not marginal to its mission and emphasise the important contribution women have made to the church historically. But how can women be considered central to the mission of the church when they cannot lead the liturgies upon which this mission is founded and through which it is enacted? It is in the light of this question that I begin with a study of a women's liturgy, insisting that *in terms of liturgical practice* it is marginal while recognising that this may not be (as many feminist women and the Roman Catholic hierarchy - albeit for different reasons - insist) an appropriate categorisation in terms of ecclesiology. In terms of liturgical practice they are marginal because: they cannot participate fully in the normative liturgy; the alternative liturgies they create are not recognised as valid by the normative church (nor even by all feminist Christians[38]); and the number of women involved in feminist liturgy groups is a small percentage of Roman Catholic women.

---

[37] See M. Collins, 'Is the Eucharist Still a Source of Meaning for Women?' in P.J. Philbert, ed., *Living in the Meantime* (Mahwah: Paulist Press, 1994).

[38] Mary Collins, in a lecture given to the National Assembly of the Leadership Council of Women Religious in August 1991, called alternative feminist Eucharists and other feminist liturgies which draw on Neopagan sources or neoclerical models 'fool's gold'. For a discussion of her comments see S.A. Ross, *Extravagant Affections: A Feminist Sacramental Theology* (New York: Continuum, 1998) 88 - 90.

Hannah Ward and Jennifer Wild, reacting against the caricature of the marginal as home to the oppressed-turned-prophet comment that, 'Being on the margins has become a vocation for some. It is certainly more often than not the place of the self-styled martyr.'[39] It seems a cynical view that can coalesce political oppression with an eccentric embrace of self-pity in this way. So, the argument goes, a claim of marginality is an exposure of a voluntarily victimised location. As far as the broad-based Christian church is concerned, this point of view only adds to the practice of blaming the abused for their abuse.

Diann Neu, co-founder and co-director of WATER[40] challenged me in an interview to check her liturgical, trinitarian, references to wisdom literature, asserting that they were, 'All theologically correct'. She said she wanted to be seen to be theologically correct because she did not want to be ex-communicated from the Roman Catholic communion: her grandmothers had participated in those rituals, put money on that plate, been part of that work, not some other work, not some other community; that one was her church. I include this snippet of her generous interview to illustrate the following point: the churches to which groups such as hers are marginal are, at a deep level, 'home' to those whom they have marginalised. Truly to 'claim the centre' would mean the theology emerging from one's own community would be a sufficient barometer of correctness. No-one wants to adhere to a more-oppressed-than-thou plea in order to be thought credible, and none of the cases presented in this study is making such a plea; they are marginal not by virtue of self-identification as 'marginal' but by virtue of the fact that they are not like the mainstream, they are in a minority, they are not liked by the mainstream and often not wanted by it either. They may just be different, they may be merely overlooked or they may be the butt of derision, but that in no way diminishes the political sense in which they are marginal. Their bodies are excluded from conventional liturgy, their voices are not included when the theology is written.

Ward and Wild propose the vocabulary of 'threshold' and 'liminality' as an alternative to that of marginality, an image of being '*between* here and there.'[41] If one agrees with Michael Drumm that all Christian ritual is a threshold activity,[42] that all Christian ritual is a case of being between here and there, then Ward and Wild's analysis subsumes the marginal into the centre and runs the risk of overlooking the ways, actual and potential, in which the centre may be operating as an oppressive power. It allows institutional blindness. The trouble with being '*between* here and there' is that one is actually '*neither* here nor there' and, whether

[39] H. Ward and J. Wild, *Guard the Chaos* (London: Darton, Longman and Todd, 1995) 29.
[40] WATER is the Women's Alliance for Theology, Ethics and Ritual in Silver Spring, MD.
[41] Ward and Wild, *Guard the Chaos*, 31.
[42] M. Drumm, *Passage to Pasch: Revisiting the Catholic Sacraments* (Dublin: Columba Press, 1998). Drumm, however, should be challenged for this assertion, as it seems to elide a Turnerian notion of liminality with events whose embodiment make present not just the past and the journey but, as we saw in Chapter Four, the end also.

the concern is the centre or the margins, such a location is incompatible with a claim to being part of the presence of the body of Christ or the realm of God: they put one somewhere.

However, while rejecting Ward and Wild's analysis, it is nevertheless important to remain alert to the fact that 'marginal' does not necessarily mean 'wholly downtrodden'. Marginal is an entirely relative term: a group may not be marginal in terms of its relation to certain social structures (for example, the gay community in Ireland is not, in general, economically marginal) while remaining marginal in terms of others (gays within the church). Moreover, individuals and groups can function as both 'target and vehicle'[43] of marginalisation: this has been most recently highlighted in theological circles by womanist theologians who claim that the liberationist agenda of early feminists may have addressed the ways that Black women were oppressed as women but actually served to reinforce the ways in which they were oppressed for being Black.[44]

According to Swigonski's analysis of the communication strategies of women in American society, women in situations of anti-female discrimination exhibit a 'double vision':[45] they can simultaneously access the perspectives of both the dominant group and their own. The outcomes of her research support a recent growth in acknowledgement[46] that non-dominant groups know the ways of the dominant group because their very survival has depended on such knowledge, while the opposite is not equally the case: members of the dominant group therefore have only a 'partial view of reality.'[47] Mark Orbe argues that it is for this reason that research, which has traditionally excluded marginalised perspectives, ought to deliberately seek the 'outsider-within' insights that only those groups can offer. Orbe suggests that, in order to reflect the 'notion that no one culture in our society is inherently superior to other co-existing cultures',[48] marginalised groups should be termed 'co-cultural'. This terminology is helpful in avoiding the 'inferior' associations inscribed in 'sub cultural' or 'minority' and Orbe's methodology is important in that it insists on assessing the efficiency of communication 'from the perspective of co-cultural group members'[49] rather than from the mainstream. However, it assumes the possibility of dialogue between

---

[43] The phrase is Foucault's. See, for example: M. Foucault, *Discipline and Punish: The Birth of Prison* (New York: Random House, 1979).

[44] See, for example: D. Williams, *Sisters in the Wilderness: The Challenge of Womanist God-Talk* (Maryknoll, NY: Orbis Books, 1993).

[45] M.E. Swigonski, 'The Logic of Feminist Standpoint Theory for Social Work Research', *Social Work* 39 (1994) 390.

[46] See for example: R. Frankenberg, *White Women, Race Matters: The Social Construction of Whiteness* (Minneapolis: University of Minnesota Press, 1993).

[47] M.P. Orbe, *Constructing Co-Cultural Theory: An Explication of Culture, Power and Communication* (Thousand Oaks, CA: SAGE Publications, 1998) 29.

[48] Ibid., 2.

[49] Ibid.

dominant and non-dominant groups which, in situations of serious oppression, may not always be the case.

While this study has used the pattern of worship in Ireland to establish a 'centre', it has gone beyond Ireland in presenting case studies for that which is 'marginal'. There are feminist Christian and ecumenical groups in Ireland, but they are very new. The intention behind the inclusion of material about examples of such communities in America was, therefore, to gain the perspective of groups that were formed as a result of a similar impetus to that underlying nascent Irish groups, but which are well established. Such examples were sought as a counterweight to the criticism which has been levelled at the Irish groups that these types of liturgy are 'one-off' worship events, not the continuing work of a ritual body.

The way in which the case studies are presented in the text is itself a form of analysis. No description can be 'pure', with interpretation coming as entirely subsequent to it; every description of a ritual inevitably reflects a high degree of pre-stated analysis. What was looked for during fieldwork (instances of dialogue) has inevitably conditioned what was found. Hence, the format of the case studies presented below eschews traditional ways of writing up liturgies, where there is an order of service augmented with 'stage directions'. This is a deliberate measure, an attempt to develop a ritual-reporting style that is consistent with the change in focus that Habermas's philosophy demands of theology; that is, one wherein liturgy is not described as the text of liturgy but as the communicative actions of the persons there gathered.

What matters, as was demonstrated in Chapter Four, is not what is prescribed to be said, but what is actually said; and hence it is essential for the interpreter to attend the actual ritual rather than merely read the text prescribed to be followed in it. A witness to a liturgy can report where 'responses' were full, partial or absent and where there was hearty singing or where there was silence, in a way that would be impossible if studying written words alone. Chapter Four thus highlighted a crucial flaw in the way that Christian scholars have traditionally operated: they are trained to study what is prescribed, what has been established as a norm, but not to study how that is *enacted*. The limitations of such an approach were exposed when the application of an alternative epistemology discovered many instances where none of the words the congregation was supposed to say were actually said, or where the presider omitted certain words he was supposed to say.

In the case studies presented below it is, however, not simply dialogue (who said what) that is reported. Reportage of the atmospheric elements, as the observer experienced them, is included in order to reflect awareness of Irwin's dictum that one cannot treat liturgical 'text' without context. It is not yet possible to analyse this context;[50] rather, it is included to remind the reader that this, like all

---

50 This is a major limitation of Irwin's work: while insisting on the articulation of contextual factors he ignored the crucial question of how these are to be accessed for the purposes of interpretation. See K. Irwin, *Context and Text: Method in Liturgical Theology* (Collegeville, MN: Pueblo Press, 1994).

discursive exercises, is an essentially intersubjective one and the idea of observer as somehow detached, able to distil the dialogue from the atmosphere in which it appears, is impossible. It is also included as an indicator of the compromises that emerged in the outcomes of Chapter Four's analysis: studying verbal communication cannot be a complete way of conducting a study of liturgy as it relies so heavily on the non-verbal for the context of the verbal; and much of what the verbal creates is non-verbal in form.

Influencing the choice of the particular case studies used, were certain personal as well as empirical factors. While it is not essential to include these, the first paragraph of each report gives a short account of the reasons for my selection of each community as an indication of the 'marginality' understood to be operative in each case. The report of each ritual is followed by an extrapolation of several verbal exchanges from within each account. These are then interpreted in terms of communicative action, according to the Habermasian model developed in Chapter Four.

The case studies are recorded in the past tense. Janet Walton, one of very few liturgical scholars to include first-hand reports of full liturgies in her work, describes liturgies in the present tense, arguing that this gives a sense of immediacy.[51] The past tense is preferred in the following accounts because where Walton's agenda is to encourage the reader to realise for themselves how the principles of feminist liturgy that she presents can be integrated into their own experiences, this study's agenda is to present these case studies as fieldwork, as data to which a theory can be applied.

A Case Study of Feminist Liturgy

Feminist and womanist critiques of mainstream liturgy expose the way mainstream forms of worship support patriarchy and alienate women. They do this in a great variety of ways, which include, for example, the exclusive use of male imagery for God, the use of androcentric structures (forms of interaction and leadership) and the elimination of women from leadership roles. Over the past thirty years many women have gathered to create liturgies that work as liturgy but which avoid the problems named above.

What follows is a description of a ritual to which I was invited by Diann Neu, co-founder and co-director of WATER (Women's Alliance for Theology, Ethics and Ritual) in Washington, DC who described it as 'our feminist liturgy group'. The group consists of about thirty friends, with a core fifteen or so who meet regularly. All are women, most are highly educated (with Ph.D.'s), many were previously members of religious communities and a large proportion is therapists. All devote considerable time to social action and were acutely aware of issues of

---

[51]   J.R. Walton, *Feminist Liturgy: A Matter of Justice* (Collegeville, MN: Liturgical Press, 2000) 49.

poverty and justice. They retain their original name, SAS (Sisters against Sexism), despite describing it as 'very dated'. It was obvious from the way I was greeted that the group were used to welcoming visitors and they spoke of the way they valued their decision to be 'open', contrasting this with other women's liturgy groups which preserve stricter rules regarding who can attend.

It was 6.30pm on a wintry Sunday night in the suburbs of Washington DC. Thirteen women and a baby arrived at the home of Jessica and Louise. They greeted one another with hugs in the hall and kitchen and put the food they had brought with them on the table in the dining room. The wooden room was lit with lamps, wrapped in bookcases and smelling of fennel. On the table were two loaves of homemade bread, salads, cheese, fruit, and wine. We stood around the dining table, linked hands, and the host, Louise, welcomed us and invited us to keep silence for a moment. She then asked for a word of blessing from any one of the group and the baby squealed loudly and joyfully; 'I'll take that' said Louise, the women laughed and said 'yes!', and with a squeeze of the hands the circle split up and everyone helped themselves to food and drink and sat around eating and talking, catching up with events in one another's day-to-day lives.

After half an hour we were all invited by the host to make our way into the living room. Extra seats were drawn up in the gaps between the sofas to make a large circle around the central coffee table. On this table were a candle and several small bowls of fruit. Each person was handed a glass with some white wine in it and was told it was 'for the ritual'. The general dinner conversation continued until the ritual-leader, Jessica, took her seat in front of the fireplace, made sure we each had some wine and a napkin and handed each person a piece of paper containing the words of a blessing we are to use in the ritual. Jessica briefly described the ritual. One of the group interrupted her to ask her to repeat the name of the ritual - *'Tu B'Shvat'* - which she did and, asked what it meant, translated it as 'The New Year of the Trees' and explained how, in her native Jewish tradition this ceremony falls at this time each late winter. Tu B'Shvat Seders have been around for centuries, if not millennia, she said, feminists and Reconstructionist Jews having revived the idea in recent years. She explained that she used many sources in preparing the ritual, both feminist and not, plus a couple of concepts of her own. Another woman turned to me and explained that Jessica is both Jewish and Catholic.

Jessica held in her lap a large flat basket containing bright oranges and invited us to join her in a prayer of blessing to 'open' the ritual: all but three of us read the Hebrew transliteration fluently, *'Bruchat et elilah, shekhina, malkat ha'olam, shehechiyatnu, vikiysmstnu, vihigianu lazman hazeh.* Blessed are you, Goddess, queen of the Universe, who has blessed us and kept us and allowed us to reach this day.' As the basket of oranges was passed around the circle and we each took one, there was the following dialogue:

Jessica: 'You should try to think, really think, concentrate, when you're peeling the orange, because it's meant to be about the hard shell, our hard shells, think what it means if you're peeling away your hard shell, Jews talk of the inside like your soul, a sweet soul. Don't eat it just yet, we have to say a blessing.'

Another: 'Boy, these smell good. So good.'

Jessica: 'Yes, they're Israeli; they're at their best this time of year I think.'

Another: 'It's one of the best things about winter, when the oranges come in, the real oranges.'

Jessica: 'This ritual celebrates what Jewish people call the four worlds and marks the links between them, the movement from winter to summer, transformation, and gives us a chance to pause and think at the start of the cycle of it all. So we're going to say a blessing over the fruit.'

Everyone held her peeled orange and said, '*N'varech et ein ha-hayyim matzmihat p'ri hagafen v'nishzor et sarigei hayyeinu b'masoret ha-am*. Let us bless the source of life that nurtures fruit on the vine as we weave the branches of our lives into the tradition' and proceeded to eat the orange. One woman said jokily 'What does it mean to be eating my soul?' Several replied, 'I know!'. Jessica invited us to raise our glasses, remarking that the white wine represented the cold weather of winter, and we repeated the blessing. The speech volume increased as everyone became accustomed to the Hebrew words and everyone then drank. It was good, cold and clear wine.

Jessica announced, 'We can now enter *Olam Hayetzira*, the World of Formation, where we honour things where the raw material is transformed, such as clay making a pot. And to symbolise this we eat fruits with a large central pit, such as olives, dates and apricots.' She passed around ceramic dishes of olives and dates. Both tasted delicious and this prompted another conversation about origins: the olives Jessica told us were Greek, the dates Israeli. Jessica asked a woman to fetch a bottle of red wine from the dining room and as this was passed around Jessica instructed us to pour just a drop or two of it into the remaining white wine, as this was to symbolize the coming of spring. Following Jessica we raised our glasses 'To *Olam Hayetzira*', drank and began to chat to our neighbour as the many small dishes were passed. The chat was about the ritual itself, including other stories of *Tu B'Shvat* experiences. Jessica brought us back quickly from these one-to-one conversations to a conversation among the whole group by asking 'What are your raw materials? What are the things with which you work, the things you work to transform?'

There was a thoughtful silence for a few moments before people started volunteering their reflections. It started as a series of single words: People. Ideas. Wood. Computer languages. Music. Dirt. Children. But it then became more of a conversation after one woman asked 'How do you mean?' when another had said 'Ideas'. More and more people commented as the conversation questioned what in fact it meant to transform anything. Jessica asked that the wine be passed again, while we were still talking, and instructed us to 'get a mix of mostly red with a bit of white in, because it's meant to show the *warmth* of spring'. We were still talking about raw materials and what it means to say we transform them when Jessica began to pass grapes – 'They're Chilean, people!' – blueberries and raspberries which provoked widespread expression of awe and excitement to taste these summery fruits in the dead of winter. We raised our glasses as Jessica hailed '*Olam Haberiah*, the world of Creation, where we think now about large created things, like whole landscapes, the big picture, and so we're going to pass around fruits that can be eaten whole.'

The mood was jolly. Conversation was happening in small groups and there was a lot of laughter in the room. Jessica again asked for the attention of the whole group and asked us to tell one another about our tree. Not everyone spoke, but most did. Some were very brief, like the woman who told us about the maple at the end of the garden in her childhood home, others told us whole stories about trees that were particularly old or had survived (or not) particular urban developments. The first four people just spoke, but in response to the fourth a woman asked, 'What happened to that tree? Do you still go there?' and the other woman replied. Another then said, 'That reminds me of a man I work with who...' and the sharing became a conversation rather than just a litany of tree-stories, with every contributor getting a response to their story, even if it was just an affirmative 'uh-huh'. There were several moments of silence and it was in the last of these that Jessica intervened to 'move us to the *Olam Ha'atzilut*, the world of emanation, which is truly wonderful, worth the wait, and really beyond expression, so no fruit can capture it, so fill your glasses with just red wine for the heat of summer and the full blossoming of nature and...'

She stopped, called her partner over and whispered something in her ear; the partner disappeared into the kitchen and Jessica said, 'I just thought of something; usually you use something that smells wonderful to give that hint of wonderfulness, to arouse it, like spice, so we were going to pass around these two teas, cinnamon and almond; but we have these chocolates (Louise appears with a box of chocolates) and I think they'd be a great way of representing this level'. There was a lot of laughter as the chocolates were passed along with the teas, especially when one women asked 'what is *their* origin?!' But they did have a known origin, which caused even more laughter: another woman in the group explained that she had a recent business trip to Switzerland and had brought these back for Jessica and Louise 'They are ok; they're genuine Swiss'. After a moment another woman asked if it was really appropriate to use chocolate in this way and received a quick reply, 'No justice without chocolate!' and she laughed.

Shortly after passing the teas and chocolates, Jessica asked us to 'be still for a moment and gather any prayers we have tonight, remember those who aren't able to be with us and...' She was cut off as a mixture of prayers and announcements started. Some people had sent apologies. Most of those same people were prayed for in different contexts. One woman who had been remembered then arrived late (due to work) and everyone laughed because it was as if she had heard her cue and entered. Jessica gave thanks for Marcia Falk, whose translation of the *Tu B'Shvat* prayers she had used. Several people asked for prayers for different causes, most of them stemming from their work or family. One woman asked us to remember those affected by the Indian earthquake. A prayer was said, and subsequently added to by others, for Louise's sister who had just had a brain tumour removed; Louise replied with thanks to the group for their prayers and help. It was then Louise who, after a moment's silence suggested the group 'should calendar'. Jessica led us all in saying again the words of blessing with which the ritual had opened ('*Bruchat at elilah....*').

Everyone then went to their bags and found their diaries and, sitting back in the circle, with much negotiation, fixed one meeting for this 'Sunday Eucharist' every three weeks for the next six months, one weekend retreat at Pentecost and a seder meal on Maundy Thursday. For each event one of the women offered to be host and another to organise the ritual. By 9pm everyone had left, taking the leftover food with them.

Analysis as Communicative Action

Louise welcomed us and invited us to keep silence for a moment. She then asked for a word of blessing from any one of the group and the baby squealed loudly and joyfully; 'I'll take that' said the host, the women laughed and say 'yeah!'

The women have gathered together and eaten together according to this pattern for twenty-three years. The host nearly always asks for a blessing but on this night the baby was interpreted as challenging the *rightness* claim that the host had raised. This is reflected in the host's response: 'I'll take that' which makes explicit the fact that she has the ability to discern what does and does not constitute blessing. She is supported by the affirming words of her friends, in whose 'yeah' comes a further acceptance of the baby's squeal as (an appropriate) blessing'.

CPU 1:   *A blessing is (only) made through interaction.*
CPU 2:   *Spontaneity must be accepted.*

Jessica briefly described the ritual. One of the group interrupted her to ask her to repeat the name of the ritual -'Tu B'Shvat' - which she did. Asked what it meant, she translated it as 'The New Year of the Trees' and explained how, in her native Jewish tradition, this ceremony falls at this time each late winter. Another woman turned to me and explained that Jessica is both Jewish and Catholic.

Two validity claims are raised and redeemed here: to *truth* and to *trustworthiness*. Jessica was asked to repeat the words she had used but the answer did not satisfy and so she was asked again, specifically, to give grounds for the words she had used, which she then did. The woman sitting next to me, aware that I am a guest, turns to me and seeks to justify Jessica's choice of a ritual from Jewish tradition, arguing that it is appropriate for her to be using the material in this way. What interests me is that I did not prompt this justification by anything I said; it was understood to be challenged by virtue of there being an outsider witnessing an argumentation in the group. It was the trustworthiness of the group (in having Jessica lead this ritual) that was being asserted.

CPU 1:   *Personal identity authorises certain ritual acts (a lack of identification with the ritual may trigger imperialism).*

CPU 2:   *Who, exactly, is present conditions the worship that can be done - it is not a ritual that would 'work' with any random selection of people.*

One woman said jokily 'What does it mean to be eating my soul?' Several replied, 'I know!'.

This is a complex argumentation. The 'joky' tone is irrelevant to our Habermasian schema, which instructs us to look only at what was said. Moments earlier, the ritual planner had said, 'think what it means if you're peeling away your hard shell; Jews talk of the inside like your soul, a sweet soul' and the woman's remarks represent a challenge to the *rightness* of this claim. Instead of receiving a literal justification for the metaphor, she receives a statement of assent to the asking of the question, 'I know'. The speakers did not 'know' what it meant to be eating one's soul; what they knew was the strangeness of the image and the rightness of the challenge. It functioned as a critique of the ritual symbolism.

CPU: *Participants must critically reflect on the symbolism of the ritual within it.*

Jessica brought us back quickly from these one-to-one conversations to a conversation among the whole group by asking 'What are your raw materials? What are the things with which you work, the things you work to transform?' There was a thoughtful silence for a few moments before people started volunteering their reflections. It started as a series of single words: People. Ideas. Wood. Computer languages. Music. Dirt. Children. But it then became more of a conversation after one woman asked 'How do you mean?' when another had said 'Ideas', more and more people commented as the conversation questioned what in fact it meant to transform anything.

Here the person who has been the main speaker turns the tables on the other participants and asks them to provide grounds. She is effectively stating that, having given their consent to proceed to this point, the burden of speaker-ship can no longer remain with her alone and it is for them now to engage with the core question. When met with silence, she does not jump in to fill it; she waits to hear her question answered. Never again in the ritual after this point is Jessica the lead-speaker. In subsequent argumentations, the group asks one another to provide grounds as issues arise in the wider conversation in the group. The resulting question - What does it mean to transform anything? - emerged from several people almost simultaneously and was directed to the group as a whole; it was a questioning of its own assumptions as a group that had a history associated with the concept of transformation.

CPU 1:   *Argumentation must include all, equally (not arise as reactions to a leader).*
CPU 2:   *A previously agreed consensus must be open to challenge.*

She stopped, called her partner over and whispered something in her ear; the partner disappeared into the kitchen and Jessica said, 'I just thought of something; usually you use something that smells wonderful to give that hint of wonderfulness, to arouse it, like spice, so we're going to pass around these two teas, cinnamon and almond; but we have these chocolates (Louise appears with a box of chocolates) and I think they'd be a great way of representing this level'. There was a lot of laughter as the chocolates were passed along with the spice teas, especially when one women asked 'what is *their* origin?!' But they did have an origin, which caused even more laughter: another woman in the group explained that she had a recent business trip to Switzerland and had brought these back for Jessica and Louise 'They are ok; they're genuine Swiss'. After a moment another woman asked if it was really appropriate to use chocolate in this way and received a quick reply, 'No justice without chocolate!' and she laughed.

Humour can, as noted above, harbour serious challenges and we have a whole string of them here, not all of which are redeemed: the leader herself challenges the appropriateness of the symbol she has intended to use by spontaneously introducing one that she thinks better fits the bill; someone challenges the origin of them but the humour nevertheless masks the fact that although they do have a known origin, it is not one that can be economically justified on the principles of fairtrade. [It was a fairtrade principle that lead Jessica to find, purchase and highlight the origins of the previous elements - oranges from a kibbutz not a plantation, grapes from Chile, not the boycotted Californian ones]; and there is a challenge to the rightness of using chocolate in the *Tu B'Shvat* instead of the traditional spices which, importantly, is redeemed via redress to an ethic of justice. (An ironic redress perhaps, given the non-fairtrade origins of the chocolate.)

CPU 1:   *The symbols and actions of the group have to reflect their socio-political commitments.*

CPU 2:   *Justice is the ultimate appeal.*

A Case Study of Lesbian/Gay Worship

Lesbians and gay men are 'marginal' because Irish society is, generally speaking, not tolerant of homosexual lifestyles, neither on a state level (e.g.: gay relationships are not recognised in the same way that homosexual marriages are, resulting in their being penalised in terms of tax breaks and in medical/legal next-of-kin access situations); nor on a social level (gays are often the targets of verbal and physical abuse and other forms of discrimination). Nor are they tolerated in religious settings: all the main churches in Ireland refuse to admit openly gay men to the priesthood, many adhere to official teachings that homosexuality is unnatural and wrong, all forbid the blessing of the unions of homosexual partners, and many also preach on the 'dangers' of homosexuality. I once heard a sermon arguing against the establishment of a local interdenominational school on the grounds that they would be 'teaching homosexuality'. (The school was never started). Incredible though it may read in print, it belies a practice of prejudice so deeply ingrained that homosexuality is the constant butt of 'jokes', it is often mistakenly and slanderously associated with sexual abuse, and homosexuals suffer greatly by having to conceal their identities for fear of recriminations which may be personal, verbal, violent or economic - many have lost their jobs when their sexuality was revealed.

Reach is group of homosexual and bi-sexual Christians who have been meeting in Ireland for over twenty years. The organisation was originally formed by the Legion of Mary who, responding to the vulnerability of gay men cruising along the canal in Dublin, set up a bi-weekly meeting place for gay men in the city. The group still meets every two weeks for a liturgy which is, more often than not, a Roman Catholic Eucharist but may also be a service based on the worship traditions of other Christian traditions, such as a bible-study or Quaker meeting. Members of the group also meet regularly for a variety of social events, such as mountain walks and barbecues. Although the group is open to lesbians, bisexual women and transgendered persons none currently attend. Confidentiality is a very important feature of *Reach*'s identity. The members hold a 'guest night' (when family and friends or prospective members can come along) only twice a year: once for a carol service and once for a Eucharist. It was to this event that I travelled in May 2001, one of the group having agreed to act as my host. I was the only guest on this occasion and there was one prospective newcomer.

At one end of Marianella, the Redemptorist monastery in Dublin, is the door to a set conference and teaching rooms. It is also the door to one of the city's driving test centres and through it, over the course of half an hour on a Saturday evening in May, came twenty-four gay men. In the foyer I met the person who had agreed to take me as his guest and we went down a corridor to the meeting room, at the entrance to which my host, like all the other men, paid some money to the group's secretary who was standing behind a small desk. Nothing was said about this: my companion knew the amount to pay and, presumably, what it was for, and the secretary just said 'thanks'. My host told the secretary my first name, and he made a nametag for me to put on my chest, just as he had done for all the men who had already arrived. People were standing in small groups around the room; I was introduced to everyone by their first name and, without exception, each man shook my hand and said, 'Hi, Siobhán. You're (very) welcome'. I said 'Thank you'.

After a quarter of an hour, the secretary came in and people took a seat. The room was a plain seminar-sized room, which had been decorated for this occasion with two Caravaggio prints on the wall that the wide semi-circle of chairs was facing. Between the two ends of the 'horse-shoe' of chairs was a table draped with a white cloth. On it were two ceramic goblets and a purple flowering plant. To the immediate left of the table was a tall candleholder: a rainbow-coloured candle lit atop a candle stand, with satin streamers every colour of the rainbow twisting from it down to the floor. The group's chairperson stood in front of his seat, the general chatter stopped, and he welcomed everyone, 'especially' the guests and 'especially' Fr. Tim who had come to say the mass. He then asked one of the group to say the 'Reach Preamble'. From his seat, the man read:

> Reach is a fellowship of gay people with a Christian outlook who seek to share their experience, strength and hope; affirming and supporting each other through liturgy, social contact and discussion. Our vision is to foster a sense of personal worth and self-acceptance by meeting together in a spirit of trust and friendship. The principles of confidentiality and mutual respect are essential to promote this spirit of friendship. Our aims are: to enhance our spiritual lives and to grow in the dignity God has intended for us; to reach out to those who feel isolated or alienated; to promote dialogue with the churches and with other gay groups. In the light of this let us ask God for the knowledge of his will for us and the courage to carry that out.

One of the group handed around a home-produced hymnal and the man seated behind the electric keyboard at the back of the room told us the number to turn to; the keyboard sounded and everyone, remaining seated, sang 'Be Thou My Vision', in full voice. The presider walked to the front of the space and took one of the two unoccupied seats at the end of the circle near the altar. He stood as the hymn ended and said how glad he was to be back with the group again. He (T) said 'In the name of the Father and of the Son and of the Holy Spirit' and the congregation (C) said 'Amen'. T: 'The grace of our Lord Jesus Christ and the love of God and the fellowship of the Holy Spirit be with you all,' C: 'And also with you.' T: 'The theme of tonight's mass is acceptance. And it's a great coincidence, we've, me and Michael, we've been planning this theme for a while, and it's a great coincidence it falls on the day we celebrate the feast of the Ascension, a feast when we're reminded in a very real way of the utter acceptance of the Son by the Father, and the acceptance, the love, that God, through his Son, opens out to and offers to us. So let's gather, and just sit with, our thoughts for a minute, calling to mind anything in our lives that inhibits or blocks our ability to accept this love that God offers to draw us into. After we've thought for a while, and prayed, I will offer the group a general absolution.'

Two minutes' silence followed. T: 'Let us pray'... the priest said a very brief prayer for forgiveness, followed immediately by singing, '*A Thiarna dean trocaire*'; (Lord have mercy) the congregation responded by singing the same phrase. T: 'I will now give a general absolution in the sincere hope that none of ye head off to the red house straight after this, but, well, it'll still count even if you do' (C: gentle laughter) and our penance tonight and in the coming days will be to call to mind and give thanks to God for those who have shown us acceptance in our lives'. Fr. Tim raised his right hand to the congregation and began the words of the general absolution. After the first line he stopped and said, 'You know, I've forgotten the words'. He smiled, looking at everyone, and many smiled back, keeping the eye contact until he said, 'hang on a second now...' and began it again, remembering it this time. C: 'Amen'. T: 'Great! ... Glory to God in the highest'; the congregation all immediately joined in saying the 'Gloria', at the end of which Tim said 'Let us Pray'. He sat down and read the prayer for the day, and all said 'Amen'.

T: 'We'll now have our reading; who's going to do the reading?' A man waved a piece of paper above his head, Tim smiled and said, 'And as we listen to tonight's readings, if there is any word or phrase that strikes you then let it stick in your mind; that's the thing you need to hear, so just let it speak to you in your mind and your heart.' The reader, seated, read an extract from *Ephesians*, ending with 'This is the Word of the Lord.' C: 'Thanks be to God'. Everyone sang 'All People that on Earth Do Dwell' for the psalm. When it finished, Tim sang an Irish call-and response setting of the 'Alleluia' and the congregation replied in full voice. For the first time in the liturgy, everyone stood and Tim read the gospel (the ascension story), ending with 'This is the gospel of the Lord'; C: 'Praise to you, Lord Jesus Christ'.

Everyone sat again and Tim gave a homily from his seat. He started by giving time for silent reflection then said that he was going to say a few words on how the readings had spoken to him and if anyone else would like to share any thoughts or reflections as well there would be plenty of time to do so. His reflections were a meditation on 'the love between Father and Son' as expressed in the gospel reading, weaving the experience of 'all God's daughters and sons and God's love for us' into this and ending with a prayer that 'we might avoid all useless worry'. His emphasis was not exclusively on gay experience vis-à-vis acceptance but on all our need to feel acceptance and all our need to accept others.

He then invited anyone else to 'offer their reflections on the gospel or the reading, or any other word or prayer that has come to you during our liturgy' and left a good time for people to come in. He said 'Does anyone want to speak?' Heads around the room shook. 'Is it ok, then, if I move on?' Several people said 'yes'. Tim said, 'I can't believe I'm going to have the last word on this one! Oh well, the night is young yet' and everybody laughed.

T: 'Now. Let us pray. And as we do so, let's try to hold in mind any word or phrase that has dwelt in us strongly so far, holding it in our prayers as we come before God as his beloved sons and daughters'. Three different people seated around the room read three prayer-reflections. They were quite long meditations on acceptance, loneliness and hope, written in the first person and employing a lot of urban imagery. After each one, the keyboard struck a chord and the whole assembly sang: 'Lord hear as we pray. Oh God give us your love.' Tim said a prayer at the end, in conventional address to God, giving thanks for 'all those in our lives so far who have shown us a glimpse of what it might feel like to be accepted'. He initiated the sung response again with a glance at the musician, following it with, 'Let's have the offertory.'

Two men went to the back of the room where there was a decanter on a table with wine in it and a large ceramic dish containing two very large wafer hosts. I felt a tap on my shoulder and one of the men invited me to bring up the bright yellow teddy bear with a rainbow top who was sitting on the table by the bread and wine. Meanwhile the congregation were all singing, 'All People of our God and King'. I picked up the teddy and followed the two men who walked to the front of the room with the other gifts. The priest took these from each of us, saying a few words as he did: to me he said, 'Doesn't he have a lovely top on him!' and I replied 'It's gorgeous!' Those within earshot laughed. Tim put the bread and wine on the table and put the teddy on the chair he had just vacated in the circle, pulling him round a bit so he faced the congregation. After the singing stopped, Tim said, 'I like this Teddy as a part of the offertory today because several people have said that the person they first came out to was the teddy bear. I didn't have one as a child but now, in my late fifties, I've acquired one and I find them such a great emblem of acceptance. But you know, here in the bread and wine (he moved and stood behind the altar) there is a complete symbol of acceptance' and he spoke for a few minutes on the 'fully integrated' acceptance 'of each and every one of us' that the bread and wine embody.

Tim pulled up a chair and, sitting behind the altar, said he would like to use a special Eucharistic prayer, a prayer of Jesus of Compassion. He walked over to his bag beside the keyboard to fetch the text of the prayer and, returning to the altar, sat down and set the pages by his side. The priest said his part exactly, the congregation theirs. Tim then stepped to the other side of the horseshoe-end and took the hand of the man next to him, who had stood up; everyone else stood and held hands, the last man even holding the teddy's hand. The keyboard started and everyone sang the 'Our Father', keeping their hands linked during the subsequent prayer until Tim invited everyone to say together

'Lord Jesus Christ, you said to your apostles: I leave you peace, my peace I give you. Look not on our sins but on the faith of your Church and grant us the peace and unity of your kingdom where you live for ever and ever. Amen'. T: 'Let us offer each other the sign of peace' and the congregation greeted one another with hugs. Nearly everyone in the room hugged nearly everyone else, saying '*NAME*, peace be with you'.

Tim returned to his seat behind the altar as the congregation returned to theirs. Sitting down, he said, 'Let's pass the bread around and say the invitation to communion together so that way we can all feel that this is one loaf and we're all accepted and included in it'. He broke the wafers into chunks and each person sitting in the circle passed it to the next, taking one piece each and just holding it. When everyone had taken some, Tim said 'This is the Lamb of God who takes away the sins of the world. Happy are those who are called to his supper.' And the men all said, 'Lord I am not worthy to receive you but only say the Word and I shall be healed.' Straight after this everyone ate his wafer. Tim drank some wine and invited two Eucharistic ministers to come forward and they gave each other the wine. They then turned, stood in front of the altar and offered the ceramic chalices to each person who came forward from their seats, saying '*NAME*, The blood of Christ', to which each person said 'Amen'. All but one man went up to receive from the chalice. When all were served, Tim sat down in the circle again and said 'We have a communion hymn, I think'. The keyboard started and we sang 'Gentle as Silence'.

Tim gave a few personal reflections after the hymn, tying together the theme of acceptance with the gift of the Eucharist. He complimented all those involved in planning the liturgy, suggesting the prayers of the faithful should be published so that others could use them, and he thanked the group for inviting him back, saying he always enjoyed being there. He asked if anyone else had any reflections they would like to share. No one said anything so he continued with a blessing and the dismissal.

The group's chairperson stood, thanked Tim profusely and made a long series of announcements about the group's activities and administration. These were confidential. Others chipped in at various points with corrections, suggestions and offers. At the end, my host told me that there would be a cup of tea afterwards but he was not going to stay for it and what did I think I would do? I decided not to stay, intimating from the way that the question was put that it might not be appropriate to do so. I gather the tea and cake lasted about twenty minutes and about half the group went on afterwards to a pub around the corner.

Analysis as Communicative Action

I was introduced to everyone by their first name and, without exception, each man shook my hand and said, 'Hi, Siobhán. You're (very) welcome'. I said 'Thank you, *NAME*'.

In this brief exchange, repeated as many times as there were people in the room, a basic *trustworthiness* claim was raised and redeemed. By greeting me by name and then saying I was welcome, each man challenged me to show that it was appropriate that I was there: it was a challenge to the trustworthiness of my being introduced to them. This was communicated in tone: the mere fact of saying 'you are welcome' does not of itself warrant a response, but when said with a certain tone, it does. Each man listened and continued shaking my hand while I responded (rather than, say, turning to the next person or changing the subject). This shows that the response was crucial to the exchange, as much as if I had refused to shake the hand that was simultaneously being offered to me. The response, 'Thank you' established my position as guest (and thus theirs as host). It also established my trustworthiness by demonstrating that I knew how to act appropriately, that is, that I accepted their welcome.

CPU 1:   *Group identity is based on one-to-one relationships, and not, for example, an issue.*
CPU 2a: *Ritual participants must be called by name;*
  2b: *Only your first name matters (your 'official' name is irrelevant).*
CPU 3:   *Welcome is the condition of participation.*

He stood as the hymn ended and said how glad he was to be back with the group again. He (T) said 'In the name of the Father and of the Son and of the Holy Spirit' and the congregation (C) said 'Amen'. T: 'The grace of our Lord Jesus Christ and the love of God and the fellowship of the Holy Spirit be with you all'; C: 'And also with you.'

The first exchange, the sign of the cross, is a *truth* claim. It is raised and, in the 'Amen', redeemed with consensus. Several things have been consented to: firstly, that the congregation agree that Tim is priest in this situation (he has just been welcomed, and said how glad he is to be back; now when he speaks the congregation listen first and then assent. They let him say his line, they let him lead). Secondly, the interchange functions as an affirmation that the group gathers 'In the name of' God (and specifically God as Trinity): following as it does immediately after the Reach preamble, this is an important establishing factor for the liturgy. The name of the group may be *Reach*, but it consents to meet in the name of 'the Father, the Son and the Holy Spirit'. The sign of the cross thus, thirdly, functions to demarcate the beginning of a particular, nuanced, type of gathering: one that moves beyond the greeting by name of one another and the 'preamble' greeting of the gathering in the name of Reach, to a period of liturgy when what is paramount is gathering in the name of God.

CPU: *Liturgy 'starts' by consent to interact in the name of God.*

The second exchange is a *rightness* claim. Based on the consensus just established, it establishes one thing: reciprocity. What the priest can grace the congregation with, the congregation must grace the priest with. The ability to proceed in a gathering in the name of God is dependent on the group's ability to do for one another, to grace one another, to love one another, to be fellowship for one another. What it establishes is the rightness of the priest's claim itself: by saying 'And also with you', the congregation qualifies the appropriateness of the first exchange (grace of Christ, love of God, fellowship of Spirit) in terms of the essentially reciprocal nature of grace, love and fellowship.

CPU: *For the grace, love and fellowship of God to be, there must be reciprocity.*

T: 'I will now give a general absolution in the sincere hope that none of ye head off to the red house straight after this, but, well, maybe it'll still count even if you do' (C: gentle laughter).

This is a *trustworthiness* claim. Tim knows that the 'effect' of his words is contingent on the reciprocity of the congregation; but he makes reference to, raises doubts about, the trustworthiness of his partners in interaction. He wants to speak God's absolution, but wants also to make sure that no one will abuse this by doing something they shouldn't afterwards. The congregation laughs softly. Tim's challenge to their trustworthiness is hardly redeemed by this, he has not received the assurance he sought; but, perhaps sensing that such assurance could not be spoken in this setting, he says 'maybe it'll still count' anyway. The congregation did not redeem this claim: perhaps because they did not know what he meant (the 'competent speaker' premise); perhaps because the ritual form (general absolution) did not permit them to speak (the equal opportunity to speak premise); or perhaps they did not speak because they did indeed intend to do something 'straight after this' that they did not want to admit to the priest (thus negotiating a situation where they retain an interpretation of the ritual acts that they know to be at odds with the intentions of the leader, but nevertheless wish to claim for themselves).

Whichever way one speculates, it is difficult to interpret any latent conditions of possible understanding.

The reader, seated, read an extract from Ephesians, ending with 'This is the Word of the Lord.' C: 'Thanks be to God'. Everyone sang 'All People that on Earth Do Dwell' for the psalm.

This is an exchange on several levels: the singing of the psalm is a direct response to the reading and hearing of the passage from Ephesians; it is an almighty redemption of the *truth* claims inhering in the scripture (on the challenge to conversion). However it also qualifies the interpretation the congregation have of the reading by challenging the truth claims made in it: here the people sing '*All people that on earth do dwell*', a song that emphasises the inclusivity of God's engagement in creation. The singing is also an almighty act of consensus-formation by the simple act of singing (the same words, the same tune) in unison. For one of the other hymns I noticed two people not singing; for another of them a man sitting close-by changed all the 'father' imagery to 'god' or 'creator'; so the unison, the consensus, with which this truth claim is both raised, challenged and redeemed is not to be taken for granted.

CPU 1:   *God's revelation must be for all people.*
CPU 2:   *Consensus can be expressed by singing together.*

He then invited anyone else to 'offer their reflections on the gospel or the reading, or any other word or prayer that has come to you during our liturgy' and left a good time for people to come in. He said 'Does anyone want to speak?' Heads around the room shook. 'Is it ok, then, if I move on'. Several people said 'yes'. Tim said, 'I can't believe I'm going to have the last word on this one! Oh well, the night is young yet' and everybody laughed.

Despite Tim's light-hearted tone at the end, this is a serious example of a *truth* claim raised but not redeemed. The congregation have assented to the gospel by their words 'Thanks be to God' at the end of it; however they refuse to speak about the truth of that gospel when challenged to do so. Above, with the general absolution, I speculated that perhaps the ritual form did not allow speech; here, however, the context of conversation and dialogue has been firmly introduced and invited and yet is explicitly refused by the men in the congregation. As such it is an instance of distorted communication: one party has challenged another to justify the claim they made (by affirming the gospel) and they decline to do so; they refuse to be partners in the process.

This may of course be for many reasons: a liturgical formation in scenarios where one was not allowed to speak, a lack of confidence in speaking aloud to a group, a dry throat, etc. - none of which are discernible from the evidence. However, whatever the 'reason', it functioned as a block to communicative action.

Three different people seated around the room read three prayer-reflections. They were quite long meditations on acceptance, loneliness and hope, written in the first person and employing a lot of urban imagery. After each one, the keyboard struck a chord and the whole assembly sang: 'Lord hear as we pray. Oh God give us your love.' Tim said a prayer at the end, in conventional address to God, giving thanks for 'all those in our lives so far who have shown us a glimpse of what it might fell like to be accepted'. He initiated the sung response again.

Each prayer read by the members of the congregation began 'Lord...' they were a direct address to God, a fact reflected in the posture of the speakers: they faced the altar, seated, looking at their text and not once at their fellow worshippers. In a service which has, thus far, been very much a conversation between its participants, this was striking. What was being asked of God was that God prove *trustworthy*. Each prayer directly asked, 'why the loneliness?' and 'when the acceptance?' and 'where is there hope?' and the congregation made the questions their own by further asking God to prove trustworthy by singing 'Oh God give us your love'. The claim was, however, redeemed in the final prayer of the priest which, instead of asking God a question rather thanked God for those people in whom we have glimpsed acceptance and thus hope and thus an end to loneliness. When the congregation sang 'God give us your love' this time, it was with the memory in mind of those in whom God has already given us love.

CPU: *God's trustworthiness is established through remembering how others have accepted us.*

To me he said, 'Doesn't he have a lovely top on him!' and I replied 'It's gorgeous!'

At first this may look like a straightforward truth claim, but it is actually a *rightness* claim: it is all about appropriateness. The top is a rainbow top - the rainbow being the flag of the gay community - and by drawing attention to it explicitly Tim is implicitly challenging me and others within earshot to affirm the appropriateness of bringing up as an offering this teddy bearing the gay flag. Any old ted would not have elicited the hilarity, or the question or the response. The redemption of the claim is immediately extended in Tim's explanation to the whole group of the acceptance felt to be offered by, and thus symbolised in, teddy bears.

CPU: *Any gift offered must be appropriate.*

The keyboard started and everyone sang the 'Our Father', keeping their hands linked during the subsequent prayer until Tim invited everyone to say together 'Lord Jesus Christ, you said to your apostles: I leave you peace, my peace I give you. Look not on our sins but on the faith of your Church and grant us the peace and unity of your kingdom where you live for ever and ever. Amen'.

The 'Our Father' said here is another direct address to God and another *trustworthiness* claim of God. God 'responds' and thus redeems the claim in two ways: firstly, in the words that immediately follow (said by all the people and not just the presider, as would be usual for a Roman Catholic Eucharist) where, through an act of remembering in unison, God redeems the claim through the memory of God's past behaviour ('You said to your disciples...'), God's present presence ('I leave you peace, my peace I give you') and God's future-now promise ('grant us the peace and unity of your kingdom') and timeless presence ('where you live for ever and ever'). Secondly, God redeems the claim in the exchange of the peace ('Name, peace be with you') that immediately follows.

CPU 1:   *God 'speaks' and redeems in the participants' shared remembering*
              of God.
CPU 2:   *God's trustworthiness is 'proved' through God's peace.*
CPU 3:   *Peace is personal: it is expressed one interaction at a time,*
              through the body (hugs), through calling one another by name,
              and through the gift of the interaction itself ('be with you').

When everyone had taken some, Tim said 'This is the Lamb of God who takes away the sins of the world. Happy are those who are called to his supper.' And the men all said, 'Lord I am not worthy to receive you but only say the Word and I shall be healed.' Straight after this everyone ate his wafer.

In the last exchange a direct address to God is resolved in an address one ritual participant to another; in this exchange, the opposite is the case. The *trustworthiness* claim that the presider challenges ('Happy are those...') is a direct address to those who are about to partake of this supper. The congregation respond by addressing not the presider but 'Lord', assenting their trustworthiness by declaring to God their desire for a dialogue with God ('only say the Word') through which they know they 'will be healed', and thus Happy, able to partake.

CPU: *Trustworthiness with one another is dependent on dialogue*
              with God.

They then turned, stood in front of the altar and offered the ceramic chalices to each person who came forward from their seats, saying 'NAME, The blood of Christ', to which each person said 'Amen'.

This is consensual action.

A Case Study of Ecumenical Liturgy

In 2000, as one of the co-ordinators of *Fís*, the national inter-church conference in celebration of the millennium, I had the responsibility of planning for nine ecumenical liturgies. In researching what had been done liturgically ecumenically in Ireland I was confronted with the relative absence of (recorded) attempts among the denominations to conduct sacramental worship together. In the planning stages of the liturgies I experienced a surprising amount of criticism and cynicism and it was this, combined with evidence of the scarcity of precedents, that suggested to me that ecumenical worship is more marginal than perhaps those writing in the field realise. I again chose to conduct a case study in the United States (rather than use *Fís* itself or any other Irish gathering) for the same reasons behind my choice of a feminist group, there being communities in the States that have established a tradition of worshipping ecumenically.

Every day from Monday to Thursday there is a liturgy at noon in James Chapel in Union Theological Seminary, Manhattan. Founded in the heart of the island's most economically disadvantaged area, Harlem, the vision for the seminary was that it would train theologians and ministers through immersion in the reality of urban need. Liturgy is seen as an important part of this goal, and the chapel is open to all who wish to attend services in it. The chapel, like the seminary itself, is multi-denominational and ecumenical and there is a team of liturgy experts who are employed to work with the community in the planning and evaluation of worship to ensure that its services are accessible to as many community members as possible. The chapel can hold several hundred worshippers but on most days there is a steady attendance of about sixty staff, students, faculty, neighbours and visitors. A different person - more usually group of persons - takes responsibility for leading each day's worship, although occasionally a group will take a whole week (e.g.: black caucus week). Every Thursday is Eucharist, and it was on a Thursday that I visited.

Entering through the double doors of the neo-gothic chapel I was greeted and welcomed by a woman who handed me an order of service and my eyes were instantly taken by the large mounted photograph on an easel at the entrance to the worship space: it was a picture of South American women hauling in a fishing net on a beach. Walking past it I was in a circle of chairs split with four aisles centring on a large square table, on which lay a swathe of a blue cloth (suggestive of water), a lighted candle, a large loaf, a jug of wine, a jug of grape juice and four large goblets. People entered the chapel one by one, greeted one another and most chatted quietly with their neighbour when they found a seat.

At a few minutes past noon, a man and a woman stood up and moved to each of the two lecterns on either side of the table, at the end of two of the aisles. The chattering stopped immediately and the congregation picked up their order of service sheets. The man and woman alternated leadership, starting with the man saying,

One:	'In the beginning God made the world:'
Women:	Made it and mothered it,
Men:	Shaped it and fathered it;
One:	All that is green, blue, deep, and growing,
All:	**God's is the hand that created you.**
One:	All that is tender, firm, fragrant and curious,
All:	**God's is the hand that created you.**

One:	All that speaks, sings, cries, laughs or keeps silence,
All:	**God's is the hand that created you.**
One:	All that suffers, lacks, limps, or longs for an end.
All:	**God's is the hand that created you.**
One:	The world belongs to God,
All:	**The earth and all its people.**
One:	Let us worship God.

Three different people came to the lecterns and directed the congregation in singing an alleluia in three parts: men, altos and sopranos. Everyone stood up. Following their lead, the alleluia became louder and stronger until, repeated three times, they indicated with a slight wave of the hand that we would stop.

Another person came to the lectern and said,

Christ our teacher,
you reached into our lives
Through the remembrance of story
and the promise of your presence.
Open our hearts to be attentive:
That seeing, we may perceive,
and hearing, we may understand,
and understanding, we may act upon your word, Amen.

The congregation sat down as a man approached the lectern and read Luke 5: 1-11. When he had finished, Barbara Lundblad approached the lectern wearing a brightly coloured stole around her neck and, looking just occasionally at her notes, began to tell what she described as a 'midrash', a 'filling-in the holes' in the story through further story-telling. Before long she had moved from behind the lectern and continued preaching as she moved, slowly, to different points around the table. She made direct eye contact with members of the congregation the entire time she was speaking. There were many pauses in her preaching, especially after she asked the congregation a question. Sometimes these pauses were filled with silence, other times members of the congregation would respond with a short word 'uh-huh', 'yes', 'mmm' or once or twice with gentle laughter. Barbara returned to the lectern whenever she was making a specific biblical reference, so as to read it exactly, but then returned to the space between the table and the congregation for the midrash. Most of the midrash were stories about the women involved in Luke's gospel stories. For the last part of the sermon, when she talked about the need to develop our own midrash, Barbara leant her hand on the table right beside the bread. She paused for a full 30 seconds, then started to sing, 'Come let us Worship', raising her arms high to us to indicate that we should repeat, and we did, till there was a general lead and response chant.

Barbara then took the plate holding the bread and raised them to eye-level with both hands, and said 'We all know this story, don't we. So what is it?

What is our story?' There was silence. Barbara repeated, 'We all know it. What is this story we tell today?' And from all sections of the room members of the congregation started to volunteer, some loudly, some very quietly,

'On the night before he died'
'Jesus was with his friends'
'He took bread and broke it'
'Gave thanks'
Barbara: 'And then what happened?'
'He blessed it'
'Broke it'
'He said, Do this in memory of me'
'He gave it to his friends'

Barbara lowered the bread onto the table and held the wine aloft, asking us what was the story of the wine and juice, and the story was told in the same way. When all the parts of the story had been told, Barbara invited everyone to come and share in the meal, either by taking bread and wine from the five Eucharistic ministers, whom she invited to come and stand at the table beside her, or by coming to her directly and asking for a blessing. She said that the blessing would take the form of a short passage from Isaiah. The ministers moved three to each side of the table, one with bread, another with wine, another with juice and, with organ music playing in the background, people came forward. The majority took bread and wine/juice, but there was a steady stream approaching Barbara for a blessing instead, each saying 'Amen' when offered the bread, wine and blessing.

With everyone served, the ministers placed the leftover bread and cups on the table. Barbara removed her stole and returned to her seat. A member of the congregation approached a lectern and led us in a prayer printed on the sheets:

One: From where we are
       to where you need us
All: **Jesus now lead on.**
One: From the security of what we know
       To the adventure of what you will reveal,
All   **Jesus now lead on.**
One: From the fear in our bones
       to the peace which nothing can destroy
All: **Jesus now lead on.**

A woman came to the lectern and invited us to join in the singing of *'Thuma mina.'* The words were in the hymnbooks on our seats (New Century, 360) and the woman led us in the singing of it (it had a call-and-response element too). We finished, sat down and listened to an organ improvisation for several minutes. This complete, people stood up: some left; several went to the table and ate the remaining bread, wine and juice; many stayed and chatted to one another. It was not until ten minutes after the organ postlude that the worship space was vacated and the organisers started to clear up.

On the bottom of the order of service were two written notices. The first read 'participants include' and gave the names of nine of the worship leaders. The second credited Iona's *A Wee Worship Book* and Janet Morley's *All Desires Known* for resources used in worship.

Analysis as Communicative Action

From the moment of entering the worship space to the very end of the service, the organisers sought to elicit a response in the worshippers. The photograph of fisher-women in a poorer country confronted all those who entered and this 'confrontation' was reproduced in almost every aspect of the verbal element of the liturgy, coming as it did in a format of call and response. This took two basic forms: one where a leader (or more than one) says a prescribed text and the congregation replies according to a prescribed text (as in the opening prayer, the alleluia, the 'Come let us worship', the final prayer and the final hymn); and another where the leader issues a spontaneous call and the congregation is expected to respond spontaneously (as in the sermon, the Eucharistic prayer and some of the song).

CPU 1:   *Participants must hold in mind the memory of an other.*
CPU 2:   *All must be prepared to be confronted with an other.*
CPU 3:   *Passivity in this task is not an option: it will not happen if one does not respond.*

One:	'In the beginning God made the world:'
Women:	Made it and mothered it,
Men:	Shaped it and fathered it;
F. Leader:	All that is green, blue, deep, and growing,
One:	**God's is the hand that created you.**
M. Leader:	All that is tender, firm, fragrant and curious,
One:	**God's is the hand that created you.**
F. Leader:	All that speaks, sings, cries, laughs or keeps silence,
One:	**God's is the hand that created you.**
M. Leader:	All that suffers, lacks, limps, or longs for an end.
One:	**God's is the hand that created you.**
F. Leader:	The world belongs to God,
One:	**The earth and all its people.**
M. Leader:	Let us worship God.

The first three lines went as scripted, women saying their thing, men saying theirs, but then many in the congregation continued with the next line, the

leader's line, and paused at the end instead of coming in with, 'God's is the hand that created you'. The same happened among some in the congregation with the subsequent line, although they had fitted in with the text by the second 'God's is the hand...' It would be easy to dismiss it as irrelevant because it was just nicely shambolic, or the result of a difficult-to-read order of service. However, the people in this congregation are just about as highly competent in the art of following an order of service as one could find, the majority of them being ministers or trainee-ministers in the Christian churches and so I choose not to ignore the messiness of this first prayer. Habermas's model alerts us not just to what is said but to who is saying it and here it makes a difference that a significant, audible, part of the congregation said lines assigned to the leader. They were challenging the right of the speaker to lead and were (evidenced by the fact they came round to doing it the prescribed way, rather than falling silent or carrying on doing it 'wrongly') eventually persuaded by the interaction of the congregation as a whole that the proposed 'One' was distinct from the 'All'.

CPU 1:   *Leadership is negotiated by the group within the ritual.*
CPU 2:   *Leadership is conferred through the contingencies of interaction, not prior ordination, authority or any other such pre-determined claim.*

She made direct eye contact with members of the congregation the entire time she was speaking. There were many pauses in her preaching, especially after she asked the congregation a question. Sometimes these pauses were filled with silence, other times members of the congregation would respond with a short word 'uh-huh', 'yes', 'mmm' or once or twice with gentle laughter.

Sermons are, in verbal terms, usually seen as a monologue even though those who come from preaching traditions describe them as a form of dialogue. With this sermon the congregation actually said things. They did not say full sentences or raise serious disagreements but, in a similar fashion to some Black church traditions, they uttered audible words: 'uh-huh', 'yes', 'mmm'. Yet in terms of the raising and redeeming of universal validity claims, it was a strange situation. Barbara's words were often challenging, both in subject matter (the forgotten women of the gospel stories) and form (many questions, levelled directly at the congregation) and they were punctuated by many extended pauses. These were, nevertheless, silent pauses. Apart from a few individuals saying 'Yes' or 'uh-huh', no one spoke when Barbara stopped speaking. They chose neither to challenge her, nor to provide grounds, offer justification or prove their trustworthiness in response to the challenges with which she had presented them. It was a dialogue (not just one person spoke) but one in which one person was given permission to speak a lot more than any other, as if she had been given a mandate by her conversation partners to challenge them, but to do so rhetorically, that is, in a way that suspends the requirement (or possibility) of actual debate.

Perhaps it is only possible to interpret it as communicative action in the context of what it was leading up to: the Eucharistic prayer. If the 'utterance' is taken as the Eucharistic prayer as a whole and not as the sermon as a separated fragment of the liturgy, then the above section operates as a sort of extended prologue to what was about to take place. It was a *listening* for stories (one's own and those of others) in readiness for *telling* the story (one's own and that of others).

CPU: *The whole assembly must listen (must remember the stories of others) for there to be Eucharist.*

Barbara then took the plate holding the bread and raised it to eye-level with both hands, and said 'We all know this story, don't we. So what is it? What is our story?' There was silence. Barbara repeated, 'We all know it. What is this story we tell today?' And from all sections of the room members of the congregation started to volunteer, some loudly, some very quietly,
'On the night before he died'
'Jesus was with his friends'...

[This congregation knows two things that are not evident just in a description of what happened: they know that this is not the norm (the norm in this ecumenical seminary is that the presider says these words, whether in the Protestant tradition of the words of institution or the Catholic one of a Eucharistic prayer) and they also know that this has been done before, by last year's graduating Roman Catholic women. Today they know they have a Lutheran presider who is adopting a liturgical form developed by Roman Catholic women.]

All three validity claims are in play, explicitly, here. Barbara has challenged the assembly to tell the whole story: it is a *truth* claim, a demand for grounds. The first time she asks, there is silence (as there was, for the most part, in the sermon). Barbara takes the silence as a challenge to prove *trustworthy* herself, and does so by repeating the question. The second time she asks the question she is more direct, and adds 'today', specifying the context of the interaction (and thus the *rightness* of the interaction). Randomly, people start speaking up. They listen to one another so they know what parts of the story remain to be told. There is hardly any repetition. The words peter out. Barbara asks for more. When no one has spoken for a few moments, Barbara lowers the bread. They have judged the story complete, they have provided grounds. They have told only appropriate parts. They have proved trustworthy. Barbara proceeds.

(I asked her afterwards if the members of the congregation had not told the whole story, would she have 'corrected' them, and she said she would perhaps have asked them again but she would not have intervened to fill in any gaps she alone perceived. The trustworthiness of the congregation as participants in Eucharist was therefore to be proved on its ability to tell its own story, not to have it told for them.)

CPU: *A community must be able to tell its own story; communion is*
                forged by telling its own story in the context of listening (to the
                word of God, the sermon, to one another).

Barbara invited everyone to come and share in the meal, either by taking bread and wine from the five Eucharistic ministers, whom she invited to come and stand at the table beside her, or by coming to her directly and asking for a blessing. She said that the blessing would take the form of a short passage from Isaiah..... The majority took bread and wine/juice, but there was a steady stream approaching Barbara for a blessing instead, each saying 'Amen' when offered the bread, wine and blessing.

Barbara invited all to participate in the interaction around the altar by offering a variety of ways of participating: coming forward to eat, drink or receive a blessing. This invitation, and her careful explanation of how it would be organised reflects the considerable diversity of relationship of each of the participants to the action being undertaken. So she explicitly invited us to eat bread (most Christian denominations use bread regularly in worship); and drink wine (likewise) or juice (denominations that emphasise temperance as part of a Christian lifestyle - such as Methodists and Southern Baptists - use juice instead of wine; also some people affected by alcoholism do not identify alcohol as a symbol of God's presence); or receive a blessing (some Christian denominations - such as the Brethren - take communion only twice a year and only when explicitly associated with a foot-washing or similar ritual of service; some members of the seminary do not have a Christo-centric faith e.g.: Jews - and do not wish to partake of the central symbols of Christian faith and yet want to be a part of the community's worship of God – hence it was important that she explained that the blessing was from Isaiah; finally, the official teachings of some Christian denominations - e.g.: Roman Catholic - do not recognise a Eucharist as valid if it is not celebrated by an ordained member of their own denomination and so the blessing is a way for any members of those communities to gather at the table with their community. It is, however, noteworthy that in addition to several Roman Catholic women who received communion, so did a Jesuit priest.) So her invitation was framed in such a way as to elicit the interaction of as many people present as possible.

Every single person in the room came forward to the table, and nearly all said 'Amen' to the words spoken to them as they received something from one of the ministers. 'Amen' is a word of consent, neither a claim nor a challenge. It is a moment when understanding has in fact been reached.

CPU 1:   *Interaction is conditional upon sensitivity to the participation-*
                conditions of others
CPU 2:   *Diversity must be accepted.*
CPU 3   *All must have an equal ability to engage with the central symbol:*
                the table.

CPU 4:   *Communion requires consensus.*
CPU 5:   *A body must be present(ed) for there to be consent (the Body of*
                 the community can be symbolised as bread - but it need not be:
                 here for e.g.: it can be a blessing).

A Case Study of Church of Ireland Liturgy

Since moving to Ireland in 1996, I have been astounded at the literally hundreds of times I have heard reference made to 'the church', in private, in class and in the media, only to realise that the speaker does not mean the whole church but the Roman Catholic communion alone. I have also heard very well educated people say extremely ignorant things about their 'protestant' neighbours, including in academic theological settings. The Anglican, Reformed, Free Church and Unitarian traditions may be in a minority in Ireland (just 4% according to the 1990 census) but they have long traditions of practice here. The largest of these denominations in the Republic is the Church of Ireland, with congregations in every city and most towns. It was on the grounds of accessibility that I chose a parish in the west of Ireland.

Standing just inside the door of the church were two women, who said 'Good morning' and 'Nice to see you', handed me three small books and with a motion of the arm invited me to go down the central aisle to take a seat in one of the wooden pews that faced the sanctuary. Other people were already seated, a few in each pew, and although it was late summer nearly all of them had their coats on. There was classical music playing through the stereo and everyone took a seat, saying a brief greeting to those around them.

         The rector, dressed neck to toe in a white robe with a white stole, came out of a little room at the front left of the church and walked up to the sanctuary step. Back to the congregation, he bowed at the cross on the altar in the centre of the sanctuary and walked to the large brass lectern with an eagle carving on it that stood on the floor facing the congregation and he said, 'Good morning.' The congregation responded in kind. He went on, 'You are all very welcome to today's service of holy communion. It is the tradition of the Anglican church that any Christian who is a communicant member of their own denomination is welcome to take bread and wine with us here today. So you are welcome to come forward and receive communion if you would like to. We will start today's service of holy communion by singing' and he gave the hymn number, the page number and the name of the book it was in. A recording of a choir started to play through the stereo and the congregation sang along heartily. There were three more hymns during the service and every single one was sung with equal gusto by the congregation but not by the presider who stood to the side of the sanctuary, facing the altar, each time.

         A woman from the congregation came forward and led the opening prayers. She stood in a miniature pew at the front left of the main body of pews which faced the lectern. She said the first line of the Collect for Purity, 'Almighty God, to whom all hearts are open' and the congregation came in; but they did not continue the prayer, as in a call and response pattern, they repeated the line the leader had spoken and proceeded to say the full prayer. Every other congregational prayer was undertaken this way (including the Creed, the 'Our Father' and the prayers before and after communion). As the prayer was coming to its end, children were turning around and moving to the end of their pews. As soon as it had ended, they literally sped out of the church to have their own liturgy of the word in the parish hall across the road. No mention was made of this departure, they just knew their cue and off they went. Neither was any mention made of their remarkably quiet return either when, at the start of the Eucharistic prayer, they slipped back into their seats beside their families.

Another woman came to the lectern and read the first reading from scripture. She stepped down and the first woman leader, still in her separate pew, invited us to read the psalm together 'by half verse': she read the first stanza of each verse aloud, the congregation the second. The second woman returned to the lectern and read the second reading. The women did everything exactly according to the script, and so did the congregation. The Rector, who had been sitting on the dais facing the altar returned to the lectern and the congregation stood as he read the gospel then sat down before he began his sermon.

The sermon was based on the gospel reading which had been the story of the prodigal son. The presider spoke from notes, but continually looked up to make eye contact with members of the congregation, from the back to the front of the church. He said, 'This is a story that will only work as a story, will only live, if you take it and sit with it and think it and think around it. Think of yourself as each person in the story, how would you have reacted? How would you have reacted if you were the father, the good son, the prodigal son? And think what if the characters were women, think of yourself in those terms, if you were the mother, the good sister, the prodigal sister. This story would not have been told if it was a mother who met him, because this story is set in times that are not like they are today' and he proceeded to describe the differences in inheritance issues, between father-son relationships, between that time and now. Then he said 'You see, you can't just take it in as it's read, you have to read it over and over, over several days. You actually have to read it, carefully. And that might mean you actually have to open your bibles. Now that would be a novelty, wouldn't it.' He paused for a second. Many in the congregation were looking down. He continued in this vein, a mixture of personal interpretation and biblical scholarship delivered at a quick clip with no more pauses and a return to eye-contact.

At the peace, the presider came down from behind the altar and shook hands with members of the congregation. Most congregants first shook hands with those around them, then left their pews and shook hands with everyone they met walking up and down the central aisle of the church. Everyone who shook hands with me said something, and they nearly all said something different; including what I overheard being said to others, these were 'Peace', 'Peace be with you',

'Peace, *NAME*', 'The Peace of Christ', 'Hello, *NAME*', 'Good to see you', 'Hi', and 'Nice to meet you',.

After the priest had said the 'Lamb of God', the congregation sat down. Two more women came to the front of the church, stepped onto the dais and each turned to close the gates that formed a railing around the edge of the sanctuary. A moment passed and those in the front rows of the church left their seats and moved to the railings in single file. They knelt on or stood before the step in front of the railings. The Rector came to each one and, placing a piece of bread in their up-turned palm, said '*NAME*, the body of Christ, broken for you' and each person responded 'Amen'. They remained in place, ate their bread and one of the women ministers came to each person with the chalice, presenting it to each with the words, 'The blood of Christ, bring you to eternal life'. The recipient said, 'Amen', took the cup, drank and handed it back to her. Everyone in the church came to the railings and for those who did not open their hands for communion, and young children, the priest placed his hand just above their head and gave them a blessing: 'May God bless you and keep you'. Each stayed at the railings for a few moments before returning, past the queue of people waiting for a vacant spot at the railings, to their seats.

After the final hymn and blessing, everyone slowly left, talking to one another. The Rector stood inside the back door, shook everyone's hand and had a brief chat with each person. Most people congregated outside the backdoor of church and chatted for a good 10–15 minutes.

Analysis as Communicative Action

He said, 'Good morning.' The congregation responded in kind. He went on, 'You are all very welcome to today's service of holy communion. It is the tradition of the Anglican church that any Christian who is a communicant member of their own denomination is welcome to take bread and wine with us here today...'

The opening greeting, 'Good morning', establishes a communicative interaction between presider and congregation that is more formal than the 'hello's and 'how are you's the congregation have just been using among themselves. It is a mini-*trustworthiness* claim: the presider looks for, and gets, an affirmation of his place as conversation 'leader' in this initial exchange. (Think of the converse: if no-one replied, his mandate to continue would not be coming from this community's dialogue.) He follows it up immediately with a *rightness* claim: giving reasons (the teaching of the Anglican Communion) why this congregation he is addressing in this place at this time should be able to proceed with a service in which all present are conversation partners, giving reasons to justify his own claim that all were welcome.

But who challenged him? What is revealed in the rector's remarks is an acknowledgement of the extreme controversy that surrounds intercommunion, whereby the Roman Catholic Church will allow only Roman Catholics to receive communion and advises Roman Catholics not to receive communion in another denomination's church. The rector is facing a congregation that includes tourists (of unknown origin) as well as many Roman Catholics who have married members of his parish. By saying 'Good morning' they identified themselves as partners in the conversation, and this was itself his challenge.

CPU 1:   *Diversity is welcomed.*
CPU 2:   *Leadership is assented in interaction.*

There were three more hymns during the service and every single one was sung with equal gusto by the congregation but not by the presider who stood facing the side of the altar each time.

Hymn singing featured prominently in this ritual. All of the hymns were addressed to God and every person in the congregation sang. The rector did not. It was a conversation between congregation and God which did not need a leader. Any comment that the rector felt aloof, or did not like singing, or was deep in prayer would be mere speculation: the dialogue did not involve him. The words of all four hymns included passages from scripture (God as speaker, congregation as hearer) as well as direct appeal to God, for example in 'Dear Lord and Father of mankind, forgive our foolish ways' (God as hearer, congregation as speaker).

CPU: *Dialogue is not just among persons present; it is also directly addressed to/from God to/from the body as a whole. It is, however, being done on our behalf: by the choir on record. So it is not necessary to participate. Even the presider does not.*

She said the first line of the Collect for Purity, 'Almighty God, to whom all hearts are open' and the congregation came in; but they did not continue the prayer, as in a call and response pattern, they repeated the line the leader had spoken and proceeded to say the full prayer.

This is an interesting dialogue. The woman begins the prayer, but not as a leader initiating a call and response, more as a prompt, giving the congregation their cue for the dialogue which is, again, addressed directly to God. The claim being raised is one of *trustworthiness*, it serves to establish the untrustworthiness of any leader to say this part of the dialogue, demonstrating that it is only appropriate for each person in the congregation to speak these words. It achieves this in two ways: firstly, a member of the congregation itself (not the presider) serves as 'prompt'; secondly the congregation insist on saying the whole prayer, repeating the initial words of address, thus signalling that this is a congregation-God dialogue not a presider-congregation dialogue.

CPU: *Each person has to take equal and individual own responsibility for their dialogue with God, in the context of the group. No leader can address God on our behalf.*

Then he said 'You see, you can't just take it in as it's read, you have to read it over and over, over days. And that might mean you actually have to open your bibles. Now that would be a novelty, wouldn't it.' He paused for a second. Many in the congregation were looking down. He continued in this vein, a mixture of personal interpretation and biblical scholarship delivered at a quick clip with no more pauses and a return to eye contact.

The priest's comments here, delivered as part of the sermon, betray his assumption that the people he is addressing do not read their bibles, do not ordinarily spend time 'living with' bible stories in the manner he is advocating. I say betray, because he paused afterwards. People who had been looking at him were looking down. It is one thing to challenge an assembly who have given you the mandate to preach; it is another to make assumptions about the faith practices of that assembly and deliver a sardonic rebuke on the basis of those. No-one said anything verbally, but I note that with the pause dialogue was temporarily interrupted.

The sermon is a challenge from the Christian assembly to the presider to give grounds, it is a *truth* claim. Her or his trustworthiness has already been proven; the appropriateness of their giving a sermon has already been established; what remains is for them is to justify the truth claim they have made in reading the gospel. I suggest that the loss of eye-contact marked a challenge, by speaker and hearers alike, to whether or not the truth claim was in fact being justified.

It is difficult to interpret this exchange as communicative action.

Everyone who shook hands with me said something, and they nearly all said something different; including what I overheard being said to others, this was 'Peace', 'Peace be with you', 'Peace, *NAME*', 'The Peace of Christ', 'Hello, *NAME*', 'Good to see you', 'Hi', and 'Nice to meet you'.

This was an unusual interaction, because it was not the case that one spoke while another listened, then she spoke and the other listened; rather both took one another's hand and simultaneously said their phrase. The variety of things said is also unusual, as it is a departure from the 'Peace be with you' suggested in the order of service. This too is a *truth* claim, a response to the priest's words a few moments earlier, 'Peace be with you' expressed as a desire to provide grounds to justify their response 'and also with you'. The fact that the community felt as free with their words and movement as they did (i.e.: freedom to change the script) reflects the diversity of participants (each giving a slightly different greeting) and the unity of their vision for the activity they were engaged in (each greeting not just their neighbour but as many other people as possible). As speakers they desired to say an authentic word; as hearers they desired to hear as many of their co-worshippers as they could.

CPU: *A sense of community is not taken for granted; it is known that it must be forged and affirmed through one-to-one interaction: touch, eye-contact, greeting, listening; every time, with as many fellow-worshippers as possible.*

They knelt on or stood before the step in front of the railings. The priest came to each one and, placing a piece of bread in his or her up-turned palm, said '*NAME*, the body of Christ, broken for you, bring you to eternal life' and each person responded 'Amen'.

What we see here is consent. The presider does not issue his line as a challenge or a question, but as a presentation. By juxtaposing the statement 'the body of Christ' with the person's name, the priest makes explicit that it is the relationship between the individual, the body and its brokenness that is being presented. The worshipper responds, 'Amen': i.e. it is, so be it. We are at a moment beyond negotiation.

CPU 1:   *Consent is conditional upon recognition of one's relationship to the broken body.*
CPU 2:   *The promise of eternal life is the source of hope.*

A Case Study of Geographically Marginal Worship

I was first alerted to the idea of geographical location as a marginalising force by the Donegal artist John Martin Cunningham, who curated an exhibition entitled 'Death by Geography' in his hometown of Ardara.[52] Cut off from the transport infrastructure, there are several spots on the western coastline which, like Donegal, suffer economically due to their physical location. They also, inevitably, suffer socially with higher rates of unemployment and emigration than the rest of the country. They are also marginal because of their distance from the media of communication in the east of the country, and this includes alienation from the perceived centre of the Roman Catholic church in Ireland, to the extent that several parishes lack a priest while other priests refer to a mission in an outlying parish as a

---

[52]   See A. Dunne, 'Death by Geography', *The Irish Times* (14th May 2000).

'punishment posting'.[53] Some of these communities are marginalised further by having retained Irish as their ordinary language. The parish I chose, which was in Connemara, is not served regularly by public transport, is two hours from the nearest city, is entirely Irish-speaking and loses most of its children to work in England and America, there being little industry in the area.

Every single word uttered and written and sung in this ritual was in the Irish language. For the purposes of this essay, it has been necessary to translate all but the most obvious phrases.

Coming through the door of *Teach Pobail*, (the Irish for 'the church' is 'the People's House') which stands right beside the edge of the Atlantic ocean, the assembling congregation each took a newsletter and an order of service from a pile on a tall plinth. A recording of a woman *sean-nós* singer was playing through the stereo and one could also hear the sound of water coming from the rock pool built in the sanctuary. The altar, in the centre of the nave, with pews on all four sides, contained a mass of daffodils and a large lighted candle. There were candles and daffodils in the low windows around the church and very low electric light overhead. People knelt without talking to one another, all in the pews that faced the front of the altar.

The music was turned off, the lights raised and the priest came out of the sacristy to stand behind the altar. He began by saying three times that we were very, very welcome, and invited us 'to join with the brave girls in singing'. Two women came and stood, backs to the congregation, at a microphone to the right of the altar. Music played over the stereo and they started to sing *'Fáilte Romhat'*. By the second verse, most of the congregation had quietly joined in. The words, which are about gathering beside the sea and encountering Jesus, repeat four times the refrain 'Welcome inside'.

The priest said the opening prayer and raised his hand to his forehead to begin to make the sign of the cross; as he did so the entire congregation said *'In ainm an Athar agus an Mhic agus an Spioraid Naoimh. Amen'*. In the order of service which most people were looking down at, the priest was meant to say the first part and laity just 'Amen'. A woman came to the lectern at the side of the altar and read the readings and the psalm and this was performed as dictated by the order of service, except that after the end of the second reading she said, 'It's the Alleluia' and the congregation all stood up and read together the verse prescribed for her alone to say.

The woman went to stand with her family and the priest moved to the lectern to read the gospel. The microphone suddenly did not work. He said, 'Would you look at that.' There was gentle laughter and he moved back behind the altar to read the gospel. And read it he did. He looked down at it all the time, following the words with his finger and sometimes faltering over the pronunciation. The

---

[53] Rosita Boland reports the phrase used by Fr. Kevin Hegarty. *The Irish Times Magazine* (8th April 2001).

congregation were also looking very hard at the papers in front of them, not one looking up. At the end he said, quietly, 'This is the gospel of God' and one or two people out of a gathering of about a hundred said, 'Praise to you, Christ'.

The Creed was one of the most joined-in verbal parts of the Mass, with everyone saying it out loud, but it was hard to hear the congregation because the priest was saying it aloud into the working microphone. At its end, he started the prayers of the faithful which he made up on the spot and ended each time with 'Lord hear us' to which the people said, heartily, 'Lord graciously hear us'. These complete, four people came forward with small bags and started to pass them around to collect money. There was silence apart from the sound of falling coins. The priest began the offertory prayer and the people did not say any of the three responses written for them, but the priest did. The sound of money was heard right through till the end of the prayer. It was impressive then, when the Eucharistic prayer began, that the responses to each and every part were said strongly.

It also came as a surprise, after the 'Our Father' when the whole gathering said the prayer designated for the priest to say 'Lord Jesus Christ, you said to your apostles, I leave you peace....' They said the whole thing, and offered one another a handshake before being invited to do so by the priest. They did not, however, say anything as they shook hands, but, while still handshaking, began to sing the 'Lamb of God'.

During communion, people came forward in single file to a woman Eucharistic minister who offered a small wafer host to each person and, while an altar girl held a gold plate under each person's mouth, whispered, 'Body of Christ'. No-one responded that I could hear. After communion the priest made several parish announcements, placed a Mothers' Day card made by a girl sitting in the foremost pew on the front of the altar and invited us to sing a hymn to Mary, '*A Mhuire Mháthair*.' People joined in, but very quietly.

At the end of Mass, the priest said the final blessing '*Go raibh an Tiarna libh*' to which the people replied '*Agus leat fein*'; '*Go mbeannai Dia uilechumhachtach sibh, Athair, Mac agus Spiroid Naomh*' and instead of responding with 'Amen', people picked up their coats and bags and as he continued, '*Ta an t'Aifreann thart. Imigi faoi shiochain*', the majority of people, instead of saying the '*Buichos le Dia*' scripted for them, turned and left. Half the congregation had left the building before the priest had bowed to the altar and turned to go to the sacristy. In the small narthex there was a low hum of 'hello's and 'windy night's but three minutes after the final blessing everyone had left the vicinity.

Analysis as Communicative Action

He began by saying three times that we were very, very welcome, and invited us 'to join with the brave girls in singing'. Two women came and stood, backs to the congregation, at a microphone to the right of the altar. Music played over the stereo and they started to sing '*Fáilte Romhat*'. By the second verse,

most of the congregation had quietly joined in. The words, which are about gathering beside the sea and encountering Jesus, repeat four times the phrase 'Welcome inside'.

The welcome the priest offered to the congregation is responded to with the singing of a hymn of welcome, the words of which act as a welcome on several levels: welcoming oneself, welcoming one another, welcoming Christ. It is a drawing together, a *rightness* claim and challenge to prove appropriateness, to create a way of acting 'inside' that is created by the process of welcoming. It makes explicit the knowledge that it is not possible to be an assembly if there is no welcome. And it makes explicit that it is not enough for the presider to welcome the congregation; the whole group must engage in words of welcome.

CPU 1:   *There must be welcome.*
CPU 2:   *Welcome cannot be taken for granted; must be stated, affirmed between all interacting parties: congregation and God and presider.*

the entire congregation said '*In ainm an Athar agus an Mhic agus an Spioraid Naoimh. Amen*'. In the order of service which most people were looking down at, the priest was meant to say the first part and laity just 'Amen'.

This is the first example of a feature that will be apparent in the way the liturgy is described: on several occasions the congregation said words assigned to the priest and on others neglected to say words ascribed to them. It raises a *trustworthiness* claim, a challenge to the priest having the licence to lead certain key prayers. (It can be seen again in the grace, after the 'Our Father'.) In this case, it seems resolved: priest and people say this trinitarian opening statement, and its Amen, together. The words thus stated form a consent, a statement of purpose which all bring about through stating it.

CPU: *The synopsis of faith, the sign of the cross, must be presented mutually - cannot be presented by one alone.*

She said 'It's the Alleluia' and the congregation all stood up and read together the verse prescribed for her alone to say.

It is not the priest alone whose right to say certain lines is refused. Here a laywoman is similarly challenged. The congregation all say the words, but the woman reader persists in speaking her lines through the microphone, so her voice is heard over the congregation. Habermas alerted us to look at what is said and this often directed us to look at who is saying it and the power issues that may be made manifest there; but we have not encountered before the need to look at who speaks loudest! Here it was certainly a factor worthy of note: the woman asserted her right to lead the words by using the microphone. [Incidentally, the woman said 'It's the alleluia'; does the fact of her saying that make it an alleluia despite the fact it was Lent and according to the texts prescribed for Roman Catholic worship there is no alleluia in Lent? I have no way of knowing if this 'incorrectness' between what was on their sheets and what the woman said had a bearing on the congregation's questioning the trustworthiness of this leader, or whether it is their normal practice to say the full gospel antiphon. All I can report is that she was challenged.]

CPU: *Leadership must be negotiated within the ritual.*

He looked down at it all the time, following the words with his finger and sometimes faltering over the pronunciation. The congregation were also looking very hard at the papers in front of them, not one looking up. At the end he said, quietly, 'This is the gospel of God' and two or three people out of a gathering of about a hundred said 'Praise to you, Christ'. The Creed was one of the most joined-in verbal parts of the Mass, with everyone saying it out loud.

This is a refusal of consent, a dissent. A verbal statement of consent-formation is met with little to no response. The priest is not a native-speaker of Irish (there are too few native-speaking priests to serve all the native-speaking parishes) although he is obviously trying very hard. The type of Irish spoken in this parish is not one with a history of being written, so the Irish written on the sheets is 'school Irish'. The way that many of the words look on the page is unfamiliar. The priest's pronunciation stumbles and his inflection is monotonous. Instead of telling a story he is reading some words. The fact that immediately afterwards the congregation said the Creed so heartily indicates that it was not merely a lack of voice that prevented their saying the response; rather the congregation refused to say the response because this did not count as a 'the gospel of God'.

CPU: *Resistance and critique must be negotiated within the ritual.*

The priest began the offertory prayer and the people did not say any of the three responses written for them, but the priest did. The sound of money was heard right through till the end of the prayer. It was impressive then, when the Eucharistic prayer began, that the responses to each and every part were said strongly.

The priest says both his part and the congregation's. As with the preceding fragment, here the congregation refuses their lines one minute, but says them loudly and clearly the next. This is no accident. There is a relationship between the audible collection of their money and their refusal to assent to the offertory of bread and wine. Communicative interaction breaks down at the obvious level at this point, with the priest saying the congregation's part in their place. However, the priest is maintaining communicative action in terms of audible address to God. The effect is that it becomes isolated, a private prayer of the priest to God, compared to the very public prayer that ensues as the Eucharistic responses begin.

Here the priest over-rides the congregation's resistance and speaks on their behalf. Canonically it may be perfectly legitimate, but in terms of communicative action it is an act of violation, a distortion.

a woman Eucharistic minister who offered a small wafer host to each person and, while an altar girl held a gold plate under each person's mouth, whispered, 'Body of Christ'. No-one responded that I could hear.

The fact that no one responded verbally, by saying the customary 'Amen' or anything else, leaves us with a similar situation to that experienced with the gospel: a seeming lack of consent. However, in this case it is more ambiguous, because the act of taking the host and eating it is itself a form of consent - a consent to eat. It is also ambiguous because, during the sign of peace, while people shook hands and smiled at one another, no-one that I could hear said anything to accompany the gesture, and this would indicate that this is not the only one-to-one interaction that is conducted non-verbally.

This is very hard to analyse as communicative action, not because it is non-consensual, but because the Habermasian model is insufficiently developed for non-verbal interpretation.

At the end of Mass, the priest said the final missa *'Go raibh an Tiarna libh'* to which the people replied *'Agus leat fein'*; *'Go mbeannai Dia uilechumhachtach sibh, Athair, Mac agus Spiroid Naomh'* and instead of responding with 'Amen', people picked up their coats and bags and as he continued, *'Ta an t'Aifreann thart. Imigi faoi shiochain'*, the majority of people, instead of saying the *'Buichos le Dia'* scripted for them, turned and walked to the door. Half the congregation had left the building before the priest had bowed to the altar and turned to go to the sacristy.

For this congregation, the interaction of the liturgy between themselves as a body and the priest is confirmed when he says 'The Lord be with you' and they reply 'And also with you'. This couplet is itself a *rightness* claim, affirming the appropriateness of the words of the priest, and putting in place a very direct acknowledgement of mutual interaction. Had the people not spoken their line, the priest could not have said it for them as he did above, this being a direct address by priest to people not by priest (on behalf of people) to God. Imagine: 'The Lord be with you'; 'And also with me'!

It functions as a *rightness* claim because it has indicated the appropriateness of ending at this point; it has deemed the interaction ended. This congregation which so wholeheartedly asserted a trinitarian truth claim at the start of their gathering now neglect to repeat the same at the end. Instead they say this couplet and, it having indicated the end, leave.

CPU: *It is over when it is over, when mutuality stops (and that is at different times for different people, not when a script says it should stop).*

Preliminary Outcomes

At the risk of stating the obvious, there were significant differences between the rituals of the different communities studied. It is worth this risk in order to counter any naïveté (in either the eulogising or disparaging tendencies of previous studies) which lumps all marginal peoples together. The groups encountered above were marginal by dint of differing social, cultural, individual and historic conditions vis-à-vis their relation to the broader-based Christian churches and these are, inevitably, reflected in their rites. Consequently we should not be surprised that where for feminists the notion of blessing was pivotal, the people of the Irish-speaking parish put on their coats and turned to leave while the priest offered a blessing. Likewise, the condition made explicit in this parish that the sign of the cross must be stated *en masse* was not found elsewhere.

It would be tempting, in a eulogising sort of way, to say that 'marginal communities are more spontaneous in their worship than mainstream ones' because a spontaneous thing often happened; but this would be flawed not only on the grounds that the Church of Ireland parish did not exhibit this spontaneity, but also because it is too broad a conclusion, too great a generalisation to be drawn from this study. This has not been a study of all marginal locations nor of all mainstream ones (not that either would be possible). What can be said has to be limited to these communities, to the specifics of their particular interactions and where patterns are discerned they may be used to point to potential 'universals' but they are not such of themselves.

To see these patterns more clearly, I have correlated the various emerging conditions of possible understanding which were most commonly exhibited in the following figure:

Figure 3

In and through interaction:	CofI	Ecum	Fem	IrP	Gay
Diversity is acknowledged and accepted	Y	Y	Y	X	Y
There is an emphasis on Welcome	Y	Y	Y	Y	Y
Blessing of gathering is pivotal	Y	X	Y	X	Y
Stories are told by other-than-presider	Y	Y	Y	Y	Y
Emphasis on remembrancing	Y	Y	Y	Y	Y
Emphasis on Listening (not just sermon)	Y	Y	Y	Y	Y
Ample greeting of one another	Y	Y	Y	Y	Y
Everyone is present at the table	Y	Y	Y	X	Y
'Amen' spoken at communion	Y	Y	Y	X	Y
Critique/dissent expressed	Y	Y	Y	Y	Y
Leadership negotiated within ritual	Y	Y	Y	Y	Y
Emphasis on accessibility & mutuality of symbols	Y	Y	Y	X	Y
Something involving all happened spontaneously	X	Y	Y	Y	Y
Verbal participation essential	Y	Y	Y	Y	Y
Awkward moments happened	Y	Y	Y	Y	Y

To draw these together in but one possible way I note that, in common to all cases, the predominant action was *listening* in a context of *welcome*. What was heard were *stories* and the voices of *one another*. What was required in the liturgy was *critical engagement* with the stories heard, an engagement which was prompted by a series of interactions of *remembrance* and which need not always go smoothly: it involved *awkward moments* and constant *re-negotiation of leadership* roles.

The pattern that emerges can be identified as a manifestation of radical intersubjectivity. The points in each ritual that were accessible as communicative action reveal a thoroughgoing pre-understanding that God is encountered not *primarily* in the bread or the table but in interaction with one another, that point where self and other are mutually constituting: this is the precondition of access to bread, table, word, bath, whatever, where, of course, God is also engaged. But God is not engaged in these 'elements' in the sense that God metaphysically inhabits them, rather God's is the body that is nourished by eating the bread, and this body is found (only) in the bodies of those involved in the ritual.

A Habermasian approach does not facilitate examination of the non-verbal and this presented itself as a serious constraint regarding two particular aspects of the investigation. Firstly, the emotional-intuitive aspect of faith as it is expressed in ritual is crucial to it, and this has been ignored. Secondly, particularly in the Irish-speaking church, there was an abundance of art in and around the church, all of it commissioned by, and/or actually made by, the local congregation. It was frustrating to have no means within the model of critically engaging with this; but it is equally frustrating to read studies that report visual pieces of art in religious settings but do so without accurate regard for the reactions they actually elicit in the worshipping community. In interview with community members in the Irish-speaking parish, I realised that the extraordinary abstract crucifix sculpture by Isobel Stuart that I thought expressed so much about the situation of the community will actually be removed by the time this book is printed, such is the disgust felt about it. This highlights for me that while Habermas's model, and this essay, is remiss in its neglect of such factors, we currently have no alternative method by which to make representative comment about how any non-verbal element operates interactively.

The consequence of a mandate to examine 'what was said' involves the constraint that one cannot look at *everything* that was said. While it is hoped that the analysis is representative, no claim is being made that it is in any sense exhaustive. With this point in mind, it is necessary to relate the results of this analysis to the question that is central to the methodology I have developed for redefining sacramental theology, expressed by Lathrop as, 'What does the actual worship of that assembly say about God?' The following, final, chapter attempts to answer that question.

Chapter Six

Conclusions

You are the body of Christ; that is to say, in you and through you the method and
work of the incarnation must go forward. You are to be taken, you are to be
consecrated, broken and distributed, that you may become the means of grace and
vehicles of the eternal charity.[1]

Having developed an epistemology aimed at accessing religious ritual and applied
it to the liturgies of various Christian communities, the first question that presents
itself is that of liturgical theology: what does the actual worship of these assemblies
say about God?[2] Following a summary and exposition of what the six case studies
disclosed, I will assess the implications of this liturgical theology for the
development of an interpretative framework in which to define the notion of
sacrament.

It is impossible to form a theological interpretation of the data deriving
from the Roman Catholic parish in the west of Ireland discussed in Chapter Four
because the dominant type of interaction in play was one of systematically distorted
communication. Conventional liturgical theology would look at the texts prescribed
for this service and ignore the fact that, in practice, many of them were performed
differently than scripted (or even not at all), limiting the scholar to a theology based
on what *ought* to have happened (rather than what did happen). The Habermasian
approach to language-use developed in this study was designed to access the 'is' of
a worship event instead of the 'should be' or 'could be' of it. In this case it exposed
a reality that would be obscure to textual analysis, wherein ritual participants were
involved in a damaging power-play of muting and repression. There were a few
moments of consensus-forming and several occasions of dissent-negotiation, but
these were too infrequent to provide enough evidence for any particular imagery of
relationship with God.

One might then conclude that the God of this assembly is a God of
systematically distorted communication: that the worship of this community implies
that God is a manipulative, domineering power who will not listen to the people

---

[1]   Augustine.

[2]   This is to paraphrase Gordon Lathrop, for whom liturgical theology is: 'the search for
words adequate to what the actual worship of that assembly says about God'. G.W.
Lathrop, *A Holy People: A Liturgical Ecclesiology* (Minneapolis: Augsburg/Fortress
Press, 1999) 5.

who worship. Such an analysis would profoundly challenge the Christian ideas of God as essentially 'good' and God's presence in worship as essentially emancipative. However, to draw this conclusion would be to misunderstand the most basic premise of Habermas's theory: where communicative action is blocked, *nothing* can be genuinely communicated, neither a 'good' nor a bad, nor even an 'indifferent' image of God or of anything else. When communicative action is denied, it is not accidentally so; the affect of systematically distorted communication is distortion and this is prohibitive of interpretation. Only where there is openness to the other in discourse can language mediate that which is inherently communicative within it. Systematically distorted communication in a *liturgical* context is, therefore, idolatrous: it may claim to communicate a God of compassion and love, a God of justice and forgiveness, but it is actually mediating only the hierarchical power relations of a human institution.

In the case studies examined in Chapter Five, there were several instances of breakdown in communicative action, but they were not sufficient in number, consistency or affect to warrant a perception of *systematically* distorted communication. Moreover, the people involved in the transactions that comprised these five liturgies repeatedly engaged in argumentations which, by being redeemed, made explicit several strong, mutually-composed ethics, norms and aspirations - there was communicative action. In terms of theological 'content', that is, the question of God, there were both common themes and striking variations between these communities. In common to all those assemblies studied, based on the conditions of possible understanding that were exposed as operative in their rituals (see Figure 3), was a depiction of a God who is welcoming, who embraces diversity in creation and in human politics, who is known primarily through listening (listening to the stories of others), who expects critique and dissent, who is remembered in a great variety of ways, and who is known through awkward moments and spontaneous gestures as much as through prescribed texts, movements and sounds.

Yet the most prominent common understanding made explicit in the analysis of these case studies is the assertion that God is present through (interaction with) one another. All five communities share an idea of God as a presence felt in and through the interaction of people with one another and with the things of the earth (water, bread, wine, fire, light), a presence which is affirmed in the moments when consent between those people and this earth is expressed and reached, but which is also assumed to be accessible, manifest and at play in the many consensus-forming processes that comprise these ritual practices. The conclusion to this experiment in liturgical theology is, therefore, an acknowledgement that not only is God (a) known in and through interaction, but also that (b) God *is* interaction.

Claiming that God is known in and through human interaction is not new. Rahner, for example, contended that the 'transcendental experience of God' cannot be mediated except through the 'human "Thou"',[3] leading him to posit a unity between love of God and love of neighbour.[4] Rahner's concern was to emphasise the deeply incarnational nature of God's engagement in the world, the extent to which God can only be known when understood as a *presence* in worldly encounters: 'this, however, is only present originally and totally in the communication with a "Thou".'[5] The consequence of starting with the experience of human interaction, of believing that God is mediated through others, opens up the possibility of a Christology that, like Chauvet's, starts not with the hypostatic union but with Easter.

It also accords with Peukert's proposition that, 'A theory of human intersubjective interaction in history [can become] the hermeneutical basis for a theory of the Trinity that, even as discourse on God himself, remains a theory of experience.'[6] This is possible because for Peukert human intersubjectivity is an inherently transcendent-tending activity. Perceiving a parallel between Habermas's idea of undistorted communication and his own Rahnerian 'transcendental' conception of fundamental theology, Peukert proposes that communicative action between human beings is the normative condition for doing theology because, 'The determination of the reality of God thus becomes possible in the process of transcending in interaction and in the reality experienced and disclosed within this process.'[7] And so he can conclude: 'The experience of the reality of God is mediated through others.'[8]

Yet the evidence presented by the case studies in Chapters Four and Five would suggest the need for a significant development of Peukert's conclusion. Chapter Four presented an example of a sequence of human interactions that mediated institutionalised power relations but said little of God, and this suggests that the experience of the reality of God is not *necessarily* mediated through others, and not necessarily even through worshipping with others. A more accurate account, suggested by the analysis of the case studies in Chapter Five, is that the reality of God is mediated through *communicative action with* others. Such an amendment serves to militate against the general idea that intersubjectivity is of itself necessarily liberative. This chimes with the results of recent anthropological work (reported in Chapter Two), which understands human ritual practices as essentially no different to the activities that compose the rest of human life and, as

---

3   K. Rahner, *Investigations* Vol. 6 (London: Darton, Longman and Todd, 1974) 245. By placing 'Thou' in inverted commas, Rahner is indicating Martin Büber's sense of the word: i.e., 'Thou' is a construction of the interaction between I and thou; a mere 'you' cannot suffice because it implies two singular subjects - me and you - rather than the intersubjectively construed 'Thou'.

4   Ibid., 247.

5   Ibid., 246.

6   H. Peukert, *Science, Action and Fundamental Theology: Toward a Theology of Communicative Action* (Cambridge, MA: The MIT Press, 1986) 274.

7   Ibid.

8   Ibid.

such, potentially as harmful as they may be emancipatory in effect. This revision, then, echoes Habermas's concern to emphasise that the possibility of the 'transcending' quality of language is only enacted in situations where any and all forms of domination are absent.

However, a more profound amendment is also suggested by my theological interpretations of the marginal worship services. The model of intersubjectivity suggested above by Rahner and Peukert implies a situation of extraordinary communion between interacting subjects, but it does not quite convey the radical intersubjectivity which a Habermasian set of hermeneutics alerted us to recognise in the case studies. According to Habermas, such situations (whereby human beings are presumed to be able to stand in non-objectifying relations to one another) obliterate the very notion of the individual acting subject in favour of an entirely mutually-constituted reality or, as Chauvet would have it, body.

This concept is unique neither to Habermas nor to linguistic philosophy; influenced by Husserl, Büber and Hegel, Merleau-Ponty, Wittgenstein, Mead, Schutz and Habermas have all developed an outline of what can be termed 'radical intersubjectivity'. Crossley discerns four central claims common among these authors in their attempts to propose radical intersubjectivity as a rejection of the conventional subjectivist and objectivist accounts:

> Firstly, ...human subjectivity is not, in essence, a private 'inner world' which is divorced from the outer (material) world; ...it consists in the worldly praxes of sensuous, embodied beings and ...it is therefore public and intersubjective. Secondly, ...subjectivity consists in the first instance, in a pre-reflective opening out onto and engagement with alterity, rather than an experience or objectification of it. Thirdly, ...human action, particularly speech, necessarily assumes a socially instituted form and... this form is essential to its meaningfulness. Fourthly, ...much human action and experience arises out of dialogical situations or systems which are irreducible to individual human subjects.[9]

What makes this position 'radical' is its suggestion that 'human subjectivity [is] necessarily intersubjective.'[10] As indicated in Chapter Three, the means by which Habermas sees understanding as accessible is entirely dependent on an ability to make explicit that which is ordinarily implicit at this level of intersubjectivity. This is because all speech acts are mutually-constituted. As Crossley remarks, 'language, and thus linguistic meaning are based, in the final instance, in shared agreement and understanding concerning the use of utterances. They necessarily depend upon an irreducible agreement "between" people and are always, therefore, radically intersubjective.'[11] Language used in distorted communication

---

[9] N. Crossley, *Intersubjectivity: The Fabric of Social Becoming* (London: SAGE Publications, 1996) 24.

[10] Ibid.

[11] Ibid., 43.

is no less intersubjectively formed, Crossley warns: 'power is parasitic upon intersubjectivity ...it needs intersubjectivity and draws on intersubjectivity to create its effects.'[12]

What the idea of radical intersubjectivity suggests to theology is not so much that God is mediated through communicative action with others, nor that God is the transcendent to which communicative action tends, but that God *is* intersubjectivity. Not that we know God through other people but that we know God as our very relating to each and every aspect of that to which we are related.

There are two immediate consequences to such a claim. Firstly, regarding theology, the notion of the permanent flux, or contingency, of earthly life dictates that nothing of/about God can be held as foundational or fundamental or finite.[13] By suggesting that God is that which is engaged and revealed in the radical intersubjectivity of living organisms, we are faced with the reality that our subjectivity is endlessly intersubjective and, moreover, theological. The very point at which we are formed (in a constant process of formation) is the point/locus of God's presence.

Given that language is the mediator of this formation, we can agree with Chauvet that it is the '*contingent mediation* of a language, a culture, a history' that is 'the very place where the subject comes to its truth.'[14] But the bottom line is that the 'transcendent' is only present in, can only be known through, the concrete mediations of intersubjectivity. In Habermasian terms, this is to reject the notion of context-transcendence in favour of a view of a deeply context-engaged source of transcendence; it is also to accord such a presence more of a *Jetztzeit*, or magic, than the functionality of a linguistified notion of the sacred implies. In theological terms it is to go a step further in a long tradition of incarnational confession whilst rejecting, however, any vestiges of an 'ultimate' concept of God.

By reflecting on worship in this way, the discourse on overcoming metaphysics broached in Chapter One has been extended. Perceiving in the liturgical theology of the cases studied a conclusion that God is radical intersubjectivity, I can agree with Chauvet's understanding that in 'unmasking the

---

[12]   Ibid., 127.

[13]   Maurice Wiles writes that contemporary advocates of the Trinity as, 'the given in terms of which everything else should be interpreted' can make such a claim 'because in a post-modern world you cannot be called on to justify the foundational beliefs from which you choose to begin.' Yet this study has suggested that 'belief', in terms of communicative action, can only be the product of solidarity; so while you may no longer be called on to justify your 'foundational' beliefs, you may nevertheless be called to account by the community in and through which your beliefs are formed. Either way, however, any 'doctrine' is rendered relative rather than given, and the conclusion of this study can therefore agree with that of Wiles: 'All forms of theology need to learn a greater humility, a greater readiness to acknowledge the partial and provisional character of even their most basic convictions.' M. Wiles, 'Theology in the Twenty-first Century', *Theology* 103:816 (Nov/Dec 2000) 408 - 410.

[14]   Chauvet, *Symbol and Sacrament*, 140.

never-elucidated presuppositions of metaphysics, thinkers learn to serenely acquiesce... to the prospect of never reaching an ultimate foundation, and thus orient themselves in a new direction - inasmuch as this is possible - starting from the uncomfortable non-place of permanent questioning.' The evidence from the case studies would, however, amend this with the suggestion that the place of non-questioning is as liberative as it is uncomfortable, thus avoiding any entirely pessimistic connotations. But more significantly, comparison of the outcomes of this study with those of Chauvet also raises the following question: despite rejecting the possibility of any ultimate foundation, Chauvet advances a 'fundamental' theology; it is therefore necessary to ask whether a liturgical theological acknowledgement of God as radical intersubjectivity (as beyond any singular ultimate foundation/definition) precludes 'fundamental' theological reflections?

Chauvet's proposal is for a *'foundational'* or 'fundamental theology of sacramentality'[15] which he qualifies as 'a reinterpretation of the whole of Christian life from the viewpoint of sacramentality.'[16] Yet the evidence he presents to support his claim that 'as we change our view of humanity, we necessarily and concurrently change our view of God as well'[17] seems to contradict this. The distinction Chauvet is making is that while (the symbolic mediation of) God is contingent and therefore without ultimate foundation, the actual symbolic nature of our relationship with God has a 'bottom line' in the sacraments of the church (and hence, also, in the Trinitarian Christology he perceives them to reveal) which forms the foundation of our relationship with God. Thus the proposal is made that while God has no ultimate foundation, Christian faith in God is founded on certain fixed things (the sacramental celebrations of the ecclesial body).

The outcome of the analysis of the liturgies of marginal Christian communities presented above suggested that God is intersubjectivity and this accords with Chauvet's understanding of the 'mediation of language... as the ever-open place where the true nature of what we are in relations with others and with God may become reality.'[18] Nevertheless, in the diversity of their conditions of possible understanding, the liturgies studied also present a strong challenge to the claim that any particular mode of interpretation can be fixed or 'fundamental'. It might be proposed, therefore, that the work of overcoming metaphysics will not be complete until theology itself acquiesces to the variety and contingency of God's mediation in the world and loses its desire or claims to be fundamental. However, this would be to significantly underestimate the extent to which *Christian faith*, rather than other senses of the transcendent, is founded on something specific: the

---

[15] L.M. Chauvet, *Symbol and Sacrament: A Sacramental Reinterpretation of Christian Existence* (Collegeville, MN: Liturgical Press, 1995) 1.

[16] Ibid., 4

[17] Ibid.

[18] Ibid., 41.

Pasch of Christ. It is one thing to argue that there is no ultimate foundation called God; quite another to argue that faith has no foundations.

Even still, it may be wise for Christian theologians to hold fire on issuing 'fundamental' or 'foundational' theologies when the actual *experience* of that which is foundational to Christian faith remains so varied. It has been noted several times in this study that what is fundamental to some is sexist to others (seen for example in Ross's criticisms of Chauvet above). In liturgical theology, what is 'foundational' is the experience of engaging in liturgy but, as has been demonstrated, this engagement can occur in a wide variety of ways, with the corollary of a wide variety of theologies.

Common to all accounts presented here, however, is a strong ethic of *tradition as a foundation* for liturgical celebration. Such a designation, based as it is on tradition in a broad sense, is not without conflict: what some claim as Christian tradition, others see as heresy. For example, the feminist liturgy presented in Chapter Five may be criticised by 'high' church liturgical theologians for its lack of adherence to an established *ordo* of Christian worship (i.e.: it didn't use ordinary Christian language); or the gay men's liturgy may be criticised for its separatism and secrecy (i.e.: its lack of openness to fellow Christians). Yet all the groups studied preserve a strong sense that they are operating on the basis of the Christian worshipping traditions: a particular theology may not be 'foundational', but faith has to be founded on something. If God is construed as radical intersubjectivity, this conveys a second immediate consequence: the current polarisation of tradition and invention (or 're-invention') reported in Chapter Five must be seen to represent an unhelpful and inaccurate split.

Several interpretative themes emerge from reflection on these immediate consequences, themes which may signal a direction for further study. Regarding Christology, the liturgical exposure of God as radical intersubjectivity was arrived at via an embodied encounter with a, therefore, embodied God. The God that is bodied-forth as the 'product' of these symbolically-mediated gatherings of Christians is embodied nowhere other than in the multiple intersubjective relations of those gatherings. This echoes the meditations of Augustine on the interaction, 'Body of Christ:' 'Amen'. However, where Augustine could affirm that the ecclesial body, the body of God thus identified, was identified with 'Church',[19] some of the communities studied in Chapter Five report considerable tensions with regard to ecclesiology.[20] This study suggests that the ethic of radical

---

[19]   Augustine, Sermon 272 (*PL* 38:1246 - 1248); Sermon 227 (*PL* 38:1099 - 1101).

[20]   It may be suggested that the controversy over who is or is not 'church', i.e.: over what in fact the church is, has parallels with the medieval controversy over that other central Christian symbol, the Eucharist. Concluding her survey of the practice of the Eucharist in England in the Middle Ages, Miri Rubin writes that these five centuries tell, 'a story of ongoing emergence and appropriation, of symbols which speak differently to different people. It is the story of the emptying and replenishing of meaning in symbols which were sometimes shared and sometimes divergent, and the necessity of this being so.'

intersubjectivity resolves this tension in the notion of a continuum of intersubjectivity between all who gather to worship.

Such a continuum would demand that those who are currently seen as marginal would be acknowledged as only *relatively* so, a change in perspective that would highlight a base-line of commonality and mutual connection rather than difference or heterodoxy. Practices vary, God is endlessly bodied forth in various ways, but the body that is God, the radical intersubjectivity of all that lives, has been liturgically encountered as radically inclusive. Accordingly, Christians would be accepted as entirely self-identifying: held by the authority embodied in the memories/stories they tell and listen to and the imagination (and therefore embodiment) of a world founded on the justice of God.

Accordingly, what 'saves' is that which is 'redeemed'. Redeemed universal truth claims put in place redeemed relationships. This takes on particular significance for Christian soteriology because the kind of redemption enacted in Christian worship has as its ultimate appeal an ethic of justice modelled on a life of following Christ. Thus, where the Other is encountered in the intersubjective formation of liturgy, stories, gestures, symbols, acts and prayers from the Christian tradition mediate that Other to itself in such a way that the relationship between self and Other is redeemed. The vision of relationship thus created, by being realised in language-exchange, continues and adds to the historical tradition formed by all those who have followed Christ.

This dialogical negotiation, entered into using the memories of liturgical tradition (embodied in stories, gestures, symbols and meals) but developed according to human creativity, fosters an endlessly vibrant truth claim about the presence it simultaneously creates and envisages in the world: the presence of an intersubjectivity that enables redemption. This emerged as one of the most significant outcomes of Chapter Four, a particularly Habermasian contribution to the Christian notion of eschatology: the proposition that liturgies create eschatology anew each time they are celebrated.

In terms of theology's use of ritual studies this may suggest a potential avenue for resolving the question of ritual power raised in Chapter Two. Given the fact that ritual theory was reported now to pay attention to 'ritualization' rather than to any preconceived idea of ritual, 'The power of ritual is thus far more local, strategic, messy, imprecise, ordinary, flexible, ambiguous and indeterminate'[21] than previously thought; and this raises the question of, to paraphrase Mitchell, 'how religious power, ritually expressed, can create religious truth'.[22] The Habermasian

---

Perhaps in the future we can say of the Church today as Rubin does of the Eucharist in the late Middle Ages: 'it became the receptacle of power as well as a way of challenging power'. M. Rubin, *Corpus Christi: The Eucharist in Late Medieval Culture* (Cambridge: Cambridge Univeristy Press, 1991) 361.

[21] N.D. Mitchell: *Liturgy and the Social Sciences* (Collegeville, MD: Liturgical Press, 1999) 89.

[22] Ibid.

epistemology adapted above suggests that this 'power' is in fact created dialogically, intersubjectively. And so it is neither the ritual location nor the rubrics that produce a peculiar manifestation of religious truth; it is the way people behave in that location and with those rubrics - their intersubjectivity.

In terms of cosmology, such a radically intersubjective eschatological vision, traditionally known as God's realm, necessarily involves the whole of creation (reflected in the fact that in all five marginal communities either real bread and wine were shared by all or else water could be heard, touched and drunk in the worship space. In all mainstream churches visited for this study, no fragment of the earth's sustenance, be it bread, wine or water, was honoured or consumed by the worshippers).

Finally, regarding doxology, the question that emerges is: if, as suggested above, God is present in the very intersubjective formation of identity, then what is special about worship apart from the fact that this conclusion has been reached through accessing and interpreting the worship of specific communities? Is this (an argument of convenience) sufficient to claim, following Chauvet, that the worship of the church institutes the identity of Christians or even that, as for Pickstock, only in the liturgy is there meaning? Contemporary ritual studies repeatedly assert that it is very difficult to substantiate a theory that ritual acts are, as a genre of activity, discrete from all other genres of human activity. For Grimes they are 'ordinary acts extraordinarily practiced',[23] and others will not even say so much, arguing, as reported in Chapter Two, that little is actually known about if and how ritual is separate from other practices. In a Christian context therefore, could it be proposed that all life is doxology, or is there some special way in which ritual affords an experience of radical intersubjectivity and of God?

It is perhaps here that the notion of sacrament is most useful. Contrary to those authors who collapse 'sacrament' into 'liturgy', suggesting that the distinction between the two has all but disappeared, I contend that while it is important to consider a whole network of practices (a liturgy) as the sacrament (rather than an isolated ordinance or magical moment), it is nevertheless important to retain a distinction between liturgy and sacrament. The word 'sacrament' conjures something quite particular about the level of connection or the quality of relationship between self, community, earth and God that the word 'liturgy', with its associations of doing work, does not. As Rowan Williams suggests, 'A Christian community involved in activities it calls "sacramental" is a community *describing* itself in a way that is importantly at odds with other sorts of description.'[24] The work of worship is to bring people together to do actual, concrete, symbolic work, it is a specific form of the work of human ritualising; the work of sacrament (Aquinas's question, what is it *for*?) is to move us beyond our ordinary ideas of 'work' to a presentation of a web of connectivity which was otherwise obscure.

---

[23] R.L. Grimes, *Deeply Into the Bone: Re-inventing Rites of Passage* (Berkeley, CA: University of California Press, 2000) 346.

[24] R. Williams, *On Christian Theology* (Oxford: Blackwell Publishers, 2000) 208

'The way in which [sacraments] are epiphanies of the sacred,' writes Williams, 'is by their reordering of the words and images used to think or experience social life.'[25] It is this 'reordering', with its dual sense of 'commissioning' and 'putting in place a different order', negotiated at a social level, that defines the notion of sacrament that has emerged from this study.

The word 'defines' is, however, problematic because intrinsic to the notion of sacrament as a permanent process of reordering (reordering through the mediation of words and sounds and images which are, by nature, endlessly contingent) is the implication that it cannot be 'defined': it is, rather, endlessly contingent. 'Definitions' only make sense if one adopts an instrumentalist approach to the subject - indeed only if one sees the sacraments as objects. In an early presentation of this research a colleague asked, 'What is wrong with Dix's definition: sacraments are an outward sign of inward grace ordained by Jesus Christ by which grace is given to the soul?' In brief, Chauvet would protest at the distinction made between outward and inward, noting that such a metaphysical dualism serves to mask the way in which sacramental experience, like all symbolic mediation, operates at a holistic level.[26] Segundo would almost certainly point out the way in which this definition supports a damaging 'bank deposit' economy of salvation whereby grace needs to be 'accrued' by the individual for 'the soul' to be saved. Chauvet would add, perhaps, where is the soul if not the body? Ross may ask why sacraments should be restricted to being 'ordained' by Jesus Christ when this has resulted in the ordination of men and the prohibition on the ordination of women in several churches, and she would point out the difficulties in seeing 'the' seven, or two, sacraments as normative for forming this definition. Feminist liturgical theologians may report that not all that they have experienced as sacramental in liturgy was 'ordained by Jesus Christ' in the strict sense,[27] although their identity as Christians would have been embodied in their liturgies. All points support the thesis of this study, but perhaps the most basic is that 'defining' sacraments in the first place imposes an extraordinary limitation on the potential 'epiphanies of the sacred', those moments of awareness of God's radical intersubjectivity in the world.[28]

---

[25] Ibid.

[26] 'The body is *the primordial place of every symbolic join of the 'inside' and the 'outside'*... [It] is the *binding*, the space in the middle where both identity and difference are symbolically connected under the authority of the Other.' Chauvet, *Symbol and Sacrament*, 147.

[27] Dix was referring to Christian doctrine's demand that the sacramental act is traceable to a biblical precedent. This has fostered some controversy over the years, and results in Catholics recognising seven sacraments, where many Protestants, objecting that there is no direct precedent in Christ's acts for five of these acts, recognise only two: Baptism and Eucharist. For a discussion of this subject, see: M. Hellwig, 'Christian Sacraments' in M. Eliade, ed., *The Encyclopedia of Religion* 12 (New York: Macmillan, 1986) 504 - 510.

[28] Wiles supports such a position: 'The more our theology eschews the language of confident definition and acknowledges the imaginative outreach that characterises what

Applying Habermas's communicative ethics to liturgical theology fosters an idea of sacrament which rejects any fixed notion of what a sacrament 'should be' or 'could be', preferring instead to focus on sacrament as a way of describing what 'is'. What it is, or was, for the five communities studied in Chapter Five was, necessarily, felt differently by each person in each place; however, in common to all five, the sacrament experienced in their gathering was a series of connected moments of consensus. What was being consented to in all cases was openness to the Other, acceptance of the truth of the Other, belief in the stories of the Other, and a statement of utter connectivity between one's self and that Other. It was a moment beyond ritual, a moment of redemption, a moment of radical intersubjectivity deeply and utterly expressed in terms of the ethic of justice that meeting as Christians involves.

Was it Trinitarian? It is tempting to see in these outcomes a straight and strong parallel with the Trinitarian formulations that are so emphasised at present in the theological world. Such a parallel would be evidenced not only in the fact that four of the five communities used Trinitarian metaphors for God in their worship but also that the idea of radical intersubjectivity has much in common with the notion of God as indescribable except as utter relationality: thus seen not as three separate persons but as the 'intersubjectivity' of those persons. Indeed, for most of the course of this research I expected to elaborate a Trinitarian liturgical theology as its conclusion. However, the nuanced outcomes of the study do not support such a parallel.

Firstly, and most obviously, for feminist Christians even when the actual language of Trinitarian naming (Father, Son and Holy Spirit) is translated into non-gendered or feminine vocabulary (e.g.: Source-Sophia, Christ-Sophia, Spirit-Sophia[29]), the form mimics the exclusively male form (indeed, is identical to it) and for some this renders the form itself androcentric and thus problematic.[30] However, and secondly, even though this feminist discussion has arisen largely in response to liturgical experiences, it remains at the level of doctrinal speculation. Looking not *at* the metaphor but at *how* the metaphor is *used* has suggested that often what is being communicated in its use is not about naming God at all. For example, apparent in the usage of the sign of the cross in the case studies is the fact that the 'Trinitarian formula' is spoken in order to negotiate leadership, to dissent

---

it attempts to say, the closer it stands to the proper practice of of worship and devotion.' 'Theology in the Twenty-first Century', 411.

[29] This particular synthesis is the basis of Elizabeth Johnson's construction of a feminist Trinitarian theology: *She Who Is: The Mystery of God in Feminist Theological Discourse* (New York: Crossroad, 1992) 124 - 187.

[30] Although many feminist Christians, as reported in Chapter One, do not agree with this interpretation, arguing that the relationality to which the three-fold naming points transcends any patriarchal form. See, R.C. Duck and P. Wilson-Kastner, *Praising God: The Trinity in Christian Worship* (Louisville: Westminster John Knox, 1999).

from prescribed roles in favour of more equable ones, to convey a sense of blessing/refuse a sense of blessing and to issue a request to listen.

God's presence is recognised not so much in the poetic referentiality of the words - a theological statement of relationality - but by locating God in the midst of the messy negotiations in which people are engaged as they fumble for words adequate to the task. This is not to say the use of Trinitarian formulas has nothing to do with relating to God, on the contrary; but it is to stress that the nature of that relating, the level at which it occurs, is entirely contingent on its practical, liturgical use, not its doctrinal merit.

It is also important, thirdly, to reflect the outcome that many of the moments of consensus and many of the processes of consensus were conducted through language that was not Trinitarian. This is significant because it challenges the idea that specific Trinitarian formulae are *normative* to Christian faith. The memory of Christ through the stories of his followers and the invocation of the Spirit of God are practices that tradition recognises as base-line conveyers of authority; but an *obligatory* formula is a deeply anti-intersubjective notion (and thus anti-liturgical, in this revised sense) because it says nothing of the demands communicative action will make upon it.

Having surveyed the theological outcomes of the case studies, it is necessary to assess the value and limitations of using Habermas in this endeavour. Habermas's theory of communicative action provided this research with an outline methodology which promised to afford *access* to human interaction, to make explicit that which was implicit. In the absence of any specific methodological framework, one was adapted on the basis of Habermas's description of the process of raising and redeeming validity claims in order to expose the possible conditions of universal understanding. The model was entirely appropriate to Christian liturgy, a forum in which all speech acts are observable. Considering the fact that such a modelling was unprecedented and therefore highly experimental, it produced some remarkable results: the analysis did indeed make explicit conditions of understanding that were previously implicit (considered above) and, in doing so, served the purposes of liturgical theology well.

Two serious constraints in the model were, however, repeatedly encountered: firstly, although Crossley insists that emotional information can easily be integrated into a Habermasian analysis, in practice this proved an inexact science and the emotional content of interactions remained largely obscure. It would be helpful if scholars were to develop Crossley's arguments into a workable interpretative model, as the lack of integrated emotional information renders any conclusions issuing from liturgical acts partial.

Secondly, as was reported in the interpretation of the case studies, a large proportion of the embodied reality of the liturgy (e.g.: gestures, movements, visual art, seating-style, non-linguistic symbols, smells, sounds and music) lay, frustratingly, beyond the scope of analysis. While it is acknowledged that the verbal should be studied as behaviour (and not as text), it will nevertheless be important in developing this epistemology to find an accurate way of accessing the non-verbal.

'Accurate' is emphasised as a challenge to the many liturgical theologians (high church, feminist and otherwise) who wax lyrical about the meaning of symbols or the feel of space-arrangements without addressing the question of what those things 'mean' or 'feel like' to other worshippers and the associated, essential, question of how they would access this knowledge.

A further recurring constraint in the thesis was the immaturity of theories of ritual and ritualizing. Chapter One reported the trend in theology, particularly among liturgical theologians, to privilege ritual as uniquely disclosive of Christian faith because of the purportedly different way it operates as a genre of behaviour. Chauvet, Power, Ross, Kavanagh, and Kelleher all claim that the way Christian symbols 'work' is by harnessing ritual power, that is, they work *sacramentally* because of their rituality. The underlying theory - that ritual affords a 'magic' that other genres of human interaction do not - is seriously questioned not just by the ritual theorists discussed in Chapter Two, such as Staal, Asad and Bell, but also by Habermas's contention that *all* situations of communicative action are, by virtue of their inherent ideal speech situation-forming tendencies, potential harbingers of a context-transcendent realisation.[31] Certainly the application of the Habermasian model to the fieldwork data above, while designed with Christian liturgy in mind, did not need adjustment of any sort in order to relate to a supposedly 'special' context wherein the sacramentality of relationship with God was accomplished in a peculiar way. On the contrary, such a relationship was discovered through the most familiar of human interactions: language usage.

In order for this study to consider the question of whether or not ritual as a genre affords Christian faith a unique and discrete conduit it would have had to be a comparative study (i.e.: comparing ritual contexts to others). However, even if it were comparative, it would still have encountered difficulties in advancing any such claim because cross-cultural perspectives on the issue are so various. This is largely due to ritual theory being such a new subject of discourse. Prior to the late twentieth century it was taken for granted that ritual 'did' something special; however, the development of post-colonial critiques pointed out that the evidence used to make such a claim was often based on an imperious view taken by the scholar. Liturgical theology must take heed and proceed with caution. Worship may afford access (to theology) for the scholar, just as it concurrently affords access (to God) for the believer, but, as it pertains to scholarship, this is an argument based on 'convenience' (the convenience of it being a *public* discourse; how could scholars access the theology of a person saying their bedtime prayers in their private house?) rather than, as claimed, any special properties of ritual itself. One piece of research that is therefore urgently needed, whether in a Christian or a non-Christian context, is a comparative study of the outcomes of analysing 'ritual' and non-ritual

---

[31] See also: G. Steiner, *Real Presences* (London: Faber and Faber, 1989): 'This essay argues a wager on transcendence. It argues that there is in the art-act and its reception, that there is in the experience of meaningful form, a presumption of presence.' 214.

situations; only then can more be understood about the boundaries and powers of these purportedly strange acts.

Until such a time, the (liturgical) theology of sacrament must take as its starting point, its subject, an interpretative framework rather than an instrumental reality. This revision of the very notion of sacrament has within it certain strong interpretative guidelines. While it does not take seven or two sacraments, or any other numerical objectification of them, as normative, thus allowing the possibility of seven times seventy-seven of them, the traditions of practice of the two (Baptism and Eucharist) held in common by all denominations provide an essential sense of continuity and thus authority to contingent mediations of sacrament in various liturgies. Knowledge of the remarkable and manifold ways in which these traditions have evolved over the years simultaneously elicits a reminder that the continuity and authority of practice is conditional upon its ability to be creatively mediated by each assembly.

These two guidelines themselves form an interpretative framework which can be described in various ways - tradition and evolution, faithfulness and creativity, memory and imagination. Their function as a hermeneutic pairing would have been impossible to discern without the attention given in this study to the margins of the institutional church, because it is there that the tensions between the two guidelines are at their most acute. Marginal worship does not always 'work', it may not always be 'sacrament'; but it is all the more liturgical for trying (and, as was seen in Chapter Four, mainstream worship does not always 'work' either). It is also all the more Christian for trying, as it struggles to ensure that Christianity's key institutions – the symbols by which faith is constantly formed – are prevented from becoming 'remote from the practical meaning of the Christian message'. Worship that preserves the tension between memory and imagination does this by restoring to these key institutions their self-understanding *as* the Christian message.

The ethic of memory ensures that the stories of the suffering people of history are told and heard. The ethic of imagination ensures that an appropriate, a recognisable, a 'valid' connection is being made between those stories and the contingencies of contemporary life. The dialectic between the two ensures that the Christ of history, as known through the stories of his followers, is experienced in and through interaction with the Other of the present context. Memory tempers imagination with the memory of injustice and suffering, militating against any illusion of impunity. Imagination tempers memory with the freedom to grow, to become co-creative, to embody rather than just to body-forth. Both together indicate the possibility of a radical intersubjectivity that can and does redeem. And without either the theology of liturgy cannot be experienced as sacrament.

In conclusion then, this study has located sacramental theology within liturgical theology and confirmed liturgical theology's need to continue its dialogue with the social sciences in order to understand better the nature of its medium: ritual. In this interdisciplinary context it resolved the question of access latent in liturgical theology by developing a model of Habermasian communicative ethics appropriate to the study of ritual. The application of this theory to the data compiled in fieldwork reports of Christian liturgy, particularly that occurring at the margins of the church, furnished a strong sense in which sacramental theology may be considered *as* the doctrine of God.

As such, this 'doctrine' has been rendered dependent on the contingent mediations of language and symbol, and is consequently both multi-faceted and ever-changing. While rejecting an absolute parallel with the doctrine of the trinity, this study nevertheless highlights the similarities between the radical intersubjectivity exposed in the case studies and the metaphor of relationality the trinity conveys. This study did not discover that the doctrine of God was 'entirely' contingent; on the contrary, it took as an indispensable guide the traditions of liturgical practices that the contingent mediations of language and symbol in Christian contexts embody and honour. Sacraments - and therefore doctrines - were seen to be known in practice through the twin forces of memory and imagination. The notion of sacrament thus discovered in communities at the margins of the church was one known as a moment of utter connection with a God of justice deeply embodied in the relationships of all living things. It was 'known' by an interactive, intersubjective imaginative act.

Appendix

The Case Study of a Liturgy in a Church in the West of Ireland

Methodology

I attended and recorded (in detailed note form) four liturgies in this same church over a period of four months between 2000 and 2001. I chose this particular liturgy because there was more interaction between the presider and congregation than in the other three liturgies, when, for example, several of the major congregational prayers were omitted.

To enable me to estimate the percentages of responses, given that this was a large church with a capacity of about 1,000, I divided the seats into a grid, with each block consisting of 20 seats, and positioned myself in such a way that I had a good, clear view of four blocks, since I had found that this was the maximum number of people that I could monitor when, as on this occasion, approximately half of the seats were occupied. This would then enable me to divide the number of responses by four and multiply by the total number of blocks, since the congregation was usually fairly evenly distributed, to arrive at an estimate of the total number of responses and render this as a percentage of the total number of people present (approximately 500).

I placed myself at the front of a block of seats that were in a raised position at the very front of the church and side-on to the rest of the congregation. This gave me a particularly good view of four front blocks of the congregation who were in the main body of the church. At the particular liturgy chosen these front blocks seemed to contain no more and no less people than any other blocks, with about half the seats being occupied.

In addition to what I could see, there was the information deriving from what I could hear and the acoustics in that part of the church were particularly good, so that I could easily distinguish between the voices beside and behind me and those in front of me, coming from people whose faces I could also see.

The following figure illustrates how the percentages were calculated:

Figure 3

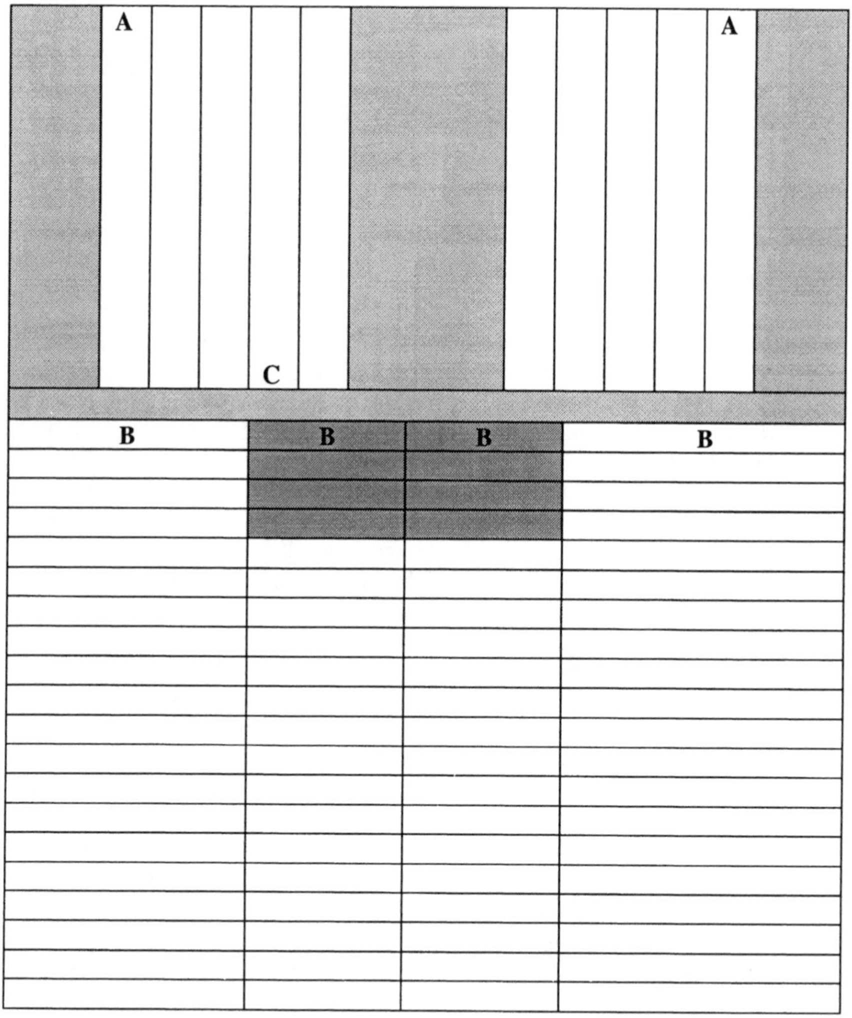

Key:
A = Each cell represents 20 people
B = Each cell represents 10 people
C = Position of observer

Altar and aisle space

People observed

Bibliography

Adams, C.J., and M.M. Fortune, eds., *Violence against Women and Children* (New York: Continuum, 1995).

Aichele, G., and T. Pippin, eds., *Violence, Utopia and the Kingdom of God: Fantasy and Ideology in the Bible* (London: Routledge, 1998).

Albright, W.F., *From the Stone Age to Christianity: Monotheism and the Historical Process* (Baltimore: John Hopkins Press, 1946).

Alexander, R.C., 'Televangelism: Redressive Ritual within a Larger Social Drama' in S. Hooker and K. Lundby, eds., *Rethinking Media, Religion and Culture* (Thousand Oaks, CA: Sage Publications, 1997).

Anderson, H., and E. Foley, *Mighty Stories, Dangerous Rituals: Weaving Together the Human and the Divine* (San Francisco: Josey-Bass Publishers, 1998).

Apel, K.O., 'Openly Strategic Uses of Language: A Transcendental-Pragmatic Perspective' in P. Dews, ed., *Autonomy and Solidarity: Interviews with Jürgen Habermas* (London: Verso, 1992).

Apostolos Cappadona, D., *Creativity and the Sacred* (New York: Crossroad 1984).

Aquinas, T., 'Treatise on the Sacraments', *Summa Theologiae* Vol. 3, Blackfriars Translation (London: Burns and Oates, 1966).

Arens, E., *Habermas und die Theologie* (Dusseldorf: Patmos Verlag, 1989).

Arens, E., *Theology after Habermas: An Introduction* (New York: Union Theological Seminary Library, 1992).

Arlen, S., *The Cambridge Ritualists: An Annotated Bibliography of the Works by and about Jane Ellen Harrison, Gilbert Murray, Francis M. Cornford, and Arthur Bernard Cook* (Metuchen, NJ: Scarecrow Press, 1990).

Asad, T., *Genealogies of Religion: Disciplines and Reasons of Power in Christianity and Islam* (Baltimore, MD: John Hopkins University Press, 1993).

Asad, T., ed., *Anthropology and the Colonial Encounter* (New York: Humanities Press, 1973).

Auer, J., *The Church: The Universal Sacrament of Salvation* (Washington, DC: Catholic University of America Press, 1993).

Aune, M.B., 'To Move the Heart' in *Rhetoric and Ritual in the Theology of Philip Melanchthon* (San Francisco: Christian Universities Press, 1994).

Aune, M.B., 'The Subject of Ritual: Ideology and Experience in Action' in M.B. Aune and V. DeMarinis, eds., *Religious and Social Ritual: Interdisciplinary Explorations* (Albany, NY: State University of New York Press, 1996) 147 - 174.

Austin, J.L., *How to Do Things with Words* (New York: Oxford University Press, 1962).

Avila, R., *Worship and Politics* (Maryknoll: Orbis Books, 1981).

Axtell, R.E., *Gestures: The Do's and Taboos of Body Language around the World* (New York: John Wiley, 1991).

Babcock, B.A., ed., *The Reversible World: Symbolic Inversion in Art and Society* (Ithaca, NY: Cornell University Press, 1978).

Balasuriya, T., *The Eucharist and Human Liberation* (Maryknoll: Orbis Books, 1979).

Barth, K., *The Epistle to the Romans* (London: Oxford University Press, 1933).

Bell, C., *Ritual Theory, Ritual Practice* (New York: Oxford University Press, 1992).

Bell, C., *Ritual Perspectives and Dimensions* (New York: Oxford University Press, 1997).

Bell, C., 'Ritual, Change, and Changing Rituals', *Worship* 63:1 (1989) 31-41.

Bell, C., 'The Authority of Ritual Experts', *Studia Liturgica* 23:1 (1993) 98 - 120.

Bell, C., 'Modernism and Postmodernism in the Study of Religion', *Religious Studies Review* 22:3 (July 1996) 179 - 190.

Bellah, R.N., *Beyond Belief: Essays on Religion in a Post-traditional World* (New York: Harper and Row, 1970).

Bellah, R.N., et al, *Habits of the Heart: Individualism and Commitment in American Life* (New York: Harper Row, 1986).

Benhabbib, S., *Critique, Norm and Utopia: A Study of the Foundations of Critical Theory* (New York: Columbia University Press, 1986).

Benhabbib, S., and F. Dallmayr, *The Communicative Ethics Controversy* (Cambridge: MIT Press, 1990).

Berger, T., *Liturgie und Frauenseele* (Stuttgart: Verlag W. Kohlshammer, 1993).

Berger, T., *Women's Ways of Worship: Gender Analysis and Liturgical History* (Collegeville, MN: Liturgical Press, 1999).

Berger, T., 'Liturgy - A Forgotten Subject-Matter of Theology?', *Studia Liturgica* 17 (1987) 10 - 18.

Berger, P.L., *The Sacred Canopy: Elements of a Sociological Theory of Religion* (New York: Doubleday, 1967).

Berger, T., 'Liturgy and Theology - An Ongoing Dialogue', *Studia Liturgica* 19 (1989) 14 - 16.

Berger, T., '"Separated Brethren" and "Separated Sisters": Feminist and/as Ecumenical Visions of the Church' in D.S. Cunningham, et al, *Ecumenical Theology in Worship, Doctrine and Life: Essays Presented to Geoffrey Wainwright on his Sixtieth Birthday* (Oxford: Oxford University Press, 1999).

Bernstein, J.M., *Recovering Ethical Life: Jürgen Habermas and the Future of Critical Theory* (London, New York: Routledge, 1995).

Bloch, M., *Ritual, History and Power: Selected Papers in Anthropology* (London: Athlone Press, 1989).

Boal, A., *Theatre of the Oppressed* (New York: Theatre Communications Group, 1985).

Boff, C., *Theology and Praxis: Epistemological Foundations* (Maryknoll: Orbis Books, 1987).

Boff, L., *Sacraments of Life, Life of the Sacraments* (Beltsville, MD: Pastoral Press, 1987).

Bohmann, J., 'On Political Theology' in H. Peukert, *Science, Action and Fundamental Theology: Toward a Theology of Communicative Action* (Cambridge, MA: MIT Press, 1986) vii - xxii.

Borgmann, A., *Crossing the Postmodern Divide* (Chicago: University of Chicago Press, 1992).

Boswell, J., *Marriage and Likeness: Same Sex Unions in Pre-modern Europe* (New York: HarperCollins, 1994).

Bourdieu, P., *Outline of a Theory of Practice* (Cambridge: Cambridge University Press, 1977).

Bourdieu, P., *In Other Words: Essays Toward a Reflective Sociology* (Stanford, CA: Stanford University Press, 1990).

Bourdieu, P., *The Logic of Practice* (Stanford, CA: Stanford University Press, 1990).

Bouyer, L., *Rite and Man: Natural Sacredness and Christian Liturgy* (Lanham, MD: University Press of America, 1963).

Bowie, F., *The Anthropology of Religion* (Oxford: Blackwell, 2000).

Braaten, J., 'From Communicative Rationality to Communicative Thinking' in J. Meehan, ed., *Feminists Read Habermas: Gendering the Subject of Discourse* (New York: Routledge, 1995).

Bradshaw, P.F., *Daily Prayer in the Early Church* (New York: Oxford University Press, 1982).

Bradshaw, P.F., *The Search for the Origins of Christian Worship: Sources and Methods for the Study of Early Liturgy* (London: SPCK, 1992).

Bradshaw, P.F., and B. D. Spinks, eds., *Liturgy in Dialogue: Essays in Memory of Ronald Jasper* (London: SPCK, 1993).

Brand, A., *The Force of Reason: An Introduction to Habermas's Theory of Communicative Action* (Sydney: Allen and Unwin, 1990).

Brown, D., and A. Loades, eds., *The Sense of the Sacramental: Movement and Measure in Art and Music, Place and Time* (London: SPCK, 1995).

Brown, D., and A. Loades, eds., *Christ: The Sacramental Word* (London: SPCK, 1996).

Brown, P., *The Cult of the Saints: Its Rise and Function in Latin Christianity* (Chicago: University of Chicago Press, 1981).

Browning, D.S., *Practical Theology: The Emerging Field in Theology, Church and World* (New York: Harper and Row, 1971).

Browning, D.S., and F. Schüssler Fiorenza, eds., *Habermas, Modernity and Public Theology* (New York: Crossroad Press, 1992).

Burghart, W. J., 'A Theologian's Challenge to Liturgy', *Theological Studies* 35 (1974) 233 - 248.

Burke, K., *Language as Symbolic Action: Essays on Life, Literature and Method* (Berkeley: University of California Press, 1966).

Bynum, C. W., *Holy Feast and Holy Fast: The Religious Significance of Food to Medieval Women* (Berkeley: University of California Press, 1987).

Cabié, R., *The Eucharist* (Collegeville, MN: The Liturgical Press, 1986).

Cannon, K.G., *Black Womanist Ethics* (Atlanta: Scholars Press, 1988).

Caron, C., *To Make and Make Again: Feminist Ritual Thealogy* (New York: Crossroad, 1993).

Casel, O., *Mystery of Christian Worship and Other Writings* (Westminster, MD: Newman Press, 1962).

Chauvet, L.M., *Symbol et sacrament: Une relecture sacramentelle de l'éxistence chrétienne* (Paris: les éditions du cerf, 1987).

Chauvet, L.M., *Symbol and Sacrament: A Sacramental Reinterpretation of Christian Existence* (Collegeville MN: Liturgical Press, 1995).

Chauvet, L.M., and F.K. Lumbala, eds., *Concilium: Liturgy and the Body* (London: SCM Press, 1995).

Cheetham, D., 'Postmodern Freedom and Religion', *Theology* 103:811 (Jan/Feb 2000) 29 - 36.

Chopp, R.S., *The Power to Speak: Feminism, Langugage, God* (New York: Crossroad, 1991).

Chupungco, A.J., *Cultural Adaptation of the Liturgy* (New York:Paulist Press, 1982).

Chupungco, A.J., ed., *Handbook for Liturgical Studies: Introduction to the Liturgy* (Collegeville, MN: Liturgical Press, 1997).

Coleman, S., and P. Collins, 'The "Plain" and the "Positive": Ritual, Experience and Aesthetics in Quakerism and Charismatic Christianity', *Journal of Contemporary Religion* 15:3 (October 2000) 317 - 329.

Collins, M., *Worship: Renewal to Practice* (Washington, DC: Pastoral Press, 1987).

Collins, M., 'An Adventuresome Hypothesis: Women as Authors of Liturgical Change', *Proceedings of the North American Academy of Liturgy*, 1993.

Collins, M., 'Principles of Feminist Liturgy' in M. Procter-Smith, and J.R. Walton, eds., *Women at Worship: Interpretations of North American Diversity* (Louisville: Westminster John Knox, 1993) 9 - 28.

Collins, M., 'Is the Eucharist Still a Source of Meaning for Women?' in P.J. Philbert, ed., *Living in the Meantime* (Mahwah, NJ: Paulist Press, 1994).

Collins, M., 'Liturgy for a Laity Called and Sent', *Chicago Studies* 39:1 (Spring 2000) 59 - 78.

Collins, M., and D.N. Power, eds., *Liturgy: A Creative Tradition* (Edinburgh: T and T Clark, 1983).

Congar, Y., *La liturgie après Vatican II* (Paris: Cerf, 1967).

Cooey, P.M., W.R. Eakin, and J.B. McDaniel, *After Patriarchy: Feminist Transformation of the World Religions* (Maryknoll, Orbis Books, 1990).

Cooke, B., *The Distancing of God: The Ambiguity of Symbol in History and Theology* (Minneapolis: Fortress Press, 1990).

Cooke, M., 'Introduction' in J. Habermas, *On the Pragmatics of Communication* (Cambridge, MA: MIT Press, 1998).

Crossley, N., *Intersubjectivity: The Fabric of Social Becoming* (London: SAGE Publications, 1996).

Crossley, N., 'Emotion and Communicative Action: Habermas, Linguistic Philosophy and Existentialism' in G. Bendelow and S.J. Williams, eds., *Emotions in Social Life: Critical Themes and Contemporary Issues* (London: Routledge, 1998).

Cunningham, D.S., R. Del Colle, and L. Lamadrid, eds., *Ecumenical Theology in Worship, Doctrine and Life: Essays Presented to Geoffrey Wainwright on his Sixtieth Birthday* (Oxford: Oxford University Press, 1999).

D'Aquili, E.G., C.D. Laughlin, and J. McManus, *The Spectrum of Ritual* (New York: Columbia University Press, 1979).

Daniélou, J., *The Bible and Liturgy* (London, Darton Longman and Todd, 1960).

David, K.A., *Sacrament and Struggle: Signs and Instruments of Grace from the Downtrodden* (Geneva: W.C.C. Publications, 1994).

de Caussade, J.P., *The Sacrament of the Present Moment* (London: Fount, 1996).

Derrida, J., *L'écriture et la différence* (Paris: Seuil, 1967).

Dews, P., ed., *Autonomy and Solidarity: Interviews with Jürgen Habermas* (London: Verson, 1992).

Dews, P., ed., *Habermas: A Critical Reader* (Oxford: Blackwells, 1999).

Dinges, W.D., 'Ritual Conflict as Social Conflict: Liturgical Reform in the Roman Catholic Church', *Sociological Analysis* 48: 2 (1987) 138 - 158.

Dix, G., *The Shape of the Liturgy* (London: Dacre Press, 1945; New York: Continuum, 2000).

Doty, W.G., *Mythography: The Study of Myths and Rituals* (University, AL: University of Alabama Press, 1986).

Douglas, M., *Natural Symbols: Explorations in Cosmology* (New York: Pantheon Books, 1982).

Douglas, M., *Purity and Danger: An Analysis of Concepts of Pollution and Taboo* (New York: Praeger, 1966).

Douglas, M., 'Deciphering a Meal' in *Implicit Meanings: Essays in Anthropology* (London: Routledge and Kegan Paul, 1975) 249 - 275.

Downey, M., and R. Fragomeni, eds., *A Promise of Presence: Studies in Honour of David N. Power* (Washington, DC: Pastoral Press, 1992).

Doyle, D.M., *Communion Ecclesiology* (Maryknoll: Orbis, 2000).

Doyle, R., *The Woman Who Walked into Doors* (London: Jonathan Cape, 1993).

Driver, T.F., *The Magic of Ritual: Liberating Rites that Transform our Lives* (San Fancisco: HarperCollins, 1992).

Duck, R.C., and P. Wilson-Kastner, *Praising God: The Trinity in Christian Worship* (Louisville: Westminster John Knox, 1999).

Duffy, R., *Real Presence: Worship, Sacraments and Commitment* (San Francisco: Harper Row, 1982).

Duffy, R., 'Justification and Sacrament', *Journal of Ecumenical Studies* 16 (1979) 672 - 690.

Duffy, R., 'The Sacraments' in J. Galvin, and F. Schüssler Fiorenza, eds. *Systematic Theology: Roman Catholic Perspectives* (Minneapolis: Fortress Press, 1991).

Durkheim, E., *The Elementary Forms of the Religious Life* (New York: Macmillan, 1915).

Durkin Dierks, S., *WomenEucharist* (Boulder: WomanWord Press, 1997).

Dussel, E., 'The Bread of the Eucharistic Celebration as a Sign of Justice in the Community', *Concilium* 152 (1989) 56 - 65.

Eagleton, T., *Literary Theory: An Introduction* (Oxford: Blackwell, 1983).

Eiesland, N., *The Disabled God: Toward a Liberatory Theology of Disability* (Nashville: Abingdon Press, 1994).

Elbogen, I., *Jewish Liturgy: A Comprehensive History* (Philadelphia: Jewish Publications Society, 1993).

Eliade, M., *The Sacred and the Profane* (New York: Harper Row, 1957).

Eliade, M., *Myth and Reality* (New York: Harper Row, 1963).

Eliade, M., ed., *The Encyclopedia of Religion* (New York: Macmillan, 1986).

Enninger, W., *An Ethnography-of-Communication Approach to Ceremonial Situations: A Study on Communication in Institutional Social Contexts; The Old Order Amish Church Service* (Wiesbaden: F. Steiner, 1982).

Erikson, E., 'Ontogeny and Ritualization in Man', *Philosophical Transactions of the Royal Society of London*, B 251 (1966).

Everrett, W.J., *The Politics of Worship: Reforming the Language and Symbols of the Liturgy* (Chicago: United Church Press, 1999).

Everrett, W.J., and T. Bachmeyer, *Disciplines in Transformation* (Washington, DC: University Press of America, 1979).

Fabella, V., and M.A. Oduyoye, eds., *With Passion and Compassion: Third World Women Doing Theology* (Maryknoll: Orbis Books, 1988).

Fagerberg, D. W., *What is Liturgical Theology?* (Collegeville, MN: Liturgical Press, 1992).

Fink, P.E., *Worship: Praying the Sacraments* (Washington DC: Pastoral Press, 1991).

Fink, P.E., 'Towards a Liturgical Theology', *Worship* 47 (1973) 206 - 220.

Fink, P.E., ed., *New Dictionary of Sacramental Worship* (Washington, DC: Michael Glazier, 1990).

Flanagan, K., *Sociology and Liturgy: Re-presentations of the Holy* (London: Macmillan, 1991).

Foucault, M., *The Birth of the Clinic: An Archaeology of the Human Sciences* (New York: Pantheon, 1973).

Fox, P.A., *God as Communion: John Zizoulias, Elizabeth Johnson, and the Revival of the Symbol of the Triune God* (Collegeville, MN: Liturgical Press, 2001).

Freire, P., *Pedagogy of the Oppressed* (New York: Continuum, 1970).

Freud, S., *Totem and Taboo* (1912) (New York: W.W. Norton, 1962).

Gaillardetz, R., 'North American Culture and the Liturgical Life of the Church: The Separation of the Quests for Transcendence and Community', *Worship* 68:5 (1994) 403-416.

Ganoczy, A., *An Introduction to Catholic Sacramental Theology* (New York, Paulist Press, 1984).

Gardner, A., *History of Sacrament in Relation to Thought and Progress* (London: Williams and Norgate, 1921).

Geertz, C., *The Interpretation of Cultures* (New York: Basic Books, 1973).

Geertz., C., *The Theater State in Nineteenth Century Bali* (Princeton: Princeton University Press, 1980).

Geertz., C., *Local Knowledge* (New York: Basic Books, 1983).

Geertz, C., *Works and Lives: The Anthropologist as Author* (Stanford, CA: Stanford University Press, 1988).

Geitz, E.R., *Gender and the Nicene Creed* (Harrisburg, PA: Morehouse, 1995).

Girard, R., *Violence and the Sacred* (Baltimore: John Hopkins University Press, 1972).

Glebe-Möller, J., *A Political Dogmatic* (Philadelphia: Fortress Press, 1987)

Glen, J., 'Twenty Years Later: A Reflection on the Liturgical Act', *Assembly* 12:4 (1986) 44 -46.

Goffman, E., *Interaction Ritual* (Garden City, NY: Doubleday, 1967).

Goffman, E., *Frame Analysis: An Essay on the Organization of Experience* (New York: Harper and Row, 1974).

Goodman, F.D., 'A Trance Dance with Masks: Research and Performance at the Cuymaungue Institute', *The Drama Review* 34:1 (1990) 102-114.

Goody, J., 'Against "Ritual": Loosely Structured Thoughts on a Loosely Defined Topic' in S. Falk Moore, and B. Myerhoff, eds., *Secular Ritual* (Amsterdam: van Gorcum, 1977).

Graham, E., 'Words Made Flesh: Women, Embodiment and Practical Theology', *Feminist Theology* 20 (May 1999) 111 - 120.

Granfield, P., *The Church and Communication* (Kansas City, M.O.: Sheed and Ward, 1994).

Grimes, R.L., *Beginnings in Ritual Studies* (Washington, DC: University Press of America, 1982).

Grimes, R.L., *Ritual Criticism: Case Studies in Its Practice, Essays on Its Theory* (Columbia: University of South Carolina Press, 1990).

Grimes, R.L., *Deeply Into the Bone: Re-inventing Rites of Passage* (Berkeley, CA: University of California Press, 2000).

Grimes, R.L., *Reading, Writing and Ritualizing: Ritual in Fictive, Liturgical and Public Places* (Washington, DC: Pastoral Press, 1993).

Grotowski, J., *Towards a Poor Theatre* (New York: Simon and Schuster, 1968).

Grüber, F., *Diskurs und Konsens im Prozess theologischer Wahrheit* (Innsbruck, Wien: Tyrolia, 1993).

Guardini, R., *The Spirit of the Liturgy* (New York: Herder and Herder, 1998).

Guardini, R., 'A Letter', *Herder Correspondence*, Special Issue (August 1964) 237 - 239.

Gunton, C., 'Editorial', *International Journal of Systematic Theology* 2:1 (Mar 2000) 1 - 4.

Gurrieri, J.A., 'Sacraments Shaping Faith: The Problem of Sacramental Validity Today', G. Austin ed., *Fountain of Life* (Washington, DC: Pastoral Press, 1991).

Habermas, J., *Knowledge and Human Interests* (Boston: Beacon Press, 1971).

Habermas, J., *Theory and Praxis* (Boston: Beacon Press, 1973).

Habermas, J., *Communication and Evolution of Society* (Boston: Beacon Press, 1979).

Habermas, J., *The Theory of Communicative Action*, Vol. 1: *Reason and the Rationalization of Society* (Boston: Beacon Press, 1984).

Habermas, J., *The Past as Future* (Cambridge: Polity Press, 1989).

Habermas, J., *Moral Consciousness and Communicative Action* (Cambridge, MA: MIT Press, 1990).

Habermas, J., *The Theory of Communicative Action*, Vol. 2: *Lifeworld and System: A Critique of Functionalist Reason* (Cambridge: Polity Press, 1992).

Habermas, J., *Post-metaphysical Thinking: Philosophical Essays* (Cambridge, MA: MIT Press, 1993).

Habermas, J., *On the Pragmatics of Communication* (Cambridge, MA: MIT Press, 1998).

Habermas, J., *The Inclusion of the Other: Studies in Political Theory* (Cambridge, MA: MIT Press, 1998).

Habermas, J., 'Wahrheitstheorien' in H. Fahrenbach, ed., *Wirklichkeit und Reflexion* (Pfüllingen: Neske, 1973) 256. Translation by S. Benhabbib, *Critique, Norm and Utopia: A Study of the Foundations of Critical Theory* (New York: Columbia University Press, 1986)

Habermas, J., 'Transcendence from Within, Transcendence in this World' in D.S. Browning, and F. Schüssler Fiorenza, eds., *Habermas, Modernity and Public Theology* (New York: Crossroad Press, 1992) 226 - 250.

Habermas, J., ed., *Observations on the Spiritual Situation of the Age* (Cambridge, MA: MIT Press, 1987).

Haring, B., *Trent on the Blessed Sacrament: A Reprint of the Catechism of Trent Dealing with Conciliar Definition* (London: Faith Press, 1920).

Haring, B., *The Sacrament of Reconciliation* (Slough: St Paul Publications, 1980).

Harrison, B.W., *Making the Connections: Essays in Feminist Social Ethics* (Boston: Beacon Press, 1985).

Harrison, J., *Art and Ritual* (New York: Henry Holt, 1913).

Harrison, J., *Epilegomena to the Study of Greek Religion and Themes: A Study of the Social Origins of Greek Religion* (New Hyde Park: University Books, 1927).

Hauerwas, S., 'The Self as Story: Religion and Morality from the Agent's Perception', *Journal of Religious Ethics* 1:1 (1973) 73 -85.

Heidegger, M., *Apprôche de Hölderlin* (Paris: Gallimard, 1962).

Heidegger, M., *Being and Time* (New York: Harper, 1962).

Heidegger, M., 'Dépassement' in *Essais et conférences* (Paris: Gallimard, 1958).

Heidegger, M., 'L'être-essentiel d'un fondement ou "raison"' in *Essais et conférences* (Paris: Gallimard, 1958).

Heidegger, M., 'L'homme habite en poète' in *Essais et conférences* (Paris: Gallimard, 1958).

Hellwig, M., *The Eucharist and the Hunger of the World* (Chicago: Theological Book Service, 1992).

Hellwig, M., 'Christian Sacraments' in M. Eliade, ed., *The Encyclopedia of Religion* 12 (New York: Macmillan, 1986) 504 - 510.

Hellwig, M., 'Twenty-five Years of a Wakening Church: Liturgy and Ecclesiology' in L.J. Madden, ed., *The Awakening Church: Twenty-five Years of Liturgical Renewal* (Collegeville, MN: Liturgical Press, 1992).

Henley, N., *Body Politics: Power, Sex and Nonverbal Communication* (New York: Simon and Schuster, 1977).

Hess, D.J., 'The New Ethnography and the Anthropology of Science and Technology', *Knowledge and Society* 9 (1992).

Hesser, G., and A.J. Weigert, 'Comparative Dimensions of Liturgy: A Conceptual Framework and Feasibility Application, *Sociological Analysis* 41:3 (1980) 215 - 229.

Hillman, J., *The Myth of Analysis* (New York: Harper and Row, 1972).

Hobsbawm, E., and T. Ranger, eds., *The Invention of Tradition* (Cambridge: Cambridge University Press, 1983).

Hodgson, P., *God in History: Shapes of Freedom* (Nashville: Abingdon Press, 1989).

Hoffman, L.A, *Beyond the Text: A Holistic Approach to Liturgy* (Indianapolis: Indiana University Press, 1987).

Hoffman, L.A., *The Art of Public Prayer: Not for Clergy Only* (Washington, DC: Pastoral Press, 1988).

Holmes, U.T., 'Theology and Religious Renewal', *The Anglican Theological Review* 62 (1980) 3 - 19.

Honneth, A., and H. Joas, eds., *Communicative Action: Essays on Jürgen Habermas's The Theory of Communicative Action* (Cambridge: Polity, 1991).

hooks, b., *Teaching to Transgress: Education as the Practice of Freedom* (New York: Routledge, 1994).

Horton, R., *Patterns of Thought in Africa and the West* (Cambridge: Cambridge University Press, 1993).

Houssiau, A., 'La liturgie, lieu privilegie de la theologie sacramentaire', *Questions liturgiques* 54 (1973) 2 - 14.

Houssiau, A., 'La redécouverte de la liturgie par la theologie sacramentaire (1950 - 1980)', *La Maison-dieu* 149 (1982) 27 - 52.

Hovda, R., *Strong, Loving and Wise* (Washington, DC: Liturgical Conference, 1976).

Hughes, K., *Finding Voice to Give God Praise: Essays in the Many Languages of the Liturgy* (Collegeville, MN: Liturgical Press, 1998).

Hughes, K., ed., *How Firm a Foundation.Vol. 1: Voices of the Early Liturgical Movement* (Chicago: Liturgy Training Publications, 1990).

Humphrey, C., and J. Laidlaw, *The Archetypal Actions of Ritual* (Oxford: Oxford University Press, 1994).

Hus, J., 'On Simony' in M. Spinka, ed., *Advocates of Reform: From Wyclif to Erasmus* (Philadelphia: Westminster, 1953).

Ingram, D., *Critical Theory and Philosophy* (New York: Paragon House, 1990).

Ingram, D., *Habermas and the Dialectic of Reason* (New York: Paragon House, 1987).

Irwin, K., *Liturgical Theology: A Primer* (Collegeville, MN: Liturgical Press, 1990).

Irwin, K., *Context and Text: Method in Liturgical Theology* (Collegeville MN: Pueblo Press, 1994).

Irwin, K., 'Sacramental Theology: A Methodological Proposal', *The Thomist* 54:2 (April 1990) 311 - 342.

Isasi-Díaz, A.M., '*Mujerista* Liturgies and the Struggle for Liberation' in L.M. Chauvet, and F.K. Lumbala, eds., *Liturgy and the Body* (London: SCM Press, 1995).

James, W., *The Varieties of Religious Experience* (Cambridge: Cambridge University Press, 1902).

Jay, N., *Throughout Your Generations Forever: Sacrifice, Religion and Paternity* (Chicago: University of Chicago Press, 1992).

Jennings, T.W., *Life as Worship: Prayer and Praise in Jesus's Name* (Grand Rapids: Eerdmans, 1982).

Jennings, T.W., *The Liturgy of Liberation: The Confession and Forgiveness of Sins* (Nashville: Abingdon Press, 1988).

Johnson, E.A., *She Who Is: The Mystery of God in Feminist Theological Discourse* (New York: Crossroad, 1992).

Johnson, E.A., *Friends of God and Prophets: A Feminist Theological Reading of the Community of Saints* (New York: Continuum, 1998).

Johnson, M.E., ed., *Between Memory and Hope: Readings on the Liturgical Year* (Collegeville, MN: Liturgical Press, 2000).

Jones, G., *Critical Theology: Questions of Truth and Method* (Cambridge: Polity Press, 1995).

Jung, C.J., 'The Mass and the Individuation Process', *The Black Mountain Review* 5 (Summer 1955) 90 - 147.

Jungmann, J., *The Mass of the Roman Rite: Its Origins and Development* 2 Vols (New York: Benzinger, 1950).

Jungmann, J., *The Mass* (Collegeville, MN: Liturgical Press, 1974).

Kapadia, K.M., 'Hindu Marriage as a Sacrament' in *Marriage and Family in India* (Oxford: Oxford University Press, 1966).

Kavanagh, A., *The Shape of Baptism: The Rites of Christian Initiation* (New York: Pueblo Books, 1978).

Kavanagh, A., *Elements of Rite: A Handbook of Liturgical Style* (New York: Pueblo Books, 1982).

Kavanagh, A., *On Liturgical Theology* (Collegeville, MN: Liturgical Press, 1984).

Kavanagh, A., 'The Role of Ritual in Personal Development' in J. Shaughnessy, ed., *The Roots of Ritual* (Grand Rapids: Eerdman, 1973) 145 - 160.

Kavanagh, A., 'Liturgy and Ecclesial Consciousness: A Dialectic of Change', *Studia Liturgica* 15:1 (1982) 2 - 17.

Kearney, R., *The Poetics of Imagining: From Husserl to Lyotard* (London: Harper Collins, 1991).

Kelleher, M.M., 'The Communion Rite: A Study of Roman Catholic Liturgical Performance', *Journal of Ritual Studies* 5:2 (Summer 1991) 99 - 122.

Kelleher, M.M., 'Liturgy as Source for Sacramental Theology', *Questions Liturgiques* 72 (1991).

Kelleher, M.M., 'Sacraments as the Ecclesial Mediations of Grace', *Louvain Studies* 23 (1998) 180 - 197.

Kertzer, D.I., *Ritual, Politics and Power* (New Haven: Yale University Press, 1988).

Kilmartin, E., *Christian Liturgy: Theology and Practice. I: Systematic Theology of Liturgy* (Kansas City: Sheed and Ward, 1988).

Kirby, E.T., *Ur-Drama: The Origins of Theatre* (New York: New York University Press, 1975).

Kotkavirta, J., ed., *Problems of the Communicative Rationality: Proceddings of the Habermas Colloquium in Jyväskylä* (Jväskylä yliopisto: Filosofian laitos, 1987).

Kristeva, J., *Language - The Unknown: An Initiation into Linguistics* (New York: Columbia Univeristy Press, 1989).

LaCugna, C.M., *God For Us: The Trinity and Christian Life* (San Francisco: Harper San Francisco, 1991).

Ladriere, J., 'The Performativity of Liturgical Language', *Concilium: Liturgical Experience of Faith* (New York: Herder and Herder, 1973) 50 - 56.

Laing, R.D., *The Politics of Experience* (New York: Ballantine Books, 1967).

Lakeland, P., *Theology and Critical Theory: The Discourse of the Church* (Nashville: Abingdon Press, 1990).

Lane, D.A., *Keeping Hope Alive: Stirrings in Christian Theology* (Dublin: Gill & Macmillan, 1996).

Lang, A., *Magic and Religion* (London: Longmans, 1901).

Lang, A., *The Making of Religion* (1898) (New York: AMS Press, 1968).

Lardner, G.V., 'Communication Theory and Liturgical Research', *Worship* 5 (1977) 299 - 306.

Lash, N., 'Conversation in Gethsemane' in W. Jeanrond and J. Rike, eds., *Radical Pluralism and Truth: David Tracy and the Hermeneutics of Religion* (New York: Crossroad, 1991)

Lathrop, G., *Holy Things: A Liturgical Theology* (Minneapolis: Fortress Press, 1993).

Lathrop, G., *Holy People: A Liturgical Ecclesiology* (Minneapolis: Augsburg/Fortress Press, 1998).

Lawler, M.G., *Symbol and Sacrament: A Contemporary Sacramental Theology* (New York: Paulist Press, 1987).

Leach, E., *Culture and Communication: The Logic by Which Symbols are Connected* (Cambridge: Cambridge University Press, 1976).

Leeming, B., *Principles of Sacramental Theology* (Westminster, MD: Newman, 1960).

Lévi-Strauss, C., *Structural Anthropology* (Garden City, NJ: Doubleday, 1967).

Levinas, E., *Autrement qu'être* (The Hague: M. Nijhoff, 1974).

Lincoln, B., *Discourse and the Deconstruction of Society: Comparative Studies of Myth, Ritual and Classification* (Oxford: Oxford University Press, 1989).

Lincoln, B., *Death, War and Sacrifice: Studies in Ideology and Practice* (Chicago: University of Chicago Press, 1991).

Lincoln, B., *Emerging from the Chrysalis: Studies in Rituals of Women's Initiation* (Cambridge, MA: Harvard University Press, 1991).

Lincoln, B., 'Two Notes on Modern Rituals', *Journal of the American Academy of Religion* 45:2 (1977) 147 - 160.

Lonergan, B., *Method in Theology* (New York, Herder and Herder, 1972).

Luckmann, T., *The Invisible Religion: The Transformation of Symbols in Industrial Society* (New York: Macmillan, 1967).

Lukken, G., 'Liturgy and Language: An Approach from Semiotics', *Questions Liturgiques* 73 (1992).

Macy, G., *The Theologians of the Eucharist in the Early Scholastic Period: A Study of the Salvific Function of the Sacrament According to the Theologians, c. 1080 -1220* (Oxford, Clarendon Press, 1984).

Madden, L.J., ed., *The Awakening Church: Twenty-five Years of Liturgical Renewal* (Collegeville, MN: Liturgical Press, 1992).

Malinowski, B., *Magic, Science and Religion and Other Essays* (1925) (Glencoe, IL: Free Press, 1974).

Marcus, G.E., and M.M.J. Fischer, *Anthropology as Cultural Critique: An Experimental Moment in the Human Sciences* (Chicago: University of Chicago Press, 1986).

Marion, J.L., *God without Being* (Chicago: University of Chicago Press, 1991).

Markham, I.S., *Plurality and Christian Ethics* (New York: Seven Bridges Press, 1999).

Martos, J., *Doors to the Sacred* (New York: Doubleday, 1981).

Masuzawa, T., *In Search of Dreamtime: The Quest for the Origin of Religion* (Chicago: University of Chicago Press, 1994).

Mauss, M., *The Gift: Forms and Functions of Exchange in Archaic Societies* (1925) (London: Cohen and West, 1970).

McCabe, H., *God Matters* (London: Cassell, 1987).

McCarthy, T.A., 'A Theory of Communicative Competence', *Philosophy of Social Sciences* 3 (1973) 135 - 156.

McCarthy Brown, K., '"Plenty Confidence in Myself": The Initiation of a White Woman Scholar into Haitian Voodou', *Journal of Feminist Studies in Religion* 3:1 (1987) 67 - 76.

McCutcheon, R.T., *The Outsider/Insider Problem in the Study of Religion: A Reader* (London: Cassell, 1999).

McFague, S., 'Eschatology: A New Shape for Humanity' in *The Body of God: An Ecological Theology* (Minneapolis: Fortress Press, 1993).

McKenna, J.H., 'Eucharistic Presence: An Invitation to Dialogue', *Theological Studies* 60:2 (June 1999) 294 - 319.

McKenna, M., *Rites of Justice: The Sacraments and Liturgy as Ethical Imperatives* (New York: Orbis, 1997).

McPartlan, P., *The Eucharist Makes the Church: Henri de Lubac and John Zizioulas in Dialogue* (Edinburgh: T. and T. Clark, 1993).

Meehan, J., ed., *Feminists Read Habermas: Gendering the Subject of Discourse* (New York: Routledge, 1995).

Merleau-Ponty, M., *Phenomenology of Perception* (1945) (London: Routledge, 1962).

Metz, J.B., *Faith in History and Society: Toward a Fundamental Theology* (New York: Seabury Press, 1980).

Metz, J.B., *A Passion for God: The Mystical-Political Dimension of Christianity* (New York: Paulist Press, 1998).

Metz, J.B., 'Communicating a Dangerous Memory' in F. Lawrence, ed., *Communicating a Dangerous Memory* (Atlanta: Scholars Press, 1987).

Metz, J.B., and J. P. Jossua, eds., *Concilium 85: The Crisis of Religious Language* (New York: Herder and Herder, 1973).

Milbank, J., *The Word Made Strange: Theology, Language, Culture* (Oxford: Blackwell Publishers, 1997).

Miles, M., *Image as Insight: Visual Understanding in Western Christianity and Secular Culture* (Boston: Beacon Press, 1985).

Miles, M., *Carnal Knowing: Female Nakedness and Religious Meaning in the Christian West* (Boston: Beacon Press, 1993).

Miller, V.J., 'An Abyss at the Heart of Mediation: Louis-Marie Chauvet's Fundamental Theology of Sacramentality', *Horizons* 24:2 (1997) 230-247.

Mitchell, N.D., *Cult and Controversy: The Worship of the Eucharist outside Mass* (New York: Pueblo Publishing, 1982).

Mitchell, N.D., *Eucharist as Sacrament of Initiation* (Chicago: Liturgy Training Publications, 1994).

Mitchell, N.D., *Real Presence: The Work of Eucharist* (Chicago: Liturgy Training Publications, 1998).

Mitchell, N.D., *Liturgy and the Social Sciences* (Collegeville, MN: Liturgical Press, 1999).

Mitchell, N.D., 'Americans at Prayer', *Worship* 66:2 (1992) 177 - 184.

Moltmann, J., *Theology of Hope: On the Ground and Implications of a Christian Theology* (New York: Harper Collins, 1991).

Moltmann, J., *Experiences in Theology: Ways and Forms of Christian Theology* (London: SCM Press, 2000).

Moltmann-Wendell, E., *I Am My Body: A Theology of Embodiment* (New York: Continuum, 1995).

Moore, S.F., and B. Myerhoff, eds., *Secular Ritual* (Amsterdam: van Gorcum, 1977).

Morgan, J.H., *Understanding Religion and Culture: Anthropological and Theological Perspectives* (Washington, DC: University Press of America, 1979).

Morrill, B.T., *Anamnesis as Dangerous Memory: Political and Liturgical Theology in Dialogue* (Collegeville, MN: Liturgical Press, 2000).

Morrill, B.T., *Bodies of Worship: Explorations in Theory and Practice* (Collegeville, MN: Liturgical Press, 2000).

Müller, M., *Chips from a German Workshop* (1869) (Chico, CA: Scholars Press, 1985).

Myerhoff, B., *Number Our Days* (New York: Simon and Schuster, 1978).

Myerhoff, B., 'A Death in Due Time', in J.J. McAloon, ed., *Rite, Drama, Festival, Spectacle* (Philadelphia: Institute for the Study of Human Issues, 1984).

Neill, S., 'Liturgical Continuity and Change' in D. Martin and P. Mullen, eds., *No Alternative: The Prayer Book Controversy* (Oxford: Blackwells Publishers, 1981).

Newman, D.R., 'Observations in Method in Liturgical Theology', *Worship* 57 (1983) 309 - 321 .

Nichols, A., *Looking at the Liturgy: A Critical View of its Contemporary Forms* (San Francisco: Ignatius Press, 1996).

Nichols, A., 'Hymns Ancient and Postmodern: Catherine Pickstock's After Writing', *Communio* 26:2 (1999) 429 - 445.

Northup, L.A., *Women and Religious Ritual* (Washington, DC: The Pastoral Press, 1993).

Northup, L.A., 'Claiming Horizontal Religious Space: Women's Religious Rituals', *Studia Liturgica* 25:1 (1995) 86 - 102.

O'Callaghan, P., *Fides Christi: The Justification Debate* (Dublin: Four Courts Press, 1998).

O'Doherty, C., *Church as Sacrament: The Need for Self-Questioning* (Dublin: Columba Press, 1994).

O'Donovan, O., *Liturgy and Ethics* (Bramcote: Grove, 1993).

Oliver, K., *Ethics, Politics and Difference in Julia Kristeva's Writing* (New York: Routledge, 1993).

Ortner, S.B., 'On Key Symbols' in W.A. Lessa, and E.Z. Vogt, eds., *Reader in Comparative Religion: An Anthropological Approach* (New York: HarperCollins, 1979) 92 - 98.

Otto, R., *The Idea of the Holy* (New York: Oxford University Press, 1929).

Outhwaite, W., ed., *The Habermas Reader* (Cambridge: Polity Press, 1996).

Panniker, R., *Worship and Secular Man* (New York: Orbis, 1973).

Parsons, T., *The Social System* (New York: Free Press, 1951).

Penner, H., 'Language, Ritual and Meaning', *Numen* 32:1 (1985) 1 - 16.

Peukert, H., *Science, Action and Fundamental Theology: Toward a Theology of Communicative Action* (Cambridge, MA: MIT Press, 1986).

Phan, P.C., 'Woman and the Last Things: A Feminist Eschatology' in A. O'Hara Graff, ed., *In the Embrace of God: Feminist Approaches to Theological Anthropology* (Maryknoll: Orbis, 1995) 206 - 228.

Pickstock, C., *After Writing: On the Liturgical Consummation of Philosophy* (Cambridge: Cambridge University Press, 1997).

Pinker, S., *The Language Instinct* (New York: William Morris, 1994).

Power, D.N., *Unsearchable Riches: The Symbolic Nature of Liturgy* (New York: Pueblo, 1984).

Power, D.N., *Sacrament: The Language of God's Giving* (New York: Crossroad, 1999).

Power, D.N., 'Cult to Culture: The Liturgical Foundations of Theology', *Worship* 54 (1980) 482 - 494.

Power, D.N., 'Liturgy as an Act of Communication and Communion: Cultural and Practical Implications in an Age Becoming Digital', *Mission* 3:1 (1996) 43-62.

Power, D.N., 'Sacrament: An Economy of Gift', *Louvain Studies* 23 (1998) 143-158.

Procter-Smith, M., *In Her Own Rite: Constructing Feminist Liturgical Tradition* (Nashville: Abingdon Press, 1990).

Procter-Smith, M., *Praying With Our Eyes Open: Engendering Feminist Liturgical Prayer* (Nashville: Abingdon Press, 1995).

Procter-Smith, M., and J.R. Walton, eds., *Women at Worship: Interpretations of North-American Diversity* (Louisville: Westminster/John Knox, 1993).

Radcliffe-Brown, A.R., 'Religion and Society', *Journal of the Royal Anthropological Institute of Great Britain and Ireland* 75 (1945) 33 - 43.

Radford Reuther, R., *Sexism and God-Talk: Toward a Feminist Theology* (Boston: Beacon Press, 1983).

Radford Reuther, R., *Woman-Church: Theology and Practice of Feminist Liturgical Communities* (San Francisco, Harper and Row, 1986).

Rahner, K., *The Church and the Sacraments* (New York: Herder and Herder, 1963).

Rahner, K., *Theological Investigations* (London: Darton, Longman and Todd, 1974).

Rahner, K., *Meditations on the Sacraments* (London: Burns and Oates, 1977).

Rahner, K., *Foundations of Christian Faith* (New York: Seabury, 1978).

Rahner, K., 'What is a Sacrament?', *Worship* 47 (1973) 206 - 220.

Ramshaw, G., *God Beyond Gender: Feminist Christian God-Language* (Minneapolis: Fortress Press, 1995).

Ramshaw, G., *Liturgical Language: Keeping it Metaphoric, Making it Inclusive* (Collegeville, MN: Liturgical Press, 1996).

Ramshaw, G., *Under the Tree of Life* (Minneapolis: Augsburg/Fortress Press, 1998).

Rappaport, R.A., *Ecology, Meaning and Religion* (Richmond, CA: North Atlantic Press, 1979).

Ratzinger, J., *The Feast of Faith: Approaches to a Theology of the Liturgy* (San Francisco: Ignatius Press, 1986).

Reynolds, R.E., *Law and Liturgy in the Latin Churches, Fifth to Twelth Centuries* (Aldershot: Variorum, 1994).

Ricoeur, P., *The Symbolism of Evil* (New York: Harper and Row, 1967).

Robertson Smith, W., *Lectures on the Religion of the Semites: The Fundamental Institutions* (1889) (New York: KTAV Publishing House, 1969).

Rorty, R., *Contingency, Irony and Solidarity* (Cambridge: Cambridge University Press, 1989).

Rorty, R., *Objectivity, Relativism and Truth* (Cambridge: Cambridge University Press, 1991).

Ross, S., *Extravagant Affections: A Feminist Sacramental Theology* (New York: Continuum, 1998).

Rowland, C., 'Eucharist as Liberation from the Present' in D. Brown, and A. Loades, eds., *The Sense of the Sacramental: Movement and Measure on Art and Music, Place and Time* (London: SPCK, 1995) 200 - 215.

Rubin, M., *Corpus Christi: The Eucharist in Late Medieval Culture* (Cambridge: Cambridge Univeristy Press, 1991).

Ruby, J., ed., *A Crack in the Mirror: Reflexive Perspectives in Anthropology* (Philadelphia: University of Pennsylvania Press, 1982).

Sahlins, M., *Culture and Practical Reason* (Chicago: University of Chicago Press, 1976).

Saliba, J., 'The New Ethnography and the Study of Religion', *Journal for the Scientific Study of Religion* 13 (1974).

Saliers, D.E., *Worship as Theology: Foretaste of Glory Divine* (Nashville: Abingdon Press, 1994).

Saliers, D.E., 'On the "Crisis" of Liturgical Language', *Worship* 44:7 (1970).

Saliers, D.E., 'Prayer and Emotion' in J. Gallen ed., *Christians at Prayer* (Notre Dame: University of Notre Dame Press, 1977).

Saliers, D.E., 'Prayer and the Doctrine of God in Contemporary Theology', *Interpretation* 30 (1980) 265 - 278.

Saliers, D.E., *The Soul in Paraphrase: Prayer and the Religious Affections* (New York: Seabury, 1980).

Sawicki, M., *Seeing the Lord: Resurrection and Early Christian Practices* (Minneapolis: Fortress, 1994).

Schechner, R., *Essays on Performance Theory, 1970 - 1976* (New York: Drama Book Specialists, 1977).

Schechner, R., *Between Theater and Anthropology* (Philadelphia: University of Pennsylvania Press, 1985).

Schechner, R., *Performance Theory* (London: Routledge, 1988).

Schechner, R., *The Future of Ritual: Writings on Culture and Performance* (London: Routledge, 1993).

Schechner, R., and W. Appel, eds., *By Means of Performance* (Cambridge: Cambridge University Press, 1990).

Schillebeeckx, E., *Christ the Sacrament of Encounter with God* (London: Sheed and Ward, 1957; New York: Sheed and Ward, 1963).

Schillebeeckx, E., *Christ: The Experience of Jesus as Lord* (New York: Crossroad, 1981).

Schillebeeckx, E. and B. Van Israel, eds., *Revelation and Experience: Concilium 113* (New York: Seabury, 1979).

Schmemann, A., The World as Sacrament (Crestwood: St Vladimir's Press, 1966).

Schmemann, A., *Introduction to Liturgical Theology* (Crestwood, NJ: St Vladimir's Seminary Press, 1966).

Schmemann, A., *The Eucharist: Sacrament of the Kingdom* (Crestwood: St Vladimir's Press, 1988).

Schmemann, A., 'Theology and Liturgical Tradition' in M.H. Shepherd, ed., *Worship in Scripture and Tradition* (New York: Oxford University Press, 1963).

Schmemann, A., 'Sacrifice and Worship' in T. Fisch, ed., *Liturgy and Tradition: Theological Reflections of Alexander Schmemann* (Crestwood, NY: St Vladimir's Press, 1990).

Schreiter, R.J., 'Edward Schillebeeckx: An Orientation to his Thought' in *The Schillebeeckx Reader* (New York: Crossroad, 1984).

Schüssler Fiorenza, E., *In Memory of Her: A Feminist Theological Reconstruction of Christian Origins* (New York: Crossroad, 1985).

Searle, J., *Speech Acts: An Essay in the Philosophy of Language* (Cambridge: Cambridge University Press, 1969).

Searle, M., 'The Pedagogical Function of Liturgy', *Worship* 55:4 (1981) 332 - 359.

Searle, M., 'Fons Vitae: A Case Study in the Use of Liturgy as a Theological Source' in G. Austin ed., *Fountain of Life* (Washington, DC: Pastoral Press, 1991).

Searle, M., ed., *Liturgy and Social Justice* (Collegeville, MN: Liturgical Press, 1980).

Sedgwick, T.F., *Sacramental Ethics: Paschal Identity and the Christian Life* (Philadelphia: Fortress Press, 1987).

Segundo, J., *A Theology for Artisans of a New Humanity, Vol 4, The Sacraments Today* (Maryknoll: Orbis Books, 1974).

Shaughnessy, J., ed., *The Roots of Ritual* (Grand Rapids: Eerdmans, 1973).

Siebert, R.J., *The Critical Theory of the Frankfurt School: From Universal Pragmatic to Political Theology* (New York: Morton, 1985).

Smith, D.E., and H. Taussig, *Many Tables: The Eucharist in the New Testament and Liturgy Today* (London: SCM Press, 1990).

Smith, J.E., *The Analogy of Experience: An Approach to Understanding Religious Truth* (New York: Harper Row, 1973).

Smith, J.E., *Experience and God* (New York: Harper Row, 1968).

Smith, J.Z., *To Take Place: Toward a Theory in Ritual* (Chicago: University of Chicago Press, 1987).

Sperber, D., *Rethinking Symbolism* (Cambridge: Cambridge University Press, 1975).

Sperber, D., ed., *Metarepresentations: A Multidisciplinary Perspective* (Oxford: Oxford University Press, 2000).

Spretnak, C., ed., *The Politics of Feminine Spirituality: Essays on the Rise of Spiritualist Power within the Feminist Movement* (Garden City, NJ: Doubleday, 1982).

Staal, F., 'The Meaninglessness of Ritual', *Numen* 26:1 (1979) 2 -22.

Staal, F., 'The Sound of Religion', *Numen* 33: 1 (1986) 33 - 64; 185 - 224.

Staal, F., *Rules Without Meaning: Ritual, Mantras and the Human Sciences* (New York: Peter Lang, 1989)

Stamps, M.E., ed., *To Do Justice and Right Upon the Earth: Papers from the Virgil Michel Symposium on Liturgy and Social Justice* (Collegeville, MN: Liturgical Press, 1993).

Steiner, G., *Real Presences* (London: Faber and Faber, 1989).

Taft, R., 'How Liturgies Grow: The Evolution of the Byzantine Divine Liturgy', *Orientalia Christiana Periodica* 43 (1977) 355 - 378.

Taft, R., 'The Structural Analysis of Liturgical Units; An Essay in Methodology', *Worship* 52 (1978) 314 - 328.

Tambiah, S.J., *Culture, Thought and Social Action: An Anthropological Perspective* (Cambridge: Harvard University Press, 1985).

Tambiah, S.J., *Magic, Science, Religion, and the Scope of Rationality* (Cambridge: Cambridge Univeristy Press, 1990).

Tambiah, S.J., 'The Magical Power of Words', *Man* 3 (1968) 175 - 208.

Tambiah, S.J., 'A Performative Approach to Ritual', *Proceedings of the British Academy*, 65 (1979) 113 - 169.

Taylor, M.K., *Beyond Explanation: Religious Dimensions in Cultural Anthropology* (Macon, GA: Mercer University Press, 1986).

Tillich, P., *The Dynamics of Faith* (New York: Harper and Row, 1957).

Tillich, P., 'The Religious Symbol' in R. May, *Symbolism in Religion and Literature* (New York: Braziller, 1960).

Torevill, D., 'Forgetting How to Remember: Performance, Narrative and Embodiment as a Result of the Liturgical Reforms', *Irish Theological Quarterly* 65:1 (Spring 2000) 33 - 42.

Tracy, D., *The Analogical Imagination* (New York: Crossroad, 1985).

Trible, P., *Texts of Terror: Literary-Feminist Readings of Biblical Narratives* (Philadelphia: Fortress Press, 1984).

Trocmé, E., *The Passion as Liturgy: A Study in the Origin of the Passion Narratives in the Four Gospels* (London: SCM, 1983).

Turner, V., *The Forest of Symbols: Aspects of Ndembu Ritual* (Ithaca, NY: Cornell University Press, 1967).

Turner, V., *The Ritual Process* (Chicago: Aldine Press, 1969).

Turner, V., *Image and Pilgrimage in Christian Culture* (New York: Columbia University Press, 1978).

Turner, V., 'Ritual, Tribal and Catholic', *Worship* 50:6 (1976) 504-526.

Turner, V., 'Dewey, Dilthey and Drama: An Essay in the Anthropology of Experience', V.W. Turner and E.M. Bruner, eds., *The Anthropology of Experience* (Urbana: University of Illinois Press, 1986).

Turner, V.E. Turner, ed., *On the Edge of the Bush: The Anthropology of Form and Meaning* (Tucson: University of Arizona Press, 1986).

Ugolnik, A., *The Illuminating Icon* (Grand Rapids: Eerdman's Publishing Co., 1989).

van Gennep, A., *The Rites of Passage* (Chicago: University of Chicago Press, 1960).

Vellian, J., 'Theological Dimensions of Liturgy', *Studia Liturgica* 1:13 (2000).

Villette, L., *Foi et sacrament*, 2 vols (Paris: Bloud et Guy, 1956 - 1964).

Vorgrimler, A., *Sacramental Theology* (Collegeville, MN: Liturgical Press, 1992).

Wach, J., *Comparative Study of Religions* (New York: Columbia University Press, 1958).

Wainwright, G., *Eucharist and Eschatology* (London: Epsworth, 1971).

Wainwright, G., *Doxology: The Praise of God in Worship, Doctrine and Life* (New York: Oxford University Press, 1980).

Wainwright, G., *Worship with One Accord* (Oxford: Oxford University Press, 1997).

Wallace, R.S., *Calvin's Doctrine of the Word and Sacrament* (Edinburgh: Scottish Academic Press, 1995).

Walton, J.R., *Feminist Liturgy: A Matter of Justice* (Collegeville, MN: Liturgical Press, 2000).

Walton, J.R., 'Ecclesial and Feminist Blessing: Women as Objects and Subjects of the Power of Blessing' in M. Collins and D. Power, eds., *Blessing and Power* (Edinburgh: T. and T. Clark, 1985).

Ward, G., *Theology and Contemporary Critical Theory* (London: Macmillan, 1996).

Warren, F.E., *The Liturgy and Ritual of the Celtic Church* (Woodbridge: Boydell, 1987).

Weber, M, *The Sociology of Religion* (Boston: Beacon Press, 1922).

Weil, L., *Sacraments and Liturgy: The Outward Signs: A Study in Liturgical Mentality* (Oxford: Blackwell, 1983).

Weir, A., 'Toward a Model of Self-Identity' in J. Meehan, ed., *Feminists Read Habermas: Gendering the Subject of Discourse* (New York: Routledge, 1995).

Wellmer, A., 'Communications and Emancipation: Reflections on the Linguistic Turn in Critical Theory' in J. O'Neill, ed., *On Critical Theory* (New York: Seabury, 1976).

Wendel, E.M., *I Am My Body: A Theology of Embodiment* (New York: Continuum, 1995).

White, J.F., *A Brief History of Christian Worship* (Nashville: Abingdon Press, 1993).

Wiles, M., 'Theology in the Twenty-first Century', *Theology* 103: 816 (Nov/Dec 2000).

Williams, R., *Eucharistic Sacrifice - The Roots of Metaphor* (London: Grove Books, 1982).

Williams, R., *On Christian Theology* (Oxford: Blackwell Publishers, 2000).

Wilson-Kastner, P., *Sacred Drama: A Spirituality of Christian Liturgy* (Philadelphia: Fortress Press, 2000).

Winter, M.T., *WomanWord: A Feminist Lectionary and Psalter* (New York: Crossroad, 1992).

Winter, M.T., A. Lummis, and A. Stokes, *Defecting in Place: Women Claiming Responsibility for Their Own Spiritual Lives* (New York: Crossroad, 1994).

Wittgenstein, L., *Philosophical Investigations* (Oxford: Blackwell Publishers, 1958).

Wittgenstein, L., *On Certainty* (New York: Harper Row, 1969).

Wittgenstein, L., *Culture and Value* (Chicago: University of Chicago Press, 1980).

Worgul, G.S., *From Magic to Metaphor: A Validation of the Christian Sacraments* (New York: Harper and Row, 1980).

Wybrew, H., *The Orthodox Liturgy: The Development of the Eucharistic Liturgy in the Byzantine Rite* (London: SPCK 1989).

Yeats, W.B., *Selected Poetry* (London: Macmillan, 1962).

Zimmerman, J.A., *Liturgy as Living Faith: A Liturgical Spirituality* (Scranton: University of Scranton Press, 1993).

Zitnik, M., ed., *Sacramenta: bibliographia internationalis* (Roma: Editrice Pontificia Università Gregoriana, 1992).

Index